# Truth and Objectivity

# Truth and Objectivity

Crispin Wright

Harvard University Press
Cambridge, Massachusetts
London, England

Copyright © 1992 by the President and Fellows of
Harvard College
All rights reserved
Printed in the United States of America
Second Printing, 1994

First Harvard University Press paperback edition, 1994

*Library of Congress Cataloging-in-Publication Data*

Wright, Crispin, 1942–
    Truth and objectivity / Crispin Wright.
        p.      cm.
    Includes index.
    ISBN 0-674-91086-9 (cloth)
    ISBN 0-674-91087-7 (pbk.)
    1. Realism.    I. Title.
  B835.W75      1992
  121—dc20                                    92–15025
                                                CIP

For Geoffrey and Arthur:
the Wright Brothers

# Preface

During the academic sessions 1990–91 and 1991–92, I had the good fortune to hold a British Academy Research Readership and thus at least to make a start on a project which, in my original application to the Academy, I had confidently undertaken to complete within the period of the Readership if my application was successful. That project was to bring into more explicit focus a new framework for conducting the philosophical debates about realism—a framework which I had been developing in a number of papers published in recent years—and then to apply it in detail to various specific realist/anti-realist debates, especially those concerning logical necessity, the status of scientific theories, moral judgement, and secondary qualities. My election to a Visiting Fellowship at Magdalen College for the Trinity term of 1991 gave me an invaluable opportunity, as Waynflete Lecturer, to air some of the material which I planned to include in the book in which the project was to culminate. Naturally enough, the lectures were mainly concerned with elaborating the general framework, rather than with its applications. But at their conclusion, it seemed to me, as I looked over what I had presented, that the material might justify separate publication. This short book is the result.

Several considerations invited the decision to publish it. One was that it was now clear that a proper execution of the original project would demand a very big book, at whose likely completion date I could not so much as hazard a guess. Publishing very big books in philosophy nowadays is, I suspect, almost as good a way of ensuring that most of their content will never be read as not publishing it at all. Second, it seemed to me that the main contours of the general perspective outlined here may well stand out more sharply in a short exposition than they would in the much larger effort needed to apply them in detail to a variety of different areas of discourse. If there is any merit in these ideas, then, despite all the loose ends and lacunae which I have been forced to leave in place, others will, I think, be able to judge so more easily on the basis of a concise presentation, and may wish to pursue the application of the framework to the local debates on their own account. That at any rate is my hope; philosophical research, especially on issues as fundamental and difficult as these, ought to be collaborative, even under the econometric ethos which now conditions the thinking of university administrators and pressures professional philosophers on both sides of the Atlantic. A further consideration was that some of the material in the lectures involved extended criticism of recently published work of writers such as Paul Boghossian and David Wiggins; this material would date if its publication were long delayed. Finally, my hosts at Magdalen left me, in the nicest possible way, in no doubt that publication of the lectures would be very welcome from their point of view.

Publishing lectures necessitates choosing how far to rejig the material in accordance with the needs of written rather than oral presentation. The text which follows is mostly close to that of the lectures as originally delivered. In particular, I have left in place a somewhat larger number of passages of summary than is, I suppose, now strictly necessary. These passages usually constitute the initial section of a chapter, and less patient, more experienced readers might try skipping or skimming them. That is a suggested experiment, however, rather than a recommendation. I would not have retained the summaries if I did not judge that, for most readers, they are, on balance, more likely to help proceedings than to put a brake on them.

There are, however, a number of significant additions and changes.

I have usually added brief discussion notes after a chapter, taking up some of the matters which either arose during the question period or which I had earlier edited out for reasons of time. But the "lacunae and loose ends" are mostly still very much in evidence. They include especially a host of questions concerning truth and superassertibility unbroached in Chapter 2—which is nevertheless the most reworked—and the major difficulty concerning Cognitive Command and the theoreticity of observation on which Chapter 4 concludes. Worst of all in the original text was the imbalance of a discussion in which the cruces concerning Cognitive Command and Width of Cosmological Role were explored in some detail, while those concerning Evidence Transcendence and the Euthyphro Contrast received hardly any attention. It's true, of course, that I have already had plenty to say about Evidence Transcendence and the Dummettian conception of the realist/anti-realist debate in other places. But there is almost no worthwhile published discussion, by me or anyone else, of how best to understand the Euthyphro Contrast or of its significance for the modern debate about realism. I originally planned to say a lot more about it in the lectures, and some of this material now appears as the appendix to Chapter 3. Its inclusion rounds out the description of the general framework in a way which I believe will be helpful.

I am extremely grateful to Magdalen for so congenial an opportunity to live and work in Oxford again after an absence of thirteen years. Notwithstanding the difficulties which universities in Britain and perhaps especially its academic philosophers have had to contend with over the last decade, philosophy at Oxford remains hearteningly vigorous, powerful and open-minded. The discussion periods after each lecture were unfailingly constructive and helpful, and I also learned much from informal discussions with and from the written comments of many of those who attended. I would like to express my special gratitude in this connection to Simon Blackburn, Justin Broackes, Michael Dummett, Elizabeth Fricker, Dick Hare, John McDowell, Christopher Peacocke, Mark Sacks, Richard Swinburne, Roger Teichman, Ralph Walker and Timothy

Williamson. They will be disappointed to see that not all of their best suggestions and criticisms have provoked a response in the present text.

The programme which I begin to develop here was announced in the Gareth Evans Memorial Lecture, "Realism, Anti-realism, Irrealism, Quasi-realism," which I gave at Oxford in the summer of 1987. Versions of the basic ideas provided the raw material for a graduate seminar on realism which I gave at the University of Michigan in the fall of 1988—a seminar from which I learned much, especially from the interventions of Nicholas White and Stephen Yablo. I had the chance to develop matters further in a seminar I gave at the University of Queensland while Visiting Humanities Research Professor there in the spring of 1989 when I benefited from the comments and questions of André Gallois, Roger Lamb, Gary Malinas, Graham Priest and the late Don Mannison. Thanks for more recent criticisms and reactions go to Bob Hale, Peter Clark, Leslie Stevenson, Stephen Read, Neil Cooper and Basil O'Neill, who attended a research seminar of mine at St. Andrews in the early spring of 1991 at which I tried out some of the ideas, to Bob Hale again and John Skorupski for their comments on early drafts of the lectures, and to John Divers, Jim Edwards, Christopher Martin and Pat Shaw, who took the lectures as the text for their summer reading group in Glasgow in 1991, and gave me a welter of useful reactions and suggestions. To another Michigan colleague, Paul Boghossian, go special thanks not merely for many stimulating conversations on the topics treated in the lectures but for his unfailing encouragement and confidence in the interest of the overall project.

Finally I would like to express my gratitude to the St. Andrews Philosophy Departments' secretaries, Janet Kirk, Anne Cameron and Kyle Galloway, for their usual efficiency and cheerfulness in helping to prepare the typescript, to Marguerite Nesling for help with proofreading and the index, to my editor, Maria Ascher, to St. Andrews for sponsoring my application for the Readership, to the British Academy for responding with the award, and to my other employer, the University of Michigan, for granting me a leave of absence to accept it.

# Contents

# Truth and Objectivity

# 1. Inflating Deflationism

## I. Three Anti-realist Paradigms

In this short study I want to return to a well-worked—some would
feel, no doubt, mined out—issue in recent philosophy: the question of how we should best understand the contrast between so-
called realist and anti-realist views concerning different areas of
our thought and discourse, and of how the debate between them
might most effectively be prosecuted. Of course, if there ever was
a consensus of understanding about "realism", as a philosophical
term of art, it has undoubtedly been fragmented by the pressures
exerted by the various debates—so much so that a philosopher
who asserts that she is a realist about theoretical science, for example, or ethics, has probably, for most philosophical audiences,
accomplished little more than to clear her throat. So something
preliminary needs to be said by way of intuitive anchorage for the
term.

A reasonable pretheoretical characterisation of realism about,
say, the external world seems to me that it is a fusion of two kinds
of thoughts, one kind expressing a certain modesty, the other more
presumptuous. The modest kind of thought concerns the *independence* of the external world—for example, that the external world
exists independently of us, that it is as it is independently of the
conceptual vocabulary in terms of which we think about it, and

that it is as it is independently of the beliefs about it which we do, will, or ever would form. (Of course, someone may be attracted to only some of these thoughts.) Fully fledged, modesty has it that human thought is, as it were, at best a *map* of the world. Maps can better or worse represent the terrain which they concern. But nothing about that terrain will owe its existence, or character, to the institution of cartography or to the conventions and techniques therein employed. (The comparison, of course, is Frege's.)

The presumptuous thought, by contrast, is that, while such fit as there may be between our thought and the world is determined independently of human cognitive activity, we are nevertheless, in favourable circumstances, capable of conceiving the world aright, and, often, of knowing the truth about it. Not merely is there a good measure of non-accidental fit between the external world and our thoughts about it, but we are capable of winning through to the knowledge that this is so, or at least to a perspective from which we may quite justifiably take it to be so.

Analogues of these two kinds of thought are available, of course, for all the regions of discourse—science, mathematics, ethics, aesthetics, politics, the law, literary criticism and so on—in which the expression of opinion, argument, inference and persuasion have a place. But the thoughts have rather different degrees of attraction for us as the region of discourse varies. Presumption weakens, perhaps, when we enter more abstruse branches of physical theory, or engage in the most fundamental kind of scientific cosmological speculation. And modesty tends to diminish when we are concerned, for instance, with judgements about what is comic, or revolting; and it *ought* to diminish, so philosophers have argued, in the case of discourse concerning secondary qualities of material objects, and in the case of moral, aesthetic and certain other kinds of evaluation.

In any case the combination of modesty and presumption, in any area of discourse for which a thinker finds it attractive, is potentially open to two directions of attack, naturally labelled *sceptical* and *idealistic,* respectively. A sceptical attack challenges the presumptuous thought: issue will be taken either with the truth of the claim that our cognitive powers are adequate in the way presumption takes them to be, or with our right to make that claim. An idealistic attack, by contrast, will challenge some aspect of the way in which the idea of independence features in modest thinking. Or, more radically, it may challenge the whole idea that the area of discourse in question is properly seen as geared to the expression of thoughts whose aim is to reflect an independent reality.

For all the vilification and caricature which its critics have meted out over the years, the idealist tradition in philosophy has proved sufficiently durable to encourage the belief that, at least locally, there are insights for which it is striving, but for which—its persistently controversial character suggests—we have yet to find definitive means of expression. In postwar Anglo-American philosophy three paradigms have dominated our thinking about the idealist—or, as I shall henceforward say, anti-realist—direction. The first is that developed in Michael Dummett's work, though it draws, as he has emphasised, both on the ideas of the logical positivists and on the philosophy of language of the later Wittgenstein, and exhibits important points of affinity with ideas of Hilary Putnam.[1]

According to Dummett, the proper location for the dispute between realist and anti-realist lies within the theory of meaning, and its focus should be on the question: What is the proper theoretical description of an understanding of the declarative sentences of the contested discourse? In the view of Dummett's realist, such an understanding consists in possessing an idea of what it is for any particular such sentence to be, respectively, true or false,

---

1. Dummett's ideas about realism surface all over his published work, but receive their perhaps most concentrated development in his *Truth and Other Enigmas* (London: Duckworth, 1978), essays 1, 10, 11, 13, 17 and 21; in his article "What Is a Theory of Meaning? (II)", in G. Evans and J. McDowell, eds., *Truth and Meaning* (Oxford: Oxford University Press, 1976); and in his recently published 1976 William James Lectures, *The Logical Basis of Metaphysics* (Cambridge, Mass.: Harvard University Press, 1991). Putnam's contiguous ideas are developed in the papers collected in his *Realism and Reason* (Cambridge: Cambridge University Press, 1983); also in his *Reason, Truth and History* (Cambridge: Cambridge University Press, 1981), *The Many Faces of Realism* (LaSalle, Ill.: Open Court Press, 1987), and *Realism with a Human Face*, ed. James Conant (Cambridge, Mass.: Harvard University Press, 1990).

independently of any capacity we may have to verify it as true or false, or to gather germane evidence either way. Dummett's anti-realist, by contrast, takes it to be a cardinal moral of Wittgenstein's later philosophy, crystallised in the slogan that meaning is use, that understanding a sentence cannot consist, in that way, in any conception which is underdetermined by the thinker's manifest capacities. Rather it must devolve into the essentially practical ability to *use* the sentence in appropriate ways in response to conditions whose obtaining we can recognise—centrally: conditions whose obtaining justifies the assertion or denial of the sentence.

Some critics, even if willing to allow that this opposition presents a fundamental debate within the philosophy of language, have queried its connection with any natural or intuitive understanding of the term "realism". But the connection is not actually hard to see. To conceive that our understanding of statements in a certain discourse is fixed, as Dummett's realist suggests, by assigning them conditions of potentially evidence-transcendent truth is to grant that, if the world co-operates, the truth or falsity of any such statement may be settled beyond our ken. So—the connecting thought runs—we are forced to recognise a distinction between the kind of state of affairs which makes such a statement acceptable, in the light of whatever standards inform our practice of the discourse to which it belongs, and what makes it actually true. The truth of such a statement is bestowed on it independently of any standard we do or can apply; acceptability by our standards is, for such statements, at best merely congruent with truth. Realism in Dummett's sense is thus one way of laying the essential semantic groundwork for the idea that our thought aspires to reflect a reality whose character is entirely independent of us and our cognitive operations.[2]

By contrast, Dummett's anti-realist famously—notoriously—denies that, in anything justifiably regarded as representational discourse, we can intelligibly make semantic provision for the depiction of states of affairs whose obtaining, or not, is beyond our

2. An exemplary account of the relation between Dummettian realism and realism more intuitively—ontologically—conceived is to be found in Barry Taylor, "The Truth in Realism", *Revue Internationale de Philosophie* 41 (1987), pp. 45–63.

detection. I shall not here dwell on the motives for this claim.[3] What I wish to note, and what is too seldom recognised, is that it is consistent with anti-realism in this sense to retain the idea that a discourse is representational, and answers to states of affairs which, on at least some proper understandings of the term, are independent of us. For example, in shifting to a broadly intuitionistic conception of, say, number theory, we do not immediately foreclose on the idea that the series of natural numbers constitutes a real object of mathematical investigation, which it is harmless and correct to think of the number theoretician as exploring.

This concession to realism is conspicuously not a feature of the second anti-realist paradigm prominent in modern times. According to this second kind of anti-realism, Dummett's realist may well have matters more or less right as far as the *semantics* of the contested discourse is concerned. The fundamental error incorporated in ordinary realist thought about, say, ethics or mathematics is not semantic at all but one of *metaphysical superstition.* Such is the view adopted by, for instance, John Mackie about ethics[4] and Hartry Field about pure mathematics.[5] For Field, the semantics of mathematical statements may well prepare them to receive potentially proof-transcendent truth values, conferred by the intrinsic properties of a pure mathematical realm. The trouble is: there is no such realm—there are no structures of abstract mathematical entities of the kind which a face-value construal of the singular terms and quantifiers of number theory, analysis, set theory and so on would call for. The conviction that we attain to truth in pure mathematics is simply a great mistake; there is nothing out there to make our pure mathematical statements true.[6]

---

3. For an overview of grounds for it, see the introduction to my *Realism, Meaning and Truth* (Oxford: Basil Blackwell, 1986).

4. J. L. Mackie, *Ethics—Inventing Right and Wrong* (Harmondsworth: Penguin, 1977). An important collection of papers responsive to Mackie's views is Honderich, ed., *Morality and Objectivity* (London: Routledge and Kegan Paul, 1985).

5. Hartry Field, *Science without Numbers* (Oxford: Basil Blackwell, 1980); and idem, *Realism, Mathematics and Modality* (Oxford: Basil Blackwell, 1989).

6. Save that statements whose principal operator is the universal quantifier will, of course, be vacuously true if the range of the quantifier is, as Field supposes, empty.

Mackie's view of ethics is broadly similar. According to Mackie, our ordinary understanding of moral discourse demands the existence of moral properties with something like the objectivity and autonomy possessed by the primary qualities of material objects dealt with by physical science. But when we look in detail, he argues, at the demands which moral discourse places on the distinctive qualities with which it putatively deals, we find that these demands are unsatisfiable—or at least, that they go unsatisfied in this world. The conclusion, as before, is that ordinary moral thought is guilty of a sweeping, systematic mistake: *semantically,* it is indeed representational thought, true or not according to whether certain real properties apply or fail to apply in the world. But the truth is that there are no such properties; reality is simply empty of all states of affairs whose representation would require thought of distinctively moral content.

The third anti-realist paradigm I want to focus on contests something the other two grant: that the declarative sentences of the contested discourse equip us for the expression of genuinely representational thoughts. The fundamental error of the realist, according to an anti-realist of this third stripe, is one susceptible to a broadly Wittgensteinian diagnosis: the error of being misled by merely superficial "grammatical" similarities between different regions of discourse, so that we are deceived into thinking that they are in the business of doing the same essential thing: stating facts, expressing represential thoughts "which may be about houses, pains, good or evil, or anything else you please" (*Investigations* §304). What needs to be recognised is that a discourse may have all the overt trappings of genuine assertion, expression of belief and so on, yet in reality not be in the business of making statements, literally true or false, at all.

Modern anti-realist writers in this tradition about ethics include, of course, A. J. Ayer, R. M. Hare, Simon Blackburn and Allan Gibbard,[7] for each of whom—if I may over-simplify some-

7. The loci classici are of course the famous "Critique of Ethics and Theology" in A. J. Ayer, *Language, Truth and Logic* (London: Victor Gollancz, 1936), ch. 6; and R. M. Hare, *The Language of Morals* (Oxford: Oxford University Press, 1952). An invaluable précis of Hare's current views is provided by his

what—the fundamental role of ethical "assertion" is not to state anything but to express moral attitude and (thereby) to prescribe or caution against certain specific forms of conduct. The same kind of idea surfaces in the philosophy of science in various forms of theoretical instrumentalism, in the idea of laws as "inference tickets", and in the view of theoretical statements as metaphor, associated with such writers as Hesse.[8] In each case high-level theoretical statements, despite their apparent meaningfulness and apparently assertoric syntax, are denied any truth-evaluable content. And of course similar ideas are found also in the philosophy of mathematics, in the writings of thinkers as otherwise disparate as Hilbert and the later Wittgenstein.

There, then, in broad outline, are the three paradigms. It's not my purpose here to consider in detail any specific proposals for particular regions of discourse falling under any of them. Rather I want to question their claim, individually or collectively, satisfactorily to capture the directions in which a worked-out and convincing anti-realism about any particular region of our thought would have to proceed.

## II. The Need for a New Approach

Take a very homespun case: discourse about what is funny. This is an area where, in terms of the very rough-hewn characterisation of realism I gave earlier, almost everyone's antecedent prejudice would be against modesty. The thought that something is funny is not something which we conceive as apt to map a feature of the world which is independent of human minds—of their existence,

---

"Universal Prescriptivism", in P. Singer, ed., *A Companion to Ethics* (Oxford: Basil Blackwell, 1991), ch. 40. "Evaluations, Projections and Quasi-realism", in Simon Blackburn, *Spreading the Word* (Oxford: Oxford University Press, 1984), remains the best introduction to Blackburn's view. Allan Gibbard's ideas are developed systematically in his book *Wise Choices, Apt Feelings* (Cambridge, Mass.: Harvard University Press, 1990).

8. See for instance her essay "The Cognitive Claims for Metaphor", in J. P. van Noppen, ed., *Metaphor and Religion: Theolinguistics 2* (Brussels, 1984). Also, with M. A. Arbib, *A Construction of Reality* (Cambridge University Press, 1987).

cognitive standards, powers and reactive propensities. Of course, it's consistent with this that the content of such a statement should be precisely, in some sufficiently broad sense, anthropological— that it be *about* minds. But which minds, and what is it saying about them? When I claim that something is funny, I'm not simply reporting my own reaction to it; for I can readily conceive that my reaction might be wrong—insensitive or misplaced. Nor am I reporting a majority reaction, or conjecturing the direction it might take; for the same point applies—the comic sensibilities of the majority may be blunted, "off the wall" or debased. Regarding something as funny incorporates a judgement about the *fittingness* of the comic response. A standard next move would be to try to view the comic qualities of an object as residing in a disposition to elicit the comic response in *appropriate,* appropriately situated subjects. But now, in order to be saying anything concrete at all, we'd have to say what "appropriate" means when so deployed—and of course it will be extremely difficult to venture anything which is both concretely informative yet whose detail corresponds only to elements already present in our ordinary understanding of comic concepts.

Naturally, these remarks are inconclusive—maybe statements about comedy do permit an analysis disclosing that the basis for our discomfort with a realist view of them, as originally crudely characterised, is that their subject matter is indeed somehow anthropological. Noting that possible direction of exploration— and pausing only to record my own scepticism about it—the question on which I wish to focus is: What would be the prospects for a satisfactory elucidation of an intuitive anti-realism about the comic in terms of any of the three distinguished paradigms?

Well, we can take it, I think, that the crux for an anti-realist of Dummett's sort—the admission of an epistemically unconstrained idea of truth, and a truth-conditional account of content framed in terms of it—is not the issue here. It might seem implausible to claim that the sense of humour is a faculty which enables us to track independently constituted comic qualities; but it would ascend to a quite different order of implausibility to add that the obtaining of such qualities may altogether transcend, even in principle, our abilities of recognition. A similar point applies to morals. There are, no doubt, kinds of moral realism which do have the consequence that moral reality may transcend all possibility of detection. But it is surely not essential to any view worth regarding as realist about morals that it incorporate a commitment to that idea.

In short: a global victory, on general semantic grounds, for Dummett's anti-realist would leave the moral realism which many find attractive, and the corresponding comic realism which almost nobody finds attractive, still available as apparently live options. Of course, that's an impression which might disappear on closer analysis. Still, the claim that what an adverse reaction to realism about the comic really comes down to is a recoil against verification-transcendent comic truth is, at least prima facie, merely far-fetched.

This is unremarkable, since Dummett's proposal was fashioned with the cases of mathematics and discourse concerning the past chiefly in view. What is perhaps more notable is that neither of the other two paradigms fares appreciably better. The Mackie/ Field, error-theoretic model would allow that we quest for truth, so to say, in our claims about comedy, and that we use a discourse which, as far at least as its semantics is concerned, is fitted for that project. But the world lets us down; there are no comic qualities out there, no comic facts. The great discomfort with such an account is that, unless more is said, it simply relegates discourse about the comic to bad faith. Whatever we may once have thought, as soon as philosophy has taught us that the world is unsuited to confer truth on any of our claims about what is funny, the reasonable response ought surely to be to forgo making any such claims. That would not be to forgo the right to laugh, of course. But it would, apparently, be to forgo the point of reasoned appreciation and debate of what is funny, and of criticism of others' opinions about it. And these consequences are most calamitous, of course, when they are applied, as I believe Mackie was committed to applying them, within *moral* discourse. If it is of the essence of moral judgement to aim at the truth, and if philosophy teaches that there is no moral truth to hit, how do I take myself seriously in thinking the way I do about any issue which I regard as of major moral importance?

This calamity can be somewhat mitigated if some other purpose can be disclosed for the discourse in question, some norm of appraisal besides truth at which our comic, or moral statements may be seen as aimed, and which they can satisfy. Hartry Field's play with the idea of *conservativeness* in pure mathematics precisely represents an attempt to disclose such an independent norm.[9] But the error theorist will have no advantage over the third anti-realist paradigm—the expressivist approach—unless this subsidiary norm, whatever it is, is something which *only* genuine assertions are fitted to secure. And even if the error-theorist can stabilise his view against that threat,[10] the very good question will remain why, if, among the plethora of falsehoods enunciated in comic discourse, a good distinction exists between those which are acceptable in the light of the subsidiary norm, and those which are not—a distinction which informs ordinary discussion and criticism of comic claims—why in that case truth for such claims would not better be explained in terms of satisfaction of the subsidiary norm, rather than in terms which motivate the charge of global error?

The third, expressivist paradigm is not open to precisely that difficulty, since it denies that truth is properly predicable of such "assertions" at all. But the *discipline* exhibited by comic discourse, to some degree, and by moral discourse, to a very great degree, continues to pose an analogous problem. To the extent that generally acknowledged standards of *appropriateness* inform our appraisal of, for example, moral judgement and argument, the claim that moral discourse is not genuinely assertoric will seem unmotivated in contradistinction to the idea that the truth predicate which applies within it is some sort of construct from the relevant notion of appropriateness. And the force of this complaint is greatly

9. In Field's own formulation: a mathematical theory S is conservative if and only if for any nominalistic of version A and any body of such assertions N, A is not a consequence of N + S unless A is a consequence of N alone. (*Realism, Mathematics and Modality*, p. 125.)

10. Critical destruction of the third paradigm would, of course, be one strategy.

enhanced by the consideration, so it seems to me, that we actually lack any clear and workable idea of how to construe discourses which exhibit all the overt syntactic trappings of assertion—negation, the conditional, embedding within propositional attitudes, hypothesis and inference and so on—in such a way that the contents involved are not asserted but are presented with illocutionary force of quite a different kind. Even so apparently simple a matter as the cogency of inference by modus ponens when the minor premise is a moral judgement has so far, to the best of my knowledge, been provided with no satisfactory account by any theorist attempting to make good the thought that moral discourse is not, properly speaking, assertoric.[11]

Obviously, there is much more to say about the expressivist paradigm. But the strong suspicion must be, it seems to me, that it barks up the wrong tree: making good, or indeed defeating, a basic anti-realist inclination concerning comedy should not hold out such a hostage to syntactic fortune—should not have to await a demonstration that comic discourse can, or cannot conservatively be reconstrued in such a way that all vestige of assertion disappears.

The upshot is that none of the three paradigms can confidently be regarded as promising a satisfactory interpretation and development of an original anti-realist intuition about comedy: a development which allows that intuition a sporting chance of being right, which avoids allowing it to be right too easily or for irrelevant-seeming reasons, which conserves the integrity of discourse about the comic, and avoids encumbering itself with dubiously feasible programmes of reductive paraphrase. We seem to need a quite different approach. But what scope is there for one?

A different approach will have to grant that opinions about

11. For details of this complaint in connection with Blackburn's work, see my 1987 Gareth Evans Memorial Lecture, "Realism, Anti-realism, Irrealism, Quasi-realism", in French, Uehling and Wettstein, eds., *Mid-west Studies in Philosophy*, vol. 12 (Minneapolis: University of Minnesota Press, 1988), pp. 25–49; and Bob Hale, "The Compleat Projectivist", *Philosophical Quarterly* 36 (1986), pp. 65–84. For an update of the criticism in the light of later suggestions of Blackburn's, see Hale, "Can There Be a Logic of Attitudes?" in Haldane and Wright, eds., *Reality, Representation and Projection* (Oxford: Oxford University Press, 1992).

comedy *are* properly recorded in the form of assertions, apt to be true or false; that many such assertions *are,* as we ordinarily suppose, perfectly true; and that what distinguishes such discourse from areas where anti-realist intuition would be misguided is not its having an implicitly anthropocentric subject matter, to be disclosed by reductive analysis. Clearly, if anti-realist intuition is to be accommodated by any programme which grants these points, answers have to be provided to two questions. First, how does the concession that a discourse is truth-apt, and indeed that many of what we take to be true assertions expressed in it are indeed true—how can this concession avoid giving the game to the realist straight away, at least when it is combined with an acknowledgement that the contents expressed are *sui generis* and permit of no reduction to more explicitly anthropocentric terms? Are we not immediately saddled with domains of, for example, intrinsically moral, or comic fact, the source of the truth values of our moral and comic claims?

Second, if it can indeed be explained how that is not so, then what *is* at stake between realist and anti-realist, when both are agreed that the statements of a contested discourse are irreducibly apt for truth and falsity and that many of those which we take to be true are so? Is not the debate undermined? And if it is not, what is the proper way to conduct it?

What I want to attempt in what follows, and in subsequent chapters, is to indicate at least the beginnings of lines of response to both these questions, and thereby to outline a framework for the expression and development of anti-realist intuition which, while incorporating what I regard as the insights in Michael Dummett's proposal, is more generally applicable and is free of the internal strains and implausibilities of the other paradigms considered. The first task, then, is to explain how truth need not be the exclusive property of realism.

## III. Deflationism and Its Inflation

It might be supposed that this is no very major task. Is not a notion of truth already perfectly familiar which is both appropriately tied to assertoric content yet free of the metaphysical commitments associated with realism? This notion is of course the well-known *deflationary* conception, first seriously propounded by Frank Ramsey, though something like it was a central plank in the thought of some of the Logical Positivists, and it surfaces in several places in Wittgenstein's writings too. Most recently, a conception of truth putatively belonging to this tradition has been defended in detail by Paul Horwich.[12]

It would be nice if deflationism supplied what we want. In fact, though, there is serious cause to wonder how deflationism about truth can be a stable view. Rather, as we might say, deflationism shows a tendency to inflate under pressure, to the point where its principal negative contention, that truth is not a substantial property of sentences or thoughts at all, comes to seem to run contrary to its principal explanatory contention, that the concept of truth may be regarded as fixed by the famous Disquotational Schema. However, thinking through why this is so will point us, so I shall suggest, in the direction of a conception of truth—what I shall call *minimal* truth[13]—which can, I believe, play the kind of metaphysically lightweight role needed by the sort of overall strategy with realist/anti-realist debates which I am proposing.

Deflationism contends that, at least as far as what we may call the basic case is concerned, when the truth predicate is applied to an exhibited declarative sentence, its content is wholly fixed by the principle that

"P" is true if and only if P.

12. The locus classicus is Frank Ramsey, "Facts and Propositions", *Proceedings of the Aristotelian Society*, suppl. vol. 7 (1927). Horwich's account is contained in his *Truth* (Oxford: Basil Blackwell, 1990), which also includes a useful bibliography on the topic. There are issues about the relationship between Horwich's proposal and the classical deflationist line which are briefly canvassed in footnote 15 below.

13. Horwich's brand of deflationism is likewise presented under the title of "Minimalism" about truth; and it might seem to be courting confusion, and not a little insouciant, to appropriate the title for the anti-deflationist view which I am advocating. Actually my use of the term is a matter of coincidence rather than appropriation. But I felt it appropriate to retain the terminology nevertheless because my contention is precisely that minimalism about truth, as described in this and the succeeding chapter, is just what the deflationary trend comes to (what would-be deflationists like Horwich *ought* to advocate) when it is purified of the instability focussed on in the discussion which follows.

Deflationists recognise, of course, that something more needs to be said to account for the role of the predicate as attached to a singular term (as in "Goldbach's Conjecture is true") or as it occurs in quantification over its primary bearers (as in "Everything he said is true"). Such uses of the truth predicate are, however, to be explained in terms of the basic case: its application to a sentential clause. And in the basic case, it is merely a device of "disquotation"; rather than expressing any substantial characteristic of sentences, the effect of its predication, at the metalinguistic level, is just to accomplish what, within the object language, we can accomplish by asserting the sentence in question.

It is at least an awkwardness for this general line that assertion has the following analytical tie to belief: if someone makes an assertion, and is supposed sincere, it follows that she has a belief whose content can be captured by means of the sentence used. For it would seem that no strictly metalinguistic claim can parallel that. In particular, one can fully intelligently claim that "P" is true without understanding "P". To side-step such complications, deflationism does well to restrict itself to the contention that it is, near enough, wholly explanatory of the predicate, "true", that, for one who understands a mentioned sentence, the claim that it is true comes to the same thing as its assertion. The "near enough" is called for by the need to say something about the "Goldbach's Conjecture" and "Everything he said" uses. But if we imagine, for simplicity's sake, a language in which all uses of the truth predicate are basic, then deflationism comes to the contention that, for such a language, the content of the truth predicate is exhausted by the consideration that, for one who understands the mentioned sentence, the claim made by predicating truth of that sentence is the same as the claim made by its assertoric use.

However, I don't want to spend time on the fine detail of the best formulation of deflationism. We can take it that we are concerned with a theorist who holds that, subject perhaps to certain provisos of context, the Disquotational Schema

(DS)                    "P" is T if and only if P

is (all but) a complete explanation of the truth predicate—a contention from which he infers, dubiously, that truth is not a "substantial property", whatever that means, of sentences, thoughts, and so on, but merely a device for accomplishing at the metalinguistic level what can be accomplished by an assertoric use of the mentioned sentence. My contention will be that the first part of this—the explanatory claim—is actually inconsistent with the distinctively deflationist corollary, that "true" expresses no real property but is merely a device of disquotation. (Of course, it can express a real property *and* be a device of disquotation.)

In order to see the tension, we need to ask: what can we conclude about any predicate, "T", whose content is (all but) given by the role assigned to it by the DS? And the answer, I think, is a surprising amount. I shall highlight two features in particular.

Let us characterise as a *practice* any form of intentional, purposeful activity, and as a *move* any action performed within the practice, for its characteristic purposes. And now reflect on what is, or might appropriately be meant by the claim that a certain characteristic is *normative* of such a practice. Various proposals are no doubt possible, but we should recognise straight away a distinction between *descriptive* and *prescriptive* claims about normativity. A characteristic of moves in a particular practice is a descriptive norm if, as a matter of fact, participants in the practice are positively guided in their selection of moves by whether a proposed move possesses that characteristic. Thus the characteristic of actions involved in driving a car—"tends to secure safe completion of one's planned journey"—is, fortunately, a descriptive norm for most motorists. By contrast, a characteristic of moves supplies a prescriptive norm just in case the reflection that a move has that characteristic provides a (defeasible) reason for making, or endorsing, or permitting it, even if such reasons tend, for the most part, to go unacknowledged by actual participants.

I am here speaking of positive norms. A full analysis would doubtless draw many further distinctions. To begin with, *negative* descriptive norms would be, correspondingly, characteristics such that participants in a practice treat a move's having such a characteristic as a reason for avoiding, condemning, discouraging or prohibiting it. And negative prescriptive norms would be characteristics recognition of which *ought* to provide reason for such negative responses to actual or proposed moves. Each type of norm may further be regarded as *constitutive* of a practice, or not, depending on whether its being largely observed (if it is a descriptive norm) or its supplying defeasible reason for the making, refusal and so on of moves (if it is a prescriptive norm) enters constitutively into the identity of the practice concerned.

These remarks are somewhat general. Fortunately, we shall not need to chase greater precision for our present purpose. However, one refinement is necessary. I have been speaking somewhat carelessly of the normativity of *characteristics*. But it is a thesis of classical deflationism that truth is not, properly speaking, a characteristic at all. So we must pause to refashion these ideas if we are to avoid a charge of question begging in due course. Say, then, that a *predicate*, F, is (positively) descriptively normative just in case participants' selection, endorsement and so on of a move is as a matter of fact guided by whether or not they judge that move is F—a judgement whose bare possibility is neutral, presumably, on the question whether or not the predicate expresses a substantial property. Likewise a predicate is prescriptively normative just in case the selection, or endorsement, of a move *ought* to be so guided within the practice concerned.

With these notions in place, the first observation I want to make is simply that deflationism is committed to the thesis that the T-predicate is positively normative, both descriptively and prescriptively, of any assertoric practice. To see why, reflect first that it is distinctive of sentences with assertoric content, in the sense contrasting with, say, imperative, interrogative or optative content, that they can feature without syntactic incongruity as the antecedents of conditionals. Now, even if all we understand about "T" is what the deflationist tells us, we at least know that sentences in its range of predication may all feature on the right-hand side of the Disquotational Schema, and hence as the antecedent of a conditional which goes from right to left across it. So we know that every assertoric sentence—every sentence capable of featuring as the antecedent of a significant conditional—is within the range of predication of "T". Indeed, to all intents and purposes we know that "T" is *only* predicable for such sentences, since none of the things which the deflationist will want to add to his basic explanation will involve its predicability of other kinds of sentence.

How does that connect with normativity? Well, consider the practice of the sincere and literal use of the sentences in the range of the T-predicate. In order for these sentences to be determinate in content at all, there has to be a distinction, respected for the most part by participants in the practice, between proper and improper use of them. And since they are sentences with assertoric content, that will be a distinction between cases where their assertion is justified and cases where it is not. It follows that a norm, ✳ or complex of norms, of warranted assertibility will hold sway, both prescriptively and descriptively, over sincere and literal use of the sentences to which the T-predicate applies: prescriptively, because to have reason to think that a sentence is warrantedly assertible is, trivially, to have (defeasible) reason to assert it, or endorse its assertion—the "moves" distinctive of assertoric linguistic practice; descriptively, because (or so it is plausible) unless participants in the practice for the most part try to respect the norms of warranted assertion which govern it, it is not clear in what the fact could consist that its ingredient sentences have the content which they do.

But now, given the explanatory biconditional link effected by the Disquotational Schema between the claim that a sentence is T and its proper assertoric use, it follows that "T" is likewise, both prescriptively and—in a qualified sense I shall specify in a moment—descriptively, a predicate which is normative of assertoric practice. "T" is prescriptively normative, because any reason to think that a sentence is T may be transferred, across the biconditional, into reason to make or allow the assertoric move which it expresses. And "T" is descriptively normative in the sense that the practices of those for whom warranted assertibility is a descriptive norm are exactly as they would be if they consciously selected the assertoric moves which they were prepared to make or allow in the light of whether or not the sentences involved were T. We already noted the plausible thought that a distinction between warranted and unwarranted assertion must be respected to a substantial extent by actual assertoric practice if assertions are to be determinate in content; accordingly, the biconditional dependence effected by the DS between predication of "T" and warranted assertion ensures that, to that substantial extent, any actual assertoric practice will be just as it would be if T were a self-conscious goal.

In fact, though, the conclusion we ought to draw is stronger than the claim merely that "T" is normative of any assertoric practice. Say that two predicates *coincide* in (positive) normative force with respect to a practice just in case each is normative within the practice and reason to suppose that either predicate characterises a move is reason to suppose that the other characterises it too. Then what we may conclude is that "T" and "warrantedly assertible" so coincide in (positive) normative force. For reason to regard a sentence as warrantedly assertible is, naturally, reason to endorse the assertion which it may be used to effect, and conversely; and reason to endorse an assertion is, by the DS, reason to regard the sentence expressing it as T, and conversely. So reason to regard a sentence as T is reason to regard it as warrantedly assertible, and conversely.[14]

Our finding, then, is that the deflationist is committed to regarding the truth predicate, explained as he proposes, as normative, in the senses characterised, of proper assertoric practice, and indeed as coinciding in normative force with warranted assertibility. And so far that is a finding wholly consonant with deflationism. Since the defining thesis of deflationism is that "true" is merely a device of disquotation—a device for endorsing assertions, which we need only for the purposes of indirect ("Goldbach's Conjecture is true") or compendious ("Everything he says is true") such endorsements—since that is the very essence of the view, a deflationist must of course insist that the only substantial norms operating in assertoric practice are norms of warranted assertibility, and that the truth predicate can indeed mark no independent norm. For were it normatively independent, to predicate "true" of a sentence would be to claim that sentence's satisfaction of a norm distinct from warranted assertion. No room could then remain for the contention that "true" is only grammatically a predicate, whose role is not to attribute a substantial characteristic.

The next step is to reflect that the kind of coincidence in normative force between truth and assertoric warrant which the DS

14. That reflection speaks to the matter of coincidence in *prescriptive* (positive) normative force, but the reader will readily see how to characterise a corresponding idea of coincidence between descriptively normative predicates, and why "T" and "warrantedly assertible" do indeed so coincide.

enjoins is no insurance against their divergence *in extension*. Suppose F and G are so related that, while the only kind of reason we can have for supposing that something is G is that it be F, the reason supplied is a defeasible reason. Then having reason to think that an item is G will involve having reason to think that it is F; and having reason to think it is F will amount, when so far undefeated, to reason to think it is G. Hence, if either predicate is normative with respect to some practice, the two predicates will be normatively coincident with respect to it. But, precisely because an item's being F supplies only a defeasible reason for its being G, space is left for divergence in extension between the two predicates. And not merely is this space exploited in the case of truth and assertoric warrant; it is the DS itself which enforces the split.

This is the second feature of the T-predicate to which deflationism is committed, and this time the commitment, so far from consonant with the general spirit of the account, marks, it seems to me, its demise. Although coincident in normative force in the senses indicated, "T" and "is warrantedly assertible" *have* to be regarded as registering distinct norms—distinct in the precise sense that although aiming at one is, necessarily, aiming at the other, success in the one aim need not be success in the other. So much is indeed part of our ordinary understanding of the notion of truth. But it is also something which any endorsement of the DS, whether in a deflationist spirit or not, entails.

The reason is extremely simple, and has to do with a contrast between the behaviour of "T" and "is warrantedly assertible" which the DS imposes in connection with *negated* sentences. We noted earlier that any suitable substituend for "P" in the DS will be possessed of assertoric content, in whatever sense is imposed by the capacity to feature as the antecedent of a conditional. Now, whatever sense that is, it also ensures, I suggest, that such a substituend will allow of significant negation: wherever "P" is an appropriate substituend, so will be "it is not the case that P". So, substituting the latter for the former in the DS, we have

(i)      "It is not the case that P" is T if and only if it's
         not the case that P.

We may also take it that, given as premises a biconditional and the negation of either of its constituents, we may infer the negation of the other. So it is a direct consequence of the DS itself that

(ii)     It is not the case that P if and only if it is not the case that "P" is T.

So, from (i) and (ii), by transitivity of the biconditional,

(iii)     "It is not the case that P" is T if and only if it is not the case that "P" is T.

Reflect, however, that (iii) must fail, right-to-left, when "is T" is read as "is warrantedly assertible". At least, it must fail for any discourse whose ingredient statements are such that a state of information may be *neutral*—may justify neither their assertion nor their denial. For with respect to such a state of information, and such a statement P, it will be correct to report that it is not the case that P is warrantedly assertible but incorrect to report that the negation of P is warrantedly assertible. Hence, since (iii) holds good for the T-predicate, we have to acknowledge some sort of conceptual distinction between "is T" and "is warrantedly assertible".

Let's be quite clear what sort of distinction. Could we but assume the biconditional

(iv)     "P" is T if and only if "P" is warrantedly assertible,

then, in the presence of (iii), the inference from

It is not the case that "P" is warrantedly assertible

to

"It is not the case that P" is warrantedly assertible,

would of course go through, since its premise would yield

It is not the case that "P" is T,

and its conclusion could be obtained from

"It is not the case that P" is T.

So the DS, coupled with the principle that every statement has a negation, enforces a denial of the biconditional (iv) for all sub-stituends for "P" allowing of neutral states of information. And that, I take it, is tantamount to the finding that there is no general conceptual obstacle to a divergence of extension between the T-predicate and "is warrantedly assertible". So we are forced to recognise that while "is T" and "is warrantedly assertible" are nor-matively coincident, satisfaction of the one norm need not entail satisfaction of the other.

So much is implicit in deflationism. And because deflationism, in holding that, modulo a flourish or two, the truth predicate is merely a device of endorsement of assertions, is thereby committed to the idea that warranted assertibility is the *only* norm operative over assertoric discourse, the finding is, as advertised, that deflationism about truth is an inherently unstable position.[15]

15. What I have here presented seems to me a fundamental and decisive objection to deflationism as classically conceived. Readers of Paul Horwich's book, however, might wonder whether it engages the account of truth advocated there. For Horwich avows that "it is *not* part of the minimalist conception to maintain that truth is not a property" (*Truth,* p. 38, my emphasis), and *contrasts* his view with "the idea . . . that the truth predicate is not used to give descrip-tions or make statements about the thing to which it is applied, but that it is used instead to perform quite different speech acts: endorsing, agreeing, conced-ing, etc." (*Truth,* p. 40). Moreover Horwich argues (*ibid.,* pp. 63ff.) against any form of identification of truth with idealised assertibility, and should there-fore be taken to recognise, presumably, a contrast between truth and simple assertibility. Do not these features of his account effectively acknowledge the principal moral of the argument developed in the text: that, on any view which accepts the DS, there is no option but to regard "true" as ascribing a property to sentences, propositions and thoughts etc., and to regard the property in question as contrasting with warranted assertibility?

The matter deserves a more extended discussion than I shall venture here, but let me swiftly explain why I think Horwich is vulnerable to the argument

However, the result, that truth and warranted assertibility, while normatively coincident, are potentially extensionally divergent, is of course equally implicit in any conception of truth which is prepared to endorse the DS as incorporating something conceptually correct about the nature of truth, even if not as a whole account of the concept. One will not avoid the result if one disagrees with deflationism merely by addition, as it were—by

---

developed. The immediate question is why, in view of these features of it, Horwich regards his account as deflationist at all. On three counts, it seems:

(i) Although he is willing to grant that truth is a property, it is not, for Horwich, a "complex property"—not "an ingredient of reality whose underlying essence will, it is hoped, one day be revealed by philosophical or scientific analysis" (*Truth,* p. 2). There is, for Horwich, nothing to say about what truth really consists in; no real question for, e.g., Correspondence and Coherence accounts to address themselves to. Rather—

(ii) ". . . the truth predicate exists solely for the sake of a certain logical need", to wit, the need to express attitudes to propositions whose content is unspecified and to whole classes or propositions simultaneously (*Truth,* pp. 2–3). This is the familiar consideration about the "Goldbach's Conjecture" and "Everything he said" uses of "true". Horwich is insistent that, but for these constructions, there would be no work for the truth predicate to do. Finally,

(iii) it is possible, he contends, on the basis of a theory containing as axioms all and only "uncontroversial instances of the equivalence schema

(E)      It is true that P if and only if P,
         . . . to explain *all* the facts involving truth" (*ibid.,* p. 7),

where explaining all "facts involving truth" is a matter of giving a systematic account of all legitimate uses of "true". This is not, *per se,* something which, e.g., a Correspondence theorist would need to deny. But Horwich's contention is that (E) encodes a *complete* account of the concept of truth; so the point is, I take it, that since such a theory could be common ground between the classical Correspondence, Coherence and Pragmatist antagonists, there is no genuine further matter for them to dispute—point (i) again.

Horwich's brand of deflationism initially concerns a predicate of propositions, rather than sentences, with claim (iii) about the Equivalence Schema supplanting the part more usually assigned to the DS. But it should be evident enough that the combination of claims (i)–(iii) will fall to essentially the objection developed in the text, since that objection can as well be developed with the Equivalence Schema as the centre of attention as with the DS. The explanatory claim, (iii), about (E) will entail, by reasoning exactly parallel to adding substantial, non-deflationary further features to the characterisation of truth. Since anything that aspires to be a competitive account of truth will presumably respect the DS, our finding has a claim to generality.

Why does it seem that any competitive account of truth must respect the DS? Relatedly, why just that starting point for the deflationary conception? The answer, I suggest, is that standing just behind the DS is the basic, platitudinous connection of assertion and truth: asserting a proposition—a Fregean thought—is claiming that it is true. The connection is partially constitutive of

---

that developed in the text, that truth and assertibility coincide in normative force with respect to the acceptance and assertion of propositions; and an endorsement of (E) will likewise entail that "it is not the case that" and "it is true that" will commute as propositional operators—which is not the situation with "it is not the case that" and "it is assertible that". Point (iii) forces an admission, therefore, that the truth predicate registers a property of propositions which, while normatively coincident with assertibility, is potentially extensionally divergent from it. Since this norm would be in operation anyway, even if we never went in for the kind of construction which generates the "logical need" adverted to in point (ii), the contention, that meeting that need is *all* the truth predicate accomplishes for us, is implicitly inconsistent with (iii); on the contrary, the predicate serves to express a basic norm of propositional thought and expression. And once that much is granted, claim (i) looks merely dogmatic: any normative property may or may not allow illuminating analysis—it remains to be argued whether, or why, there is, or is not, scope for further philosophical insight in this case. The correctness of (iii) imports no presumption on the matter.

Even so I would hope that Horwich might recognise in the minimalism about truth advocated in this study an account kindred to the spirit of his own. At any rate, we are agreed in the root idea that truth is not *intrinsically* a metaphysically substantial notion and that nothing qualifies an expression as a truth predicate beyond its satisfaction of certain basic platitudes, like (E) or the DS. The most important difference, I think, concerns the space for a *pluralism* about truth provided by the account I want to propose. Horwich's ambition is to say the right thing about a single truth predicate assumed to be operative everywhere. However, if the only essential properties of a truth predicate are *formal*—a matter of its use complying with certain very general axioms (platitudes)—then such predicates may or may not, in different areas of discourse, have a varying *substance,* a substance which may *sometimes* carry the kind of "metaphysical" payload against which Horwich sets his own account, and sometimes not. But more about that in due course.

the concepts of assertion and of truth, and it entails the validity of the analogue of the DS for propositional contents (sometimes called the Equivalence Schema):

It is true that P if and only if P,

The DS proper—the schema for sentences—is then an immediate consequence, provided we have determined that a sentence is to count as true just in case the proposition it expresses is true, and are so reading the quotation marks that each relevant instance of

"P" says that P

holds good.

The features of truth which we have elicited from the DS for sentences are thus ultimately traceable to a pair of platitudes: first that asserting a proposition is claiming that it is true, and second that every proposition has a significant negation. It is these which ultimately ensure that truth and warranted assertibility coincide in normative force but are potentially extensionally distinct—at least, they do so in the case of any class of propositions which allow the possibility of neutral states of information. The truth predicate for sentences merely inherits these features, once it is introduced in the natural and obvious way noted.

## IV. Minimalism

All of this ensures that nothing can deserve the title of a truth predicate unless it coincides in normative force with warranted assertibility but is potentially divergent in extension. But, conversely, I now want to canvass sympathy for the view that, provided they originate in the right kind of way, these features also *suffice*. I want to commend, in other words, a kind of *minimalism* about truth—a species of deflationism, if you will, but unencumbered by the classical deflationist's claim that truth is not a substantial property. The minimalist view is that when a predicate has been shown to have the relevant features, and to have them for the right reasons, there is then no further question about the propriety of regarding it as a truth predicate. Minimalism is thus at least in principle open to the possibility of a *pluralist* view of truth: there may be a variety of notions, operative within distinct discourses, which pass the test.

To this suggestion, however, there is a natural and immediate objection. It is of the essence of truth, the objection says, that true propositions, or sentences, are *representations* of aspects of reality. So much is the basis for all correspondence accounts of truth, and whatever they go on to add to it, it too is hardly more than a platitude. Yet both classical deflationism, and the sort of minimalism just prefigured, leave it quite out of account.

The answer is that they do not. Deflationism (as well as minimalism) has the resources to accommodate what is genuinely platitudinous about the idea of truth as correspondence, though the way in which the accommodation is effected will hardly satisfy the objector (and the question how properly to formulate the residual dissatisfaction will be of great importance to us in later chapters). Let it be indeed a platitude that

> "P" is true if and only if "P" corresponds to the facts.

Is anything lost by paraphrasing this as

(CP)    "P" is true if and only if things are as "P" says they are?

Presumably not (so long at least as we stick to platitudes and do not go in for more fine-grained interpretation of the idea of correspondence). But then reflect that, wherever we may affirm that

> "P" says that P,

it follows that

> Things are as "P" says they are if and only if P.

Put the last together with the DS and, hey presto, the correspondence platitude ensues!

A likely objection is that all this brings out is that

(CP)    "P" is true if and only if things are as "P" says they are, is not after all an acceptable paraphrase of the correspondence platitude. But then what is? A comparison is instructive here with Paul Horwich's treatment of essentially the same issue. Horwich argues, likewise, that deflationism has no difficulty in accommodating the "correspondence" aspect of the concept of truth. [16] But what he considers is the stronger-looking formulation typified by

(CP⁺)     "Snow is white" is true *because* snow is white,

and the objection may continue that this explanatory formulation does indeed echo an essential aspect of the ordinary concept of truth, so that consideration of the weaker (CP) is not to the purpose. This changes nothing, of course, if Horwich's attempt to make a home for (CP⁺) succeeds. But that seems not to be so. (CP⁺), Horwich argues, is perfectly consistent with deflationism because

> In mapping out the relations of explanatory dependence between phenomena we naturally and properly grant ultimate explanatory priority to such things as basic laws and the initial conditions of the universe. From these facts we deduce, and thereby explain, why, for example
>
> Snow is white.
>
> And only then, given the [deflationary] theory, do we deduce, and thereby explain, why
>
> "Snow is white" is true.
>
> Therefore, from the [deflationary] point of view, [the claim that "snow is white" is true *because* snow is white] is fine. We can be perfectly comfortable with the idea that each truth is made true by the existence of a corresponding fact. [17]

This train of thought, it may well seem, is just beside the point. The challenge was to legitimate the idea of a state of affairs (snow's being white) being the *source* of the truth of the sentence "snow is white"—the idea of a state of affairs transmitting a truth value, as it were, across a substantial relation, the converse of correspon-

16. Horwich, *Truth*, chapter 7, §35.
17. *Truth*, pp. 111–112.

dence. But all that Horwich points to is the possibility of explaining why snow is white in terms of basic physical laws and the initial conditions of the universe, and then transferring that explanation, across the Disquotational Schema, into an explanation of why "snow is white" is true. That is, evidently enough, not to explain why "snow is white" is true in terms of *snow's being white;* it is rather (quite a different thing) to explain why "snow is white" is true in terms of the physical laws and initial conditions which also explain snow's being white. The challenge, however, was to provide an account of the explanatory relationship adverted to by

"Snow is white" is true *because* snow is white,

—a relationship which would obtain, the objector will conceive, even if there was no possible physical explanation of snow's being white at all.

This is fair comment. But, as the alert reader will have spotted, there is no difficulty, once CP is secured, in saving (CP$^+$) for  minimalism (or deflationism) as well. For, given that "P" says that P, the question why things are as "P" says they are is quite properly—if rather trivially—answered by citing its being the case that P. Whence, given (CP), the truth of "P" can quite properly be explained by citing the fact that P.

The moral is that deflationism, and hence minimalism, have no difficulty in accommodating intuitions about the relationship between truth and correspondence so long as doing so is held to require no more than demonstrating a right to the *phrases* by which those intuitions are characteristically expressed. Of course, there may be an intended further substantive content which minimalism cannot so easily make its own. Again, that's a matter for later attention.

I promised a notion of truth aptitude whose applicability within a contested discourse could be neutral ground between realists and anti-realists. As a first approximation, then, my suggestion is that since any predicate should be accounted a truth predicate which has just the features highlighted by minimalism, any discourse may count as truth-apt on which it is possible to define a predicate with just those features. And the condition for the definability of such a predicate is merely that the discourse be one of assertion, that its utterances be governed by norms of warranted assertibility. That will ensure that they have the right kind of content to allow of embedding as both antecedent and consequent of conditionals, and hence that we can lay down the DS as (partially) characteristic of the truth predicate for the sentences of the discourse. But it will also ensure that they possess significant negations, and hence— only assuming that neutral states of information are a possibility— will entail that the truth predicate so characterised has the features which minimalism regards as both necessary and sufficient.

But need any of this provoke a proponent of the third anti-realist paradigm—the paradigm of expressivism, or "quasi-realism"—to disagree? In effect, I have argued that there is a notion of truth aptitude which is carried in train by possession of assertoric content, and have highlighted features of the notion of truth for which assertions are *eo ipso* apt which are destructive of the classical deflationist line. But I have so far ventured nothing about possession of assertoric content as such; in particular, nothing at variance with the suggestion, integral to the expressivist tradition, that possession of genuine assertoric content is a relatively *deep* feature of the sentences of a discourse, which its overt syntax can serve to mask, or merely to simulate. The final ingredient in any conception of truth and truth aptitude which can be common ground between realist and anti-realist is that this is not so.

An analogy may help. Elsewhere[18] I have argued that Frege's platonism about number is best interpreted as based on the view that an expression's candidacy to refer to an object is a matter of its syntax: that once it has been settled that a class of expressions function as singular terms by syntactic criteria, there can be no further question about whether they succeed in objectual reference which can be raised by someone who is prepared to allow that appropriate contexts in which they do so feature are true. There is, that is to say, no *deep* notion of singular reference such that an

18. In *Frege's Conception of Numbers as Objects* (Aberdeen: Aberdeen University Press, 1983; revised and augmented 2nd edition to be published by Basil Blackwell, 1993). See also my "Field and Fregean Platonism", in A. D. Irvine, ed., *Physicalism in Mathematics* (Dordrecht: Kluwer, 1990).

expression which has all the surface syntactic features of a Fregean proper name, and features in, say, true contexts of (by surface syntactic criteria) predication and identity, may nevertheless fail to be in the market for genuine—"deep"—reference. So too, in the present context, the claim must be there is no notion of genuine—deep—assertoric content, such that a discourse which exhibits whatever degree of discipline (there are firmly acknowledged standards of proper and improper use of its ingredient sentences) and which has all the overt syntactic trappings of assertoric content (resources for—apparent—conditionalisation, negation, embedding within propositional attitudes, and so on)—no notion of genuine assertion such that a discourse with all this may nevertheless fail to be in the business of expressing genuine assertions. Rather, if things are in all these surface respects as if assertions are being made, then so they are.

On reflection, it is possible to be a little less combative. It is not necessary to insist that there is *no* suitable notion of deep assertoric content. It suffices that there is, at any rate, at least a more superficial one, carried by surface syntactic features; and that a minimal truth predicate is definable on any surface-assertoric discourse. If we can go on to explain what, after they have agreed that claims about what is funny are apt for truth and falsity in the minimalist sense, could still be at issue between realists and antirealists about the comic, perhaps that will supply a sense in which minimally truth-apt claims can yet fail to be *deeply* assertoric. But I don't think that will be the happiest way of expressing the significance of the points of debate which will later concern us.

## DISCUSSION NOTES

*1. Surely the nerve of deflationism about truth is the contention that truth is not a property in this sense: there is no single thing which true sentences have in common. To say that "Grass is green" is true iff grass is green, "Snow is white" is true iff snow is white and so on is no commitment to the idea that there is some one property which "Grass is green" and "Snow is white" share just in case grass is green and snow is white. How is this point touched by the "inflationary" argument?*

Deflationism is actually something of a potpourri—compare footnote 15 on Horwich's version—and it is a moot point what should be regarded as its "nerve". The inflationary argument takes the crucial contentions to be two:

(a) that "true" functions purely as a device for endorsing assertions, beliefs and so on—a device of which we have explicit need only in order to express attitudes to sentences/propositions whose content is unspecified or to whole classes or sentences/propositions simultaneously, and which therefore registers no norm distinct from justified endorsability—that is, assertibility;

(b) that the DS incorporates (all but) a complete explanation of the meaning of the word.

This package is refuted by the reflection that—assuming the inflationary argument is good at all—we can run it for *each instance* of the DS. The argument shows that the truth predicate defined via the DS for any particular sentence is normative over the assertoric use of that sentence, indeed coincides in normative force with "is warrantedly assertible" as applied to that sentence, but is potentially extensionally divergent from "is warrantedly assertible". So the consideration whether or not "Snow is white" is true, while a normative consideration over that sentence's proper use, is not the same as the consideration whether it is warrantedly assertible, and verdicts on the two matters may diverge. Since (b) entails that a norm governs the use of "Snow is white" which is distinct from assertoric warrant—a norm expressed by the truth predicate as applied to that sentence, and since (a) entails that "true" is just a device of indirect assertoric endorsement, and so cannot register an independent such norm, (a) and (b) are inconsistent.

Still, it seems right that it does not directly follow that the additional norm recorded by "true" as applied to "Snow is white" is the same as that it records when applied to "Grass is green". But consider: it is only because "Grass is green" says that grass is green that it is true just in case grass is green; likewise it is only because "Snow is white" says that snow is white that it is true just in case snow is white. Given only an additional premise of the form: "P" says that P, each instance of the DS is recoverable from

(DS*)        "P" is true ↔ (∃!P){"P" says that P & P},

(where the "(∃!P)" quantifier is, of course, substitutional and the quoted occurrence of "P" is not within its scope). But DS* is a perfectly uniform account of "true", applicable to all its predications on whole sentences. If the deflationist accepts it, mustn't he accept that there *is* some one property which "Grass is green" and "Snow is white" share just in case grass is green and snow is white? And if not, why not? How does it misdescribe the concept of truth?

*2. What if the deflationist proposes (DS\*) in the first place, rather than the DS proper? Can the inflationary argument still be run?*

Presumably so. The argument that "is true" and "is warrantedly assertible" coincide in (positive prescriptive) normative force depended not on the DS having primitive explanatory status but only on its being something of which an understanding of the truth predicate ought to lead one to accept each particular instance. That is safeguarded if it is DS* which is primitively explanatory. What the coincidence requires is (i) that any reason to accept that "P" is true is reason to accept the claim that P and vice versa; and (ii) that any reason to accept the claim that P is reason to accept that "P" is warrantedly assertible, and vice versa. Clearly, the latter can hold only for one who knows that "P" says that P. But given that knowledge, (DS*) as noted entails the corresponding instance of the DS—and hence ensures (i).

Likewise, the argument for the potential extensional divergence of "is true" and "is warrantedly assertible" just required the *correctness* of instances of the DS (plus the relevant properties of negation), and so is safeguarded by any account in which the DS is sustained, primitively or otherwise.

*3. Isn't what the inflationary argument really shows merely this: that no one who thinks that the only norm operative over assertoric discourse is warranted assertibility can accept both the DS <u>and</u> the classical logic of negation?*

It is perfectly correct that the deflationist has the formal option of blocking the argument by tampering with the ordinary logic of negation. But the changes called for will be very radical. The step that has to be blocked is that from the DS to

> It is not the case that P if and only if it is not
> the case that "P" is T,

which is an instance of the principle

$$\frac{A \leftrightarrow B}{\sim\!A \leftrightarrow \sim\!B},$$

whose validity depends only on that of modus tollens—ultimately reductio ad absurdum—and conditional proof. The claim will therefore have to be that these absolutely basic and intuitive principles, uncontested in both classical and intuitionistic sentential logic, are nevertheless implicitly at odds with the correct—deflationist—understanding of the concept of truth.

# 2. Minimal Truth, Internal Realism and Superassertibility

## I. Minimalism (Continued)

The previous chapter began to outline *minimalist* conceptions of truth and assertoric content—"minimalist" in the sense that acknowledging that a discourse is possessed of assertoric content, and indeed that its practitioners frequently hit the truth, when truth is so conceived, is to be something which is neutral on the preferability of a broadly realist or anti-realist view of the discourse in question. We saw that the minimalist view of truth may be elicited from reflection on the distinctive thesis of *deflationism* about truth, that the content of the truth predicate is (all but) fully explained by the role it plays in the Disquotational Schema. This contention imposes on the truth predicate both a coincidence in (positive prescriptive) normative force with warranted assertibility, and a potential extensional divergence from it; and according to the minimalism proposed, a predicate's possessing these two features is not merely necessary if it is to be defensible to regard it as a truth predicate, but is also, when they arise in the right kind of way, sufficient. We noted the corollary that any truth predicate registers a norm for assertoric discourse distinct from warranted assertibility. Since it is essential to deflationism—its most basic and distinctive contention—that "true" is merely a device for endorsing assertions, and hence can import no norms over assertoric discourse distinct from warranted assertibility, it follows that deflationism is an inherently unstable view.

We need now to enlarge on this minimalism, and to qualify it somewhat. It is not, to begin with, most illuminatingly represented as deflationism purified of an instability, since the deflationist tradition itself stands in need of diagnosis and motivation. The root idea, I suggest, is that we should not look for more of a truth predicate than its compliance with a certain set of very general, very intuitive principles—indeed, a set of *platitudes:* the platitudes, for instance,

> that to assert is to present as true;
> that any truth-apt content has a significant negation which is
>   likewise truth-apt;
> that to be true is to correspond to the facts;
> that a statement may be justified without being true, and vice
>   versa;

—as well as, perhaps, certain platitudes linking the truth values of differently tensed statements envisaged as uttered at appropriately different times, and maybe others. If an interpretation of "true" satisfies these platitudes, there is, for minimalism, no further, metaphysical question whether it captures a concept worth regarding as truth. And my suggestion was, in effect, that we can tidy up a little: that the key platitudes involved are those connecting truth with assertion and negation. At any rate, it is they that underlie, in the presence of certain ordinarily quite uncontentious suppositions,[1] the correctness of the Disquotational Schema,

1. Specifically, we need to suppose
   (i) that the Equivalence Schema,

   > It is true that P iff P,

   may validly be inferred from the truth/assertion platitude (on which matter, see discussion note 1);
   (ii) that we may affirm each relevant instance of the schema,

   > "P" says that P,

   (iii) that a sentence may be characterised as true just in case the proposition it expresses is true,
   (iv) the validity of modus tollens, and
   (v) that it is harmless to characterise "'P' corresponds to the facts" as, e.g., "Things are as 'P' says they are".

the platitude about correspondence, and the contrast between truth and warranted assertion (justification). Maybe matters should be more complicated; perhaps there are other, independent platitudes that should be reckoned with—I shall take note of a couple of possible candidates in due course. But I propose that, *pro tem* at least, we work with the view that the proper minimalist account will enshrine satisfaction of the platitudes about assertion and negation as both necessary and sufficient for a predicate defined over a particular discourse to qualify as a truth predicate for it.

Now, what follows from this way of looking at the matter is merely that any class of sentences with *assertoric content* will sustain the definition of a predicate with the relevant features—a satisfier of the platitudes, and hence coincident in positive normative force with, but potentially extensionally divergent from, warranted assertibility. So there's no commitment so far to anything strictly inconsistent with either the error-theoretic or expressivist anti-realist paradigms. There is nothing inconsistent with the error-theoretic paradigm, because, for all that's so far been said, moral, or aesthetic, or mathematical discourse may be made out to fail even of minimal truth. It's true that error theorists typically have tended to work in terms of metaphysically rich notions of truth, but it is not so clear that they must. And minimalism does after all allow, in contrast with deflationism, that truth is a genuine property—to possess it is to meet a normative constraint distinct from assertoric warrant—which warranted assertions are therefore not guaranteed to possess. So minimalism does not immediately shut down all room for the sort of charge of massive mistake which is the error theorist's stock in trade.

And that remains true, even after the further move is made which *does* bring minimalism into conflict with the expressivist genre of anti-realism. Clearly, there need be no conflict with the expressivist line provided the notion of assertoric content used in the characterisation of minimal truth aptitude is allowed to mark a *potentially covert* characteristic of a discourse; provided, that is, the question whether a class of declarative sentences possesses assertoric content is not immediately settled just by the reflection that these sentences satisfy certain surface constraints of syntax and discipline—that they are subjected to communally acknowledged standards of proper use, and allow the kinds of embedding, par excellence as the antecedents of conditionals, with which assertoric content is distinctively associated.[2] But a theorist drawn to minimalism will reject this idea. For such a theorist, no more can be asked of a purported conditional statement, for instance, than that it should *overtly* behave like a conditional statement. Such behaviour need involve no more than, say, that a commitment to its antecedent is treated as a commitment to its consequent when the statement itself is accepted; and that the statement itself is regarded as justified when an acceptance of its antecedent is taken to enjoin acceptance of the consequent. There is no well-conceived deeper notion of a genuine conditional nor, correspondingly, any well-conceived deeper notion of assertoric content which goes along with the capacity to feature as the antecedent of a conditional.

No doubt a fuller and more precise characterisation of the surface syntactic features which are to drive the minimalised notion of assertoric content would be possible and, in some contexts, desirable. But I do not think one is needed for our present purposes. We have no difficulty in recognising conditionals and negation, for instance, recurring across all the regions of discourse about which the realist and anti-realist might wish to debate. Whatever it is that we note in recognising that recurrence, *those* are the surface features which tie into the idea of assertoric content which the minimalist proposes to deploy.

So minimalism turns its back on the expressivist anti-realist tradition. For the minimalist, there is simply nothing to achieve by the kind of syntactic-reconstructive manoeuvres which will be central to any expressivist proposal which is sufficiently sharp to admit of focussed debate. But the error-theoretic paradigm is not so easily discarded. Mightn't moral discourse, for instance, systematically fail to deserve even of a truth predicate whose signifi-

2. Indeed, even the claim that such syntactic potentialities do carry assertoric content in train can be granted by an expressivist, provided she is in turn prepared to insist on a contrast between, for instance, *genuine* conditionals (say, "If it rains tomorrow, the visit will be cancelled") and *merely apparent* ones (perhaps "If you behave badly, the visit will be cancelled")—a distinction which would have to depend, in its turn, on the "deep" status of the antecedents involved.

cant predicability of its statements is settled just by their minimally assertoric character? I will return to the matter.

## II. Minimal Truth and Internal Realism

A likely complaint about this approach is that it simply fails to
provide any substantive account of what truth *is*. It cannot, of
course, escape this obligation, as deflationism could, by pleading
that, by its lights, there is nothing substantive to say. For
minimalism differs from deflationism precisely by granting that
truth *is* a real feature of statements and beliefs—that "true"
expresses a real norm governing statement making and the formation of belief. Yet if all we are told is that truth and warranted
assertibility, while coincident in (positive, prescriptive) normative
force, are potentially extensionally divergent, we have certainly
been told too little to *identify* truth. And matters seem hardly
improved if we focus instead on the parent platitudes which constitute those features' ultimate source—the platitudes that to assert
is to present as true and that any assertoric content has a negation
which is also assertoric in content. Doesn't there have to be more
to say? And what reason is there to be confident that, when it is
said, the minimalist conception will not, as it were, "de-
minimalise" in its turn?

This line of objection betrays an important misunderstanding.
It presupposes that minimalism is offering an *account* of the
meaning of "true", in the traditional sense in which giving an
account of the meaning of a word involves provision of an
illuminating *analysis* of the concept it expresses—an account, in
this case, of what truth most fundamentally consists in. Traditional—"correspondence" and "coherence"—theories did hope for
such an account. But minimalism has no such ambition. Rather, a
proposal is being made in a spirit close to what I take to be that
of Wittgenstein's insistence in the *Tractatus* that *object* and *proposition* are *formal* concepts.[3] The proposal is simply that any predicate

3. *Tractatus* 4.126–4.1273. The same spirit is at work in the remarks, in
*Philosophical Investigations* §§134–137, on the relations of the concepts of truth
and proposition.

that exhibits certain very general features qualifies, just on that account, as a truth predicate. That is quite consistent with acknowledging that there may, perhaps *must* be more to say about the content of any predicate that does have these features. But it is also consistent with acknowledging that there is a prospect of *pluralism*—that the more that there is to say may well vary from discourse to discourse—and that whatever may remain to be said, it will not concern any *essential* features of truth. The essential features are exhausted, rather, by the platitudes.

The minimal platitudes do, however, have some cutting edge. In order to provide an illustration, and to explore a little further the prospects for pluralism opened up by the minimalist conception, we do well now to consider a well-known proposal of Hilary Putnam's. In *Reason, Truth and History*[4] Putnam too discounts any suggestion that truth might *be* warranted assertibility (what he calls "rational acceptability"). But his grounds are different from those we noted in connection with negation and the "inflationary" argument. Putnam is impressed by two considerations: first, that truth is, plausibly, timeless *(stable)*, whereas warranted assertibility varies as a function of state of information ("truth is supposed to be a property of a statement that cannot be lost, whereas justification can be lost"[5]); and second, that assertoric warrant is, whereas truth is not, a matter of *degree.* He responds as follows

> What this shows, in my opinion, is not that the externalist (or metaphysical realist) view is right after all [in holding truth to be a radically non-epistemic notion], but that truth is an *idealisation* of rational acceptability. We speak as if there were such things as epistemically ideal conditions, and we call a statement "true" if it would be justified under such conditions. "Epistemically ideal conditions", of course, are like "frictionless planes": we cannot really attain epistemically ideal conditions, or even be absolutely certain that we have come sufficiently close to them. But frictionless planes cannot really be attained either,

4. Hilary Putnam, *Reason, Truth and History* (Cambridge: Cambridge University Press, 1981).

5. *Ibid.*, p. 55.

and yet talk of frictionless planes has "cash value" because we can approximate them to a very high degree of approximation.[6]

Putnam goes on to disclaim that he is offering any strict definition of truth, rather than merely an "informal elucidation". Nevertheless, even if only in the spirit of an informal elucidation, Putnam has proposed an equivalence *(Putnam's Equivalence)* here: that

> P is true if and only if P would be justified
> under ideal epistemic circumstances.

Does this proposal, and its contrast with the metaphysical realist conception of truth, provide an illustration of how accounts of truth can be in substantial competition while each remaining faithful to the formal minimalist core?

There is a difficulty about an affirmative answer. Putnam imposes what he calls a convergence requirement on his conception of truth—that there be no statement such that both it and its negation are assertible under epistemically ideal circumstances.[7] This is to be distinguished, of course, from any requirement of *completeness*. The requirement of completeness would be that, for each statement, *either* it *or* its negation must be justified under epistemically ideal circumstances. There seems no good reason to impose any such completeness requirement—no particular reason why all questions which are empirical in content should become decidable under ideal conditions. Indeed, to take seriously the indeterminacies postulated by contemporary physical theory is to consider that there is reason to the contrary. We can expect that an internal realist would want to suspend the principle of Bivalence for statements which would find themselves beached at the limit of ideal enquiry in this way, and ought consequently, one would imagine, to want to suspend it in any case, failing an assurance that no statements are actually in that situation.

6. *Ibid.*

7. Superfluously, presumably, since a statement does not count as justified, in any sense that concerns us, unless the case in its favour dominates anything that counts in favour of its negation.

So what is the difficulty? That there is, apparently, a simple inconsistency within the triad consisting of Putnam's Equivalence, the claim that the notion of truth it concerns complies with the minimal platitudes, and the admission that certain statements may remain undecidable under epistemically ideal circumstances, neither they nor their negations being justified. For, as we have seen, the minimal platitudes impose the standard Negation Equivalence:

> "It is not the case that P" is true if and only if it
> is not the case that "P" is true.

And to allow that, even under ideal epistemic circumstances, we might yet be in a state of information which provided warrant neither for P nor for its negation would force us to reject the right-to-left ingredient in the Negation Equivalence when "true" is interpreted in accordance with Putnam's Equivalence. In other words: it seems that ideal epistemic circumstances cannot be neutral both on a statement and its negation if to assert a statement is to present it as true, if every assertoric content has a negation which is an assertoric content, and truth is warrantedness under epistemically ideal circumstances.

Simple though this train of thought is, it provides, on the face of it, a devastating blow to Putnam's informal elucidation. Leave on one side the obvious difficulties occasioned by the undecidability of mathematical examples like, say, the generalised continuum hypothesis. Surely it is not true a priori even of empirical statements that each would be decidable—confirmable or disconfirmable—under ideal epistemic circumstances. But the minimal platitudes, for their part, presumably hold true a priori. So *if* Putnam's informal elucidation were a priori correct—as, if it is correct at all, it has to be—it would have to be a priori that if a statement failed to be justified under ideal epistemic circumstances, its negation would be justified; and this is just the thing, it seems, that cannot be a priori. Invited conclusion: Putnam's principle incorporates a mistaken a priori claim about the concept of truth, and is hence mistaken as an informal elucidation. Internal realist truth cannot be guaranteed to satisfy the minimal platitudes, and its fittingness to rank as a truth predicate is therefore open to serious question.

In fact, matters are worse: a simple extension of the argument seems to tell not just against Putnam's Equivalence but against any attempt to represent truth as essentially evidentially constrained. A semantic anti-realist may, unlike Putnam, content himself with a one-way principle, for instance (Epistemic Constraint),

(EC)     If P is true, then evidence is available that it is so,

yet still be posed an embarrassment by the argument. For if no evidence is available that P, then, contraposing on EC, he ought to allow that it is not the case that P is true; whence, by the Negation Equivalence, its negation must count as true. So, in the presence even of a one-way epistemic constraint, the unattainability of evidence for a statement is bound, it appears, to confer truth on, and hence (via EC) to ensure the availability of evidential support for its negation—contrary to what, someone might very well think, the anti-realist could and should admit, namely, that some statements may be such that no evidence bearing upon them is available either way. Indeed, how do we explain the semantic anti-realist's characteristic refusal to allow the unrestricted validity of the principle of Bivalence unless it is based on precisely that admission, coupled with the insistence that truth is evidentially constrained?

What room does a semantic anti-realist have for manoeuvre here? We can take it that—unless he decides to off-load the notion of truth entirely—there is no denying the connection between asserting and claiming true. Maybe trouble might somehow be found for the move from that connection to the Disquotational Schema, and thence to the Negation Equivalence. But the prospects do not look bright.[8] What is needed is, rather, a way to reconcile the Negation Equivalence with an insistence that truth is evidentially constrained and the admission that not every issue can be guaranteed to be decidable, even under epistemically ideal circumstances. But is there any scope for such a reconciliation?

8. However, see this chapter's discussion note 1.

Yes, there is. There can be no denying that the Negation Equivalence commits someone who endorses EC to allowing:

(A)        If no evidence is available for P, then evidence is
           available for its negation.

And of course it's extremely easy to hear that as tantamount to the admission that evidence is, in principle, available either for affirming P or denying it. But there is a suppressed premise in that turn of thought: the premise, precisely, that

.

(B)        Either evidence is available for P or it is not

—an instance of the law of excluded middle. Classically, of course, the conditional, (A), is an equivalent of the disjunction

(C)        Either evidence is available for P or evidence is
           available for its negation.

But the proof of the equivalence depends on the instance of the law of excluded middle, (B). If we may not assume that evidence either is or is not available for an arbitrary statement, then the convertibility of lack of evidence for a particular statement into evidence for its negation, demanded by the Negation Equivalence when truth is evidentially constrained, need not impose (C)—and so need not be in contradiction with the a priori unwarrantability of the claim that the scales of in principle available evidence must tilt, sooner or later, one way or the other, between each statement and its negation.

## III. Two Corollaries: Revisionism and the Characterisation of Negation

If this is right, two consequences should be striking for anyone interested in the foundations of intuitionism and in semantic anti-realism generally. First, it is essential to this way with the difficulty that it is the *law of excluded middle* which should not be assertible in the relevant instance. It would not turn the trick merely to reject the associated instance of the principle of Bivalence. If

(B)        Either evidence is available for P or it is not

is unrestrictedly assertible, whether on a classical semantic basis or not, the argument will still go through and the embarrassment will recur.[9] It would therefore seem, unless some other way of blocking the argument is found, that—contrary to what I myself have argued in the past—the thesis of EC, that truth is essentially evidentially constrained, *must* enjoin a revision of classical logic, one way or another, for all discourses where there is no guarantee that evidence is available, at least in principle, to decide between each statement of the discourse concerned and its negation.

The second consequence is that when truth is essentially evidentially constrained, evidence that there is no evidence for P becomes evidence that it is not the case that P is true, and hence, across the Negation Equivalence, is directly transmissible into evidence for P's negation. Now for the mathematical Intuitionists, the negation of a mathematical statement is taken as proved just in case we have a proof that any (constructive) proof of the original statement would lead to contradiction. The natural interpretation of that understanding is that a proof of the negation of a statement is any proof of the impossibility of constructive proof of the original; and the natural generalisation of that proposal to statements which do not admit of proof, but merely of defeasible evidence, is that evidence for the negation of a statement is, again, essentially evidence that no evidence is available for the statement. This interpretation of negation is liable to seem, at best, somewhat forced. But if what I've said is right—if the Negation Equivalence is indeed imposed by mere platitudes connecting truth, assertion and negation—then the thesis that truth is everywhere an evidentially constrained notion *imposes* this general type of account of negation.

9. A qualification is needed here to allow for the case where the disjunction is assertible, but on grounds which somehow do not allow it to sustain reasoning by cases (VE); the obvious point is that in this case we have a revision of ordinary inferential practice anyway.

There is simply no option of generalising intuitionistic mathematical negation in other, intuitively more natural ways.

An application of this general form of response to the original problem is, of course, available not just to an EC theorist but to Putnam's internal realist also. The internal realist can grant that the negation of a statement is true, that is, is confirmed under ideal epistemic circumstances, just in case the original statement is not so confirmed, yet still avoid commitment to the claim that one of each pair of a statement and its negation is thus ideally confirmable. The commitment can be avoided by refusal to endorse the claim that each statement either is or is not confirmable under ideal circumstances. But what is interesting is that (so far as I can see, at least) it is *only* if the theorist is prepared to follow that line that Putnam's "informal elucidation" can avoid running into collision with the minimal platitudes and our manifest lack of any a priori guarantee that all intelligible empirical questions must ultimately succumb to empirical theorising.

In short, Putnam's claim to have elucidated a *truth* predicate—a predicate complying with the minimal constraints—must rest on a willingness to undertake broadly intuitionistic revisions. And the same will go for any epistemically constrained conception of truth, unless we are somehow assured a priori that for each statement in the range with which we are concerned, either it or its negation possesses the constraining property.

## IV. Superassertibility

Provided this way of surmounting the difficulty is accepted, Putnam's proposal remains in the field as one possible way in which a predicate satisfying the minimal constraints on truth may be constructed by idealisation out of assertibility. But satisfaction of the Negation Equivalence is not, of course, the end of the matter. And even if we can be persuaded that Putnam's notion does indeed pass muster as a truth predicate, there is cause for concern about the character of the idealisation which it would seem to involve.

As we noted, Putnam's intention was that truth, as he informally elucidates it, is, in contrast to warrant, to be a stable prop-

erty of propositions across time and a property which is absolute—
that is, which is not applicable in varying degree. Plainly, this
intention can be fulfilled only if to have warrant for a proposition
under "epistemically ideal circumstances" involves having a case
for it which *cannot be defeated* (else we wouldn't have stability) *or
improved* (else we wouldn't have absoluteness) *by any further information.* And the only way of ensuring that both points are met would
seem to be to require that circumstances count as epistemically
ideal with respect to a particular statement just in case no further
information relevant to it exists to be had.

The force of that idea obviously depends on what "relevant"
should mean in such a context. In fact, though, it is difficult to
see that the term can impose any real restriction at all. For, as is
very familiar, warrant is a highly systematic—holistic—property
of beliefs: the status of a body of information as support for a
particular belief turns not simply on the character of the information and the content of the belief but on what beliefs are held as
background. A flash of grey glimpsed in the woods may be evidence of the presence of a squirrel, if you take yourself to be in
New Jersey, say, but evidence of a wood pigeon, if you take yourself to be in Scotland. It is no exaggeration to say that any piece
of information may, in the context of an appropriate epistemic
background, be relevant to any particular belief. How, in consequence, are we to understand the idea of possessing *all* information
relevant to a particular proposition? Doesn't it just have to mean:
possessing *all empirical information,* period?

Putnam's internalism is, of course, usually regarded as incorporating exactly this idea: the Peircean idea that truth is what is
justified at an *ideal limit* of enquiry, when all empirical information
is in. To be sure, Putnam's Equivalence may seem to say rather
less; and indeed the discussion in *Reason, Truth and History* is
inexplicit on the point. Putnam himself has protested against a
Peircean reading of his discussion.[10] But what we have just seen is,

10. See the preface to his collected essays, *Realism with a Human Face,* ed.
James Conant (Cambridge, Mass.: Harvard University Press, 1990). Readers
familiar with Putnam's text will note, however, that the gloss(es) there offered
on "epistemically ideal circumstances" won't ensure the stability and absolute-

in effect, that if truth is to be both stable and absolute, then its identification with warrantedness under epistemically ideal circumstances pre-empts any 'other conception of what such circumstances are. Yet the notion of a state of information which comprises *all* information relevant to any empirical hypothesis is far from obviously the kind of harmless idealisation of the states of information which we occupy, day by date, in the way that, to use Putnam's own example, frictionlessness harmlessly idealises ordinary mechanical conditions. Let me give just one reason for this. We understand what it would be for a mechanical system to operate under conditions of frictionlessness just to the extent that the laws of mechanics issue in determinate assignments to other parameters on the assumption of zero friction. To that extent, the hypothesis that—*per impossible*—a particular system was frictionless might well allow of experimental corroboration. By contrast, it is hard to see how a subject who somehow accomplished a Peircean state of comprehensive empirical information, could have any intimation that she had done so. By what principle could such a subject discount the idea that there was still more to learn? But that reflection sets up a tension within any account of truth of the Peircean sort. For the idea that what is true is what a subject meeting certain conditions, C, would be in position to acknowledge directly requires that a subject who was actually in conditions C—a subject of whom it was *true* that she was in conditions C—would be in position to acknowledge the fact. If such an acknowledgement would be impossible, then the antecedents of the subjunctive conditionals which, on a Peircean view, explicate what it is for a thought to be true, are uniformly false on purely conceptual grounds. Since the status of subjunctive conditionals with conceptually impossible antecedents is, by and large, extremely moot, that is bad news for Peircean views of truth.[11]

---

ness of any truth predicate for which Putnam's Equivalence is to hold. My own view is that the Equivalence is, in effect, retracted in Putnam's more recent thinking, being survived only by the vague idea that truth is not "radically non-epistemic".

   11. There is a distinct worry concerning the implicit assumption that epistemically ideal circumstances are *unique,* so that the internal realist conception of truth ensures convergence at the limit of ideal enquiry. Given that the rela-

I think that the Peircean conception idealises in quite the wrong way, for Putnam's purposes. But can it be improved on? Warranted assertibility is assertibility relative to a state of information. That can make it seem as if there is only one direction for a truth-like idealisation of assertibility to assume: to wit, we have to idealise the state of information involved. And then the quest for stability and absoluteness seems to ensure that a Peircean notion will be the result. But this is an oversight. Rather than ask whether a statement would be justified at the limit of ideal empirical investigation, or under ideal empirical circumstances, whatever they are, we can ask whether an ordinary carefully controlled investigation, in advance of attaining any mythical limit, justifies the statement, and whether, once justified, that statement continues to be so no matter how much further information is accumulated.

More carefully: another property constructible out of assertibility which is both absolute and, so it is plausible to think, may not be lost is the property of being justified by some (in principle accessible) state of information and then *remaining* justified no matter how that state of information might be enlarged upon or improved. Like Peircean truth, the characterisation of this property presupposes that we understand what it is for one state of information to enlarge upon or otherwise improve another. But it does not presuppose that we grasp the idea of a limit to such improvement—a state of information that is itself beyond all improve-

---

tion of evidence is holistically conditioned by background empirical theory, what a priori obstacle is there to the possibility that *conflicting* sets of beliefs be arrived at under epistemically ideal conditions, as a result of theorists having successfully maintained distinct theoretical backgrounds throughout the information-gathering process—so that the extension of "all relevant information" in relation to a particular statement can vary as a function of the way in which, so to say, the process of accumulating it is approached? This thought is amplified, in rather a different context, in Chapter 4 below.

Putnam himself (see the preface to *Realism with a Human Face*) emphasises a different line of criticism of the Peircean conception, connected—though he does not so express it—with the "Conditional Fallacy": roughly, the Peircean account must misconstrue the truth conditions of any proposition (say, "We shall never know P") whose truth depends precisely on the fact that we never will attain the Peircean ideal. There is further discussion of the "Conditional Fallacy" in the appendix to Chapter 3 below.

ment—or even have any general conception of what it would be for epistemic circumstances to be ideal. So it need not raise the questions about the intelligibility and coherence of the idea of such a limit to which Putnam's conception, as standardly interpreted, gives rise.

Elsewhere I have called this property *superassertibility*.[12] A statement is superassertible, then, if and only if it is, or can be, warranted and some warrant for it would survive arbitrarily close scrutiny of its pedigree and arbitrarily extensive increments to or other forms of improvement of our information.

In this admittedly vague characterisation, I am making purely formal use of the notions of "state of information", "improvement", and so on. It's natural to wonder how more specific, yet generally applicable accounts of these notions might be given. But I do not think we need to take these issues on. It's enough for our purposes if the notion of superassertibility is *relatively* clear—clear, that is, relative to whatever notion of warranted assertion is in play in the particular discourse with which we may happen to be concerned. Provided, as I have suggested is presupposed by the very idea of assertoric content, there are generally acknowledged standards of proper and improper assertion within the discourse, there must be sense to be attached to the idea of a statement which under certain circumstances meets the standards of proper assertion, and then will or would continue to do so unless the considerations which led to its downfall were open to objection in some way. In short, wherever our discourse displays some measure of convergence about what is warrantedly assertible, a corresponding notion of superassertibility has to be intelligible to us. This notion may be unclear in various respects, but they will be respects in which the relevant notion of warranted assertibility was already unclear.

## V. Is Superassertibility a Truth Predicate?

It is actually quite a subtle matter how, under the aegis of minimalism, candidacy to be a truth predicate should be assessed. Let's

12. See my *Realism, Meaning and Truth* (Oxford: Basil Blackwell, 1987), pp. 295–302.

explore some of the twists, continuing to focus on the example of superassertibility. We already noted that superassertibility is, plausibly, both absolute and stable.[13] It is uncontroversial that it is potentially divergent in extension from assertibility proper. But it merits consideration whether superassertibility and assertibility coincide in normative force. And the question, anyway, is not merely whether superassertibility has these features but whether they issue in the right kind of way, from its sustaining the key platitudes about assertion and negation characteristic of a minimal truth predicate.

The question may seem easy. Is not all claim of superassertibility to be such a predicate confounded as soon as we consider the platitude connecting assertion and truth? For the link between truth and assertion is that it is part of the *content* of the assertion that P that one thereby claims that P is true—"P and it is not true that P" is a contradiction. By contrast, "P and it is not superassertible that P" is at worst a *Moorean* paradox, comparable to "P and there is no reason to believe it".

That seems solid. But the champion of superassertibility may challenge the claim that the platitude about assertion has to be construed as one about *content*. Plausibly, it is also a platitude that to assert a statement is to present it as justified, and that to assert a statement is to present it as believed—this is why the Moorean paradoxes are *paradoxes*. If we want to say that it is not strictly part of the content of what is asserted that it is, respectively, justified or believed, well and good; the question is then whether it is merely a second-order platitude that the platitude linking truth and assertion concerns content in that strict sense. And what is the argument for that?

It would be frustrating if the discussion could not be prevented

13. In fact it is stable provided the range of the "states of information" quantifier in its definition is stable. That's an assumption that would be questioned, for instance, by an anti-realist about the past, or future, who contested whether we should think of the totality of states of affairs as eternal. But, of course, such an anti-realist would regard the truth predicate as unstable in any case, so that, in the view of such a theorist, instability stemming from that source would not disqualify superassertibility as a truth predicate. For further reflections on the matter, see *Realism, Meaning and Truth*, pp. 300–302.

from bogging down immediately over the interpretation of the platitudes. Fortunately, there is a strong reply to the challenge. The opponent of superassertibility should counter that what shows that the content of the assertion that P embraces neither the claim that P is justified, nor that P is believed, is the simple reflection that neither of the principles,

> The proposition that P is justified if and only if P,

or

> It is believed that P if and only if P,

holds good a priori—at least not without restrictions on the range of "P". By contrast, the reason why the assertion/truth platitude has to be taken as concerning assertoric content is that it directly entails, as we have observed, that the Equivalence Schema,

> It is true that P if and only if P,

holds good a priori for any assertible content P.[14] A predicate's relevantly satisfying the platitude about assertion must therefore be taken to demand the unrestricted validity of the corresponding Equivalence Schema. In particular, the proponent of superassertibility needs to argue for the validity of

($E^s$)        It is superassertible that P if and only if P.

(And if he is successful, that will of course settle the issue whether superassertibility and assertibility coincide in normative force.)

Reflect in addition that matters will also be settled positively as far as negation is concerned if superassertibility satisfies the appropriate version of the Disquotational Schema,

($DS^s$)          "P" is superassertible if and only if P,

from which, as we well know, the required Negation Equivalence,

> "It is not the case that P" is superassertible if and
> only if it is not the case that "P" is superassertible,

14. Again, see discussion note 1.

will follow by recourse only to utterly uncontroversial properties of negation. But assuming that superassertibility, like truth, may be predicated of sentences just when it may be predicated of the propositions which they express, (DS$^s$) is enjoined by (E$^s$). So the crucial issues in connection with both assertion and negation turn on the status of the latter.

And again, the matter may seem easily resolved, at least to anyone sympathetic to the idea that, for a wide class of admissible substitutions for "P", it may be that P although no evidence is available to that effect. Such a theorist will want to object that (E$^s$) cannot be valid, since it conflates right across the board the obtaining of a certain kind of high-grade evidence for P with the obtaining of the fact. A suitably chosen proposition (Goldbach's  Conjecture, say) may be undetectably true, and hence not superassertible; and a suitably chosen superassertible proposition (perhaps that we are not brains-in-a-vat) may be undetectably false. Since (E$^s$) is hostage to counterexample, and so not a priori true, superassertibility has no case to be a truth predicate.

But the friend of superassertibility may rejoin that—quite apart from any doubt about the semantical (Dummettian) realism on which it depends—there is something unsatisfactory about the *shape* of this objection. Its claim is that there is no assurance that there are no counterexamples to (E$^s$). But what does it take a counterexample to be? Is it a true proposition which may not truly be claimed to be superassertible? In that case the objection asserts, in effect, that superassertibility potentially lacks—but ought, as a putative truth predicate, to be guaranteed to have—the property of generating a valid equivalence when substituted for "Π" in the schema:

(F)     It is true that it is Π that P iff it is true that P.

(F), however, contains two occurrences of a truth predicate which, if interpreted as presupposed by the objection, has to be understood as *distinct* from superassertibility. If that doesn't seem evident, reflect that while—to one in the cast of mind which fuels the objection—it is a possibility that Goldbach's Conjecture be true without it being true that it is superassertible (provable), it certainly isn't evident that the conjecture might be superassertible without it being superassertible that it is. But if there really can be, as minimalism suggests, a *plurality* of truth predicates, qualifying as such by satisfying certain general principles, it is only to be expected that an *illusion* of failure may be created by selective interpretations of "true" as it occurs within those principles. It is as if someone were to argue that physical necessity fails to qualify as a genuine notion of necessity on the grounds that it fails to satisfy the principle

Necessarily (A $\leftrightarrow$ B) $\models$ Necessarily (A) $\leftrightarrow$ Necessarily (B),

and were then to try to back up that contention by selectively interpreting the final occurrence of "Necessarily" in terms of *logical* necessity. If we wish to determine whether there are counterexamples to (E$^s$), the proper question to put, the friend of superassertibility contends, is not whether superassertibility satisfies (F), but rather whether it satisfies what results when the two tendentious occurrences of "true" are replaced by ones of "Π":

(G)       It is Π that it is Π that P if and only if it is Π
          that P.

That is, in effect, whether, whenever it is superassertible that P, it is superassertible that it is so, and vice versa.

Can we arbitrate this dispute? What is suspect about the shape of the original objection can be put like this. If any genuine truth predicate has to validate (= satisfy a priori) the Equivalence Schema, then clearly *distinct* truth predicates can operate over a single discourse (or range of propositions) only if they are a priori co-extensive. Plainly, then, no predicate, F, can behave like a truth predicate with respect to any discourse in which it is made to function alongside another predicate, G, which is already assumed both to validate the Equivalence Schema and to be potentially divergent in extension from F.[15] The original objection is therefore cogent only to this extent: to show that a discourse is

15. Since it cannot be a priori that [P iff P is F] if it is a priori that [P iff P is G] but not a priori that [P is G iff P is F].

governed by an evidentially unconstrained notion of truth—G—is, for that reason, to show that superassertibility—F—is not a truth predicate *for that discourse*.[16] But no *global* conclusion is licensed. We have to distinguish the questions (i) whether a predicate's content would enable it, under certain conditions, to function as a truth predicate; (ii) whether, if so, the relevant conditions are met by any particular discourse; and (iii) whether they are met globally. The objection, drawing as it does on a range of examples where it is thought especially plausible that truth is evidentially unconstrained, is properly targeted against superassertibility's claim on a positive answer to (iii). But in failing to make any distinction among the three questions, it implicitly begs the other two.

There is, however, on the other side, a similar oversimplification in the suggestion that "*the* proper question to put" is, in effect, whether

(G$^s$)     It is superassertible that it is superassertible that
            P iff it is superassertible that P

holds a priori. The right perspective is rather this. In the presence of the Equivalence Schema, counterexamples to (E$^s$) are indeed all and only cases where

(F$^s$)     It is true that it is superassertible that P iff it is
            true that P

also breaks down. So if (G$^s$) is valid, then we know that there can be no such counterexamples, and hence that (E$^s$) is valid, provided but only provided *no competitor truth predicate* operates alongside superassertibility—no predicate, that is, which validates the Equivalence Schema but whose co-extensiveness with superassertibility is not guaranteed a priori. If there is a competitor in operation, (F$^s$) may fail, when its occurrences of "true" are suitably interpreted, even if (G$^s$) is valid without restriction on "P". If there is no competitor, (G$^s$) and (F$^s$) stand or fall together. The status of (G$^s$) is thus highly germane to question (i). If counterexamples to

16. Since, trivially, if P is superassertible, there has to be evidence for P.

it cannot be excluded a priori, then there will be no general assurance that superassertibility can function as a truth predicate even when we give it the fullest elbowroom, as it were—even when we make no initial assumption that a competitor is operating over the discourse. On the other hand, if counterexamples to (G$^S$) can be a priori excluded, irrespective of the range of "P", then we can return a positive answer to question (i); and the answers to questions (ii) and (iii) will then depend on whether and how widely competitor truth predicates should be regarded as in operation.

So: is (G$^S$) unrestrictedly valid? We may return a positive answer if it can be shown that to have warrant for P is to have warrant for the claim that P is superassertible, and conversely.[17] The converse direction seems unproblematic. If we have reason to regard a statement as superassertible, then we have reason to think that some (in principle accessible) state of information will stably justify the statement, no matter how added to or otherwise improved. And having reason to think that such a state of information exists is plausibly taken to have the same probative force as actually being in the state of information in question. For instance, proving that a (canonical) proof of a particular statement can be constructed is, so far as probative force is concerned, as good as constructing the proof; and there seems no reason why the point should not survive generalisation to the cases where we are concerned with defeasible grounds rather than conclusive ones like mathematical proof.

---

17. For suppose that to have warrant for A is to have warrant for B and vice versa, but, for *reductio,* that A is superassertible, while B is not. Let *I* be a total state of information in virtue of which A is superassertible; i.e., *I* warrants A and so does any improvement, *I\**, of *I*. By hypothesis, *I* also warrants B. Since B is not superassertible, there must therefore be some improvement, *I\**, of *I,* which fails to warrant B. Since any such *I\** warrants A, the supposition is contradicted.

This shows that (i) coincidence in assertibility conditions suffices for (ii) a pair of statements both being superassertible if either is. Clearly (i) is not also unrestrictedly necessary for (ii)—but is it so if we restrict attention to contingent statements and to cases where it is a priori that both are superassertible if either is? If so, then the unrestricted validity of (G$^S$) will not merely be established if the argument to follow succeeds but will *require* that it succeed. I leave the matter as an exercise for the reader.

What is less clear is that to have warrant to assert a statement must be to have warrant to regard it as superassertible. Doubtless, warrant to assert P cannot co-exist with warrant to *deny* that P is superassertible—since that would be to have warrant to think that the present case for P would be defeated if we pressed matters sufficiently far, and, again, that seems as much as to defeat it already. But the question to ask is, rather, whether warrant to assert P can co-exist with lack of warrant to regard it as superassertible—whether one can coherently combine *agnosticism* about P's superassertibility with regarding a present case for asserting it as sufficient.

The question is independently interesting, and connects with a complaint of P. F. Strawson's about the assertibility-conditional wing of the semantic anti-realist movement, that—to interpret somewhat [18]—it only makes sense to think of assertions as *warranted* if an assertion carries a commitment to something *beyond* its being warranted. To explore the matter fully would take us too far afield. But I'll outline an argument that the mooted combination of attitudes is not coherent—that it is precluded by certain quite basic elements in our ordinary conception of what justification for a statement or, equivalently, warrant for a belief involves. The elements involved are three. The first is that epistemic warranty does not have a sell-by date: what I am warranted in believing I remain warranted in believing *sine die* unless I acquire defeating collateral information. The second is that in warrantedly believing any statement, P, a subject is thereby warranted in believing that a sound investigation, to whatever extent one is possible, would bear her out. The third I shall introduce in a moment.

Suppose I warrantedly believe that P. Now, what counts as warrant to believe a particular statement varies, of course, as a function of time, place and background information. So what counts as corroboration of P for me if I return my attention to the matter in

---

18. Strawson's actual formulation is that, unless distinct truth conditions are also acknowledged, the assertibility-conditional conception of statement meaning "leaves one with no account of what the speaker in uttering the sentence is actually doing." See p. 19 of P. F. Strawson, "Scruton and Wright on Anti-Realism, etc.", *Proceedings of the Aristotelian Society* 77 (1977), pp. 15–22.

a year's time, say, may comprise very different considerations from those which warrant my present belief. However, by the first of the two assumptions, I will then be warranted, *ceteris paribus*, in believing P; and by the second I will thereby be entitled to expect whatever sound considerations are then available to me to be corroborative just in virtue of the warrant I possessed a year before.

That establishes a conditional: if I am warranted in believing P now, then, if I acquire no other relevant information in the meantime, I will be warranted in future in expecting then-available, sound considerations to bear P out. But this conditional is something which I may take myself to know now. So whenever I know its antecedent—which, presumably, I can whenever it is true, since possession of justification should be a decidable matter—I can know that in any case where I acquire no further relevant information in the interim, certain expectations will be warranted in future. But to know that certain beliefs will be warranted in the future is, only provided one has no present reason to view them as wrong, to be warranted in holding them now. That is the third element in our ordinary conception of justification advertised above: the firm *promise* of justification for what one has no reason  to doubt is already justification. So to be warranted in believing P involves having justification for believing that any subsequent, soundly conducted investigation, prior to which one has acquired no further relevant additional information, will corroborate P.

That doesn't quite do it, however. It will certainly suffice to justify the claim that P is superassertible if I may warrantedly claim that *any* improvement, *I\**, of my present state of information, *I*, will justify P. But what the foregoing establishes is only that if I am warranted in believing P, then I am warranted in claiming that any such *I\* prior to which I have acquired no further relevant additional information* will justify P. So there is a gap. However in order to eliminate the italicised qualification, it suffices to reflect, presumably, that any *I\** prior to entering which I *do* acquire P-relevant information additional to any possessed in *I*, must be the terminus of a finite chain, $\langle I, I^2, \ldots, I^* \rangle$, each element of which satisfies the qualification with respect to its immediate predecessor.

Naturally, the premises and detail of this argument will bear a more rigorous examination.[19] But it has some plausibility. And more generally, it is hard to see how the making of warranted assertions, and the avoidance of unwarranted ones, could have any distinctive point or consequence unless warrant is taken *per se* to license expectations about the character of subsequent states of information.[20] The contention that ($G^s$) holds a priori, without restriction on the range of "P", is thus very much in play.

## VI. Superassertibility as a Model of Truth

However, it is not necessary, in order for superassertibility to qualify, at least potentially, as a truth predicate, that we take on that contention directly and find in its favour. It will be of no less significance if superassertibility turns out to validate the minimalist's basic platitudes subject to certain *additional assumptions* which, consistently with the platitudes, may hold a priori for a particular discourse. Such a finding would put us in a position to say that, whether or not the platitudes are analytic of superassertibility when all occurrences of "true" are so interpreted, it is at least a possible *model* of them: it can be shown to have the features they collectively articulate when they are augmented with suppositions on whose status the platitudes themselves are silent. How does the enquiry fare if we let it take this direction?

One way of pursuing the matter begins by asking what is the relation between superassertibility and knowledge. It would be a tall order to argue unrestrictedly that whatever is superassertible can be known, not merely because one would have to vanquish the metaphysical-realist notion that even an empirically unimprovable theory might simply be mistaken, but—perhaps more seriously— because the superassertibility of a statement carries no implication about the *strength* of the available evidence, which though positive may be enduringly weak. By contrast, it seems to me a highly intuitive claim that anything we can know is superassertible.

19. A beginning is made in discussion note 3 at the end of the chapter.

20. For further discussion, see chapter 9, note 13, of *Realism, Meaning and Truth* and the other passages in that book there referred to.

Admittedly, this will not be so on any reliabilist conception of knowledge sufficiently extreme to abrogate all connection between knowledge and the possession of reason to believe. On such a view, one can know that P just by being a dispositionally reliable litmus of whether or not P, even if one has nothing whatever to say in support or explanation of one's believing or disbelieving P. But on any view according to which knowledge requires at least some back-up with reasons, that is, with assertibility, it is surely going to require superassertibility too. I do not deny that, in suitable circumstances, an agent may know something on the basis of information which can in fact be defeated. But if his knowledge claim is not to be undermined by the availability of such defeating information, it is surely required that the negative effect of that information, once acquired, could itself be stably overturned.

Doubtless, the matter needs more discussion. But let me propose

(K)         P is knowable → P is superassertible

as analytic of the concepts of knowledge and superassertibility. And now suppose we are dealing with a discourse in which, as we conceive, it is guaranteed a priori that each stateable truth can, in favourable circumstances, be recognised as such—a discourse for which we can make nothing of the idea that truth might lie beyond all possibility of acknowledgement. Comic and, on a wide class of views about it, moral discourse are each, for instance, in this situation: there seems no sense to be attached to the idea that the comedy of a situation might elude the appreciation even of the most fortunately situated judge, or that the moral significance of an act might lie beyond human recognition, even in principle.[21] In any case suppose that, for each assertoric content, P, in some germane class, we have it a priori that

(L)                   P ↔ P is knowable.

21. I prescind from the complication that the bearers of comic and moral predicates may be spatially or temporally remote. Naturally modifiers of time and place throw up the same prima facie barriers to the acknowledgeability of comic or moral truth, broadly conceived, as they pose for discourses in general. A similar point applies, of course, to quantification.

Had we the converse of (K),

> P is superassertible $\rightarrow$ P is knowable,

the validity for the discourse concerned of the Equivalence Schema for superassertibility,

(E$^s$)    It is superassertible that P if and only if P,

would of course be immediate. But we can skin the cat without appeal to the converse of (K). Reflect that (K) and (L) already provide the resources to establish one half, as it were, of the commutativity of superassertibility and negation; thus

| | | |
|---|---|---|
| (1) | Not [P is superassertible] | hypothesis |
| (2) | Not [P is knowable] | 1 (by K) |
| (3) | Not P | 2 (by L) |
| (4) | It is knowable that [not P] | 3 (by L, "not P" / "P") |
| (5) | It is superassertible that [not P] | 4 (by K) |

With that lemma in place, it is easy to see that (E$^s$) and the parent platitude connecting truth with assertion, taken as a claim about assertoric content, now admit interpretation in terms of superassertibility. What needs to be shown is that

> P and P is not superassertible

and

> P is superassertible and Not-P

are contradictory, just as are "P and P is not true", and "P is true and not-P". For the first, merely reflect that if P then, by (L), P is knowable; and if P is knowable, then, by (K), P is superassertible. For the second, reflect that, by the same moves, if Not-P, then Not-P is superassertible and hence, by the commutativity lemma, that it's not the case that P is superassertible, contradicting the first conjunct. Thus, granted the a priori link between knowability and superassertibility postulated by (K), it follows, for any set of contents which sustain (L) a priori, that the assertion of any of these contents is a commitment to its superassertibility and the assertion of its superassertibility is a commitment to (rejecting any denial of) the content. Plausibly, then, for discourses all of whose contents are in that case, superassertibility is a model of the truth predicate.[22] And if what I said about the essential appreciability of the moral and the comic is correct, a presumption is established that moral and comic truth can be taken as species of superassertibility.[23]

One interesting effect is the perspective in which the semantic anti-realism is now placed which generalises Michael Dummett's interpretation of mathematical intuitionism. Dummett's anti-realist, inspired by considerations concerning the acquisition and manifestation of understanding, contends that if the meaning of a statement is to be regarded as determined by its truth conditions, then truth cannot outrun our ability (in principle) to know. But then the thesis is that assumption (L), the equivalence of "P" and "P is knowable", holds globally, for *all* intelligible assertoric contents. So, granted (K), the semantic anti-realist contention becomes, in effect, that truth behaves, or ought to behave *everywhere* in a fashion which allows it to be construed as superassertibility. And to respond to the manifestation and acquisition arguments will be to explain how the currency of a notion of truth which cannot be modelled in terms of superassertibility is distinctively displayed in certain aspects of our linguistic practice, and how such a conception of truth might be arrived at in the first place.

This seems to me a helpful perspective. Semantic anti-realism now distances itself from the almost certainly doomed project of attempting a meaning theory which proceeds in terms of an index-

22. Such a conclusion can be drawn locally, of course, even if the general validity of (K) is rejected, provided that knowledge entails superassertibility in at least some discourses of which (L) is a priori true.

23. Only a presumption, though. A discourse which meets the conditions described, and so permits superassertibility to model the platitudes characteristic of its truth predicate, may yet have other features which impose differences between the two concepts. Getting clear about what such features could be is exactly what is involved in getting clear how realist/anti-realist debate is possible after minimalism about truth is accepted on both sides. But I anticipate.

ical notion of assertibility; instead, it avails itself of a notion of truth, contrasting with assertibility, and an associated truth-conditional conception of meaning. But it can do this only because superassertibility is, as any anti-realistically acceptable notion of truth must be, an essentially epistemically constrained notion—for if P is superassertible, it must be possible to alight on the (de facto) indefeasible state of information that makes it so, and then to accumulate inductive grounds for identifying it as such. Crucially, however, superassertibility is also, in a natural sense, an *internal* property of the statements of a discourse—a projection, merely, of the standards, whatever they are, which actually inform assertion within the discourse. It supplies no external norm—in a way that truth is classically supposed to do—against which the internal standards might *sub specie Dei* themselves be measured, and might rate as adequate or inadequate. In this way, it is metaphysically neutral, and betrays the metaphysical neutrality of the minimal conception of truth which, under the right circumstances, it models.

## DISCUSSION NOTES

*1. It is well known that it is inconsistent with the DS to accept failures of Bivalence, since when "P" is neither true nor false, the claim that "P" is true will presumably be false, and their biconditional therefore incorrect. Yet doubts about Bivalence are surely not inconsistent with the platitude that to assert is to claim to be true. So there must be something amiss with the thought, which has informed so much of the discussion thus far, that the assertion/truth platitude directly imposes the Equivalence Schema and hence the DS. Is not the inflationary argument against deflationism spoiled by this consideration? And is not much of the discussion of superassertibility's fittingness for the role of truth predicate rendered irrelevant?*

Let me, for the sake of argument, not dispute the coherence of a stance which, for suitable A and B, accepts that to assert A is to assert B without accepting the biconditional of A and B. Such a stance is a natural way of registering the case when A and B, necessarily and obviously, always take a *designated* value together,

but diverge in the undesignated values they sometimes take—as
for example "P" and "It is true that P" will do, if the matrix for
"it is true that . . ." is non-conservative in the way the objection
anticipates. Still, I do not think this concession does serious
damage to any aspect of the argument so far. Several observations
are in order.

(i) The point is, of course, quite useless as a defence of
deflationism against the inflationary argument, since that argument starts from deflationism's *acceptance* of the DS. If that acceptance is already an error, *tant mieux* for the opponent of
deflationism.

(ii) What *might* seem to be compromised is the contention,
which I presented as a self-standing corollary of the inflationary
argument, that it is part of the minimal nature of truth to provide
a norm over assertoric discourse prescriptively coincident with but
potentially extensionally divergent from justification. For the argument for that contention depended on viewing the entailment of
the Negation Equivalence by the DS as establishing the former's
validity, and hence involved a positive endorsement of the DS.

Reflect, however, that it is misleading to tie the noted sort of
failure of the DS, or of the Equivalence Schema, to failures of
Bivalence *simpliciter*. It all depends on what *kind* of objection to
Bivalence is envisaged. Semantic vagueness, for instance, is naturally conceived as consisting in an expression's propensity to feature
in statements which are only unhappily regarded as determinately
true or determinately false, and for which Bivalence is therefore
only unhappily accepted; but that conception of vagueness is
apparently quite consistent with the thought that the vaguenesses
of "P" and "It is true that P" will always perfectly *match,* so that,
the doubt about Bivalence notwithstanding, the DS and the
Equivalence Schema are quite unthreatened. A similar point
applies if the doubt about Bivalence is of a broadly intuitionistic
or semantically anti-realist sort: such a doubt concerns not the
possibility of statements which might somehow slip between the
poles of truth and falsity, but our *justification* for claiming that all
statements in a given class are determinately true or false when
truth is conceived as essentially evidentially constrained and we

have no method effective in every case for accumulating evidence one way or the other. It is only if reservations are entertained about Bivalence which specifically involve determinate additional truth values or determinate truth-value gaps that an issue is raised about the Equivalence Schema and the DS.

Now, even those who have argued for the theoretical utility of an apparatus of more than two truth values, or of truth-value gaps, have tended to do so only for special cases—statements containing referenceless singular terms, conditionals with false antecedents, liar-paradoxical statements, and so on. But unless it is supposed that Bivalence should be quite generally suspect on this kind of count, the argument from the assertion/truth platitude to the Negation Equivalence via the DS will succeed at least locally— indeed, presumably, almost everywhere. Once it is recognised that truth and assertoric warrant are, by the argument given, neces- sarily distinct in such localities of discourse, what possible reason could there be why they might come together again in appro- priately non-bivalent areas—even if the argument that forces the split is no longer directly applicable?

(iii) Say that a biconditional, A ↔ B, is *weakly valid* if, although A may in certain circumstances receive a different valua- tion from B, or may lack a truth value when B does not, it is not possible for either ever to be *true* unless the other is; and *strongly valid* if A and B necessarily always receive the same valuation. Then even for areas of discourse where the Equivalence Schema and the DS are viewed as suspect for the noted kind of reason, it will still be that each is weakly valid. That much is an inescapable consequence of the assertion/truth platitude. The contention that a predicate is equipped to serve as a truth predicate must thus depend on a demonstration that it sustains, either absolutely or modulo certain intrinsic features of the targeted discourse, the weak validity of the appropriate version of the Equivalence Schema. Since, although informed only by an undifferentiated notion of validity for the biconditional, the considerations about superassertibility advanced in sections V and VI of this chapter were explicitly directed against the possibility of counterexamples to $(E^s)$ in the precise sense of substituends of "P" where one half of the resulting biconditional *holds good* while the other does not, they remain, if effective at all, absolutely *a propos* when explicitly directed at issues to do with weak validity.

(iv) Finally, and to clinch matters, note that, within an apparatus of more than two determinate truth values or of determinate truth-value gaps, there can be no objection to the introduction of a polar negation operator—say, *Neg*—characterised by the stipulation that *Neg*(A) is false if A is true but is true in *all* other cases. It will readily be seen that if A ↔ B is weakly valid, so is *Neg*(A) ↔ *Neg*(B). Granted, then, that at least the weak validity of the DS is imposed by the assertion-truth platitude, and that every admissible substituend for "P" within the DS has a significant *Neg*ation—usually, of course, its ordinary negation—which is also an admissible substituend, there is no obstacle to derivation of the *Neg*ation Equivalence:

"*Neg*(P)" is true ↔ *Neg*("P" is true).

But this will fail, even as a claim of weak validity, when "assertible" is substituted for "true". Reflect in addition that the weak validity of the DS is sufficient for the normative coincidence of truth and warranted assertibility argued for in Chapter 1. It follows that the inflationary argument, the positive corollary concerning truth and assertibility, and the minimalist conception of truth could, with a little complication, all have emerged as originally orchestrated, even had we wished from the outset explicitly to leave scope for many truth values or for determinate truth-value gaps.

*2. There was more than a suspicion of legerdemain about the way the discussion in section V linked together the question of possible counter-examples to*

(E$^s$)    *It is superassertible that P if and only if P*

*and the question of the validity of*

(F$^s$)    *It is true that it is superassertible that P iff it is true that P.*

*The linkage was purportedly justified by characterising a counterexample to (E^s) as "a proposition which may <u>truly</u> be asserted but not <u>truly</u> claimed to be superassertible". But surely there is no need to mention truth in the characterisation: the objection could as well have been formulated as the claim that it cannot be excluded that, for certain substitutions for "P", the following holds:*

(H)          *P and it is not superassertible that P.*

*If Goldbach's Conjecture is a possible satisfier of (H), then it is a possible counterexample to (E^s). And since (H) contains no occurrences of "true", the claim that such counterexamples cannot be excluded a priori thus has no unavoidable dependence on "selective interpretation" of the truth predicate.*

This complaint may be answered by a simple dilemma. Are we or are we not to accept the Equivalence Schema for "true"? If not, then it can hardly be an objection to superassertibility's claim to be a truth predicate that it is not, if the objection is correct, guaranteed to satisfy (E^s), since it is no longer an accepted constraint on a truth predicate that it validate such a schema. But if the Equivalence Schema is accepted, then there can be no objection to rewriting (H) as

(J)          P is true and it is true that it is not superassertible
             that P.

Since, in the presence of the Equivalence Schema, the satisfiers of (H) are, necessarily, all and only the satisfiers of (J), and since whether a statement satisfies (J) will depend on how the occurrences of "true" are interpreted, the question whether it satisfies (H) must similarly so depend, even though (H) contains no occurrence of "true". In particular if Goldbach's conjecture qualifies as a satisfier of (J) when but only when the occurrences of "true" therein are interpreted as expressing something other than superassertibility, then such a conception of truth will be tacitly at work in underwriting the conjecture as a satisfier of (H), even though (H) makes no explicit mention of truth.

*3. Surely the lemma, argued for in connection with*

$(G^s)$        *It is superassertible that it is superassertible that P iff*
          *it is superassertible that P,*

*that, without restriction of subject matter, to have warrant to accept a statement is to have warrant to regard it as superassertible, has to be wrong. The superassertibility of P requires that some state of information justifying acceptance of P is such that every possible enlargement or other form of improvement of it continues to do so. But, at least with ordinary empirical statements, opportunities for investigation can be ephemeral, and evidence once available can cease to be so. Suppose I attend a graduation ceremony at which the university Chancellor is unable to attend, the Vice-Chancellor taking his place. Sixty years later, aged but still hale and alert, I am, by some freak, the sole survivor of the occasion. Suppose I have a clear recollection that the Vice-Chancellor presided. The remoteness of the event notwithstanding, there is no good reason for denying that I* know *that the Vice-Chancellor presided—unless we are to deny that old people ever remember, and therefore know, events in the earlier part of their lives. Still, it may well be that the only other surviving evidence on the point suggests that the Chancellor presided as usual. It may be, for instance, that the university's own records of the occasion have been destroyed in a fire, and that the only other surviving evidence consists in a report in a local paper prepared by a truant journalist who drew on a previous year's photographs and copy. In such a situation, my claim that the then Vice-Chancellor of St. Andrews, Struther Arnott, presided at the July graduation ceremony sixty years ago is not superassertible; for there is a material additional piece of information—the contents of the newspaper report—which calls my recollection into question, and no other relevant information is available to redress the balance. Accepting that, before I know of the newspaper report, I am justified in making the claim, it surely remains that my justification does not involve having reason to think that the untoward situation described does not obtain.*

*The point is perfectly general. It is part of our ordinary conception of the nature of evidence for the past that nothing ensures that the balance of evidence now available concerning some past situation should not, by misfortune, be misleading. So, at least in the case of present-tense empirical statements concerning particular objects and events, justification cannot in general be reason to suppose that such will not be their fate. Hence, justification for a statement is not, unrestrictedly, reason to regard it as superassertible. Justification cannot, in all cases, involve reason to think that the totality of subsequently available evidence will not be misleading. And principle (K), that knowledge entails superassertibility, should be rejected for the same reason.*

These issues are some of the important items of unfinished business to which I referred in the preface. I have no conclusively satisfactory responses to offer, but a number of observations are relevant. Note, to begin with, that the capacity of this kind of example to make trouble both for the cited lemma and for principle (K) turns on rather different considerations. (K) is refuted if the example provides a case of a known statement which is not superassertible; the lemma is refuted if a case is provided of a warranted statement which there is no warrant to regard as superassertible.

(i) It isn't *unquestionably* a possibility that a justified true belief be retained up to a stage when, by mischance, a decayed totality of available evidence—in the example, one old man's memory and a contemporary report in a usually reliable newspaper—becomes misleading. A question would be raised precisely by the kind of anti-realism about the past which takes centre stage in Dummett's famous paper.[24] On that view, ascriptions of truth to statements concerning the past are unintelligible except insofar as constrained by presently available evidence.

(ii) Leaving that kind of anti-realism out of account, it remains that to view the example as a case of a known statement which is not superassertible involves a tacit assumption about the range of the states-of-information quantifiers in the characterisation of what superassertibility involves. In effect, it is assumed that, for any time t and state of information $I$ then possesed, the range of "every possible enlargement or other form of improvement" of $I$ is restricted to states of information into which it is then possible to advance from $I$. Items of information which could have been col-

24. Michael Dummett, "The Reality of the Past", in his *Truth and Other Enigmas* (London: Duckworth, 1978), pp. 358–374.

lected but which there is no longer any opportunity to gather are excluded from consideration. If we assume that that is how superassertibility for tensed statements must work, we simply go past an idealised but quite natural version of the concept. The idealisation involves not that we might visit the past and investigate unrecorded, forgotten or originally unconsidered matters, but that the range of states of information to which the characterisation of superassertibility appeals should be understood as embracing everything which we should possess if, stationed in time as we are, we were nevertheless *per impossibile* to investigate everything which, at any given time, there is opportunity to investigate and if the information thereby accumulated were never to be lost. Obviously no even apparent counterexample is presented to (K) or to the lemma if this is how superassertibility is understood.

Superassertibility so idealised still contrasts with truth conceived in accordance with Putnam's Equivalence, since it involves no play with the idea of completion of all empirical enquiry. Of course, the idealisation it involves may still be found objectionable, on various counts. But it merits attention as one among a range of potential truth predicates, as do the other concepts of superassertibility which result from varying restrictions on the range of the states-of-information quantifier.

(iii) As already remarked (footnote 22), the interest (if any) of the concluding section of the chapter does not depend on the unrestricted validity of (K). It is enough if (K) holds a priori of classes of propositions for which (L) is also a priori. If the only problem for (K) is occasioned by the lapsing of opportunities for investigation, then (unidealised) superassertibility's claim to model the truth predicate may still be of significance for classes of propositions—mathematical propositions, ethical precepts, physical laws—for which investigative opportunity cannot, in the relevant sense, lapse. (Of course, matters will depend on what view is taken of (L) in such cases.)

(iv) Finally, it seems to me contestable whether the example poses a problem in any case for the lemma that warrant to assert involves warrant to regard as superassertible. Again, the matter needs a much finer-grained discussion than I shall venture here. But let me at least indicate a line of resistance.

Granted that a case is presented where—unremarkably—a warranted statement is not as a matter of fact superassertible, what is the argument for thinking that there is no warrant for the (false) claim that it *is* superassertible? The objection moved from the observation that, on our ordinary conception of the nature of evidence for the past, there can never be complete assurance that the balance of evidence now available concerning some past situation should not, by misfortune, be misleading, to the contention that possession of (memory-based) justification for a statement cannot involve reason to think that such misfortune has not occurred. If that is so, then the premise of the argument for the lemma developed in section V, that in warrantedly believing any statement, P, a subject is thereby warranted in believing that a sound investigation, to whatever extent one is possible, would bear her out, is incorrect. In fact, though, the transition is a *non sequitur*. That it cannot definitively be excluded that misfortune has occurred is one, plausible thing; that the (memory-based) justification is not *itself* a ground for thinking that misfortune has not occurred is also plausible. But it is a third matter whether the claim that misfortune has not occurred—that the balance of available evidence is not misleading—is unjustified *tout court*.

In order to see the force of this distinction, reflect that if it were reasonable, just because it is always *possible* that the balance of available evidence bearing on P is misleading, always to take an open mind on the matter, it would be quite obscure how any adjustment could *ever* be rationally imposed if evidence came to light which plausibly completed the relevant information still available and which, by standard criteria, defeated one's initial justification for P. Why, instead, should someone not reason as follows: "Well, I was justified in accepting P before this new evidence came to light, and no one has given me any reason to suppose that the complete field of available evidence is not a misleading one. Accordingly, since it is, for all the information I have, as likely that the new picture is misleading as that it is not, the rational thing is to ignore it. And if that is so, then it is as if I have no new information, and my prior justification for P remains intact." If this reaction offends our ordinary conception of what is reasonable, how is that to be explained if not as follows: the belief that the totality of evidence bearing on a question is not misleading is not something for which justification has to be earned, but stands as an indispensable default presumption, conditioning all rational enquiry?

If that is right, then the conditional

> If P, then the balance of the available evidence,
> if finite, bearing on P will be favourable,

though not a priori true, is a priori justified. Since the consequent entails P's superassertibility, it follows directly that any acquired warrant for P is transmissible, via the conditional—and in the presence, as in the example considered, of a presumption in favour of the finitude of the available evidence—into warrant to affirm that P is superassertible.

# 3. Convergence and Cognitive Command

## I. Résumé

It may be useful to rehearse, with an additional gloss or two, the four principal suggestions about truth which I have so far made.

(i) The classical deflationary conception of truth is inherently unstable. The deflationist holds that "true", although grammatically a predicate, denotes no substantial quality of statements, or thoughts, but is merely a device of assertoric endorsement, of use to us only because we sometimes wish so to endorse a single statement, referred to in a way which doesn't specify its content, or batches of statements all at once. Apart from applications of those two kinds, it is, for the deflationist, a complete explanation of the truth predicate that it satisfies the Disquotational Schema. It is a consequence of this general conception of the role of the truth predicate that it can register no norm governing assertoric discourse distinct from warranted assertibility. Yet the central place assigned to the Disquotational Schema—and thereby to the Negation Equivalence—actually clashes with that consequence, for it follows that, while normative of assertoric discourse, and indeed coincident in (positive prescriptive) normative force with warranted assertibility, "true" is nevertheless potentially extensionally divergent from warranted assertibility—and hence *has* to be accounted as registering a distinct such norm. Since its compliance or non-compliance with a norm distinct from assertoric warrant can hardly be an "insubstantial" property of a statement, and since a uniform account is possible of what it is for any particular statement so to comply,[1] deflationism collapses.

More generally: since any competitive philosophy of truth, whatever more it says, must incorporate the Disquotational Schema, it follows that the least and first thing we have to say about truth is that it is, in this way, a substantial norm which assertoric discourse essentially respects, but which is distinct from assertoric warrant.

(ii) The deflationist tradition incorporates an insight nonetheless. That insight is that truth is not intrinsically a metaphysically heavyweight notion—the mark of some especially profound form of engagement between language, or thought, and reality—for which certain areas of assertoric discourse, whatever internal discipline they manifest, may simply not be in the market. Rather, truth may properly be construed in a *minimalist* spirit—a deflationary spirit, if you will, provided we discard the errant suggestion that it is no real property. Any predicate is a truth predicate which satisfies certain basic principles. One such is the Disquotational Schema, the more or less exclusive focus of deflationism. But lurking behind the Disquotational Schema is the more fundamental thesis that to assert is to present as true. Other relevant principles include: that to every assertible content corresponds an assertoric negation; that a content is true just in case it corresponds to the facts, depicts things as they are, and so on; that truth and warrant are distinct, and—though I have laid no great weight on these—that truth is absolute (there is, strictly, no being more or less true) and, more contentiously, that it is stable (if a content is ever true, it always is).

I do not advance this list as comprehensive. Arguable additions would concern, for example, the connections between truth and transformations of tense and other indexicals, and principles concerning other connectives besides negation. The controlling minimalist thought remains that to be a truth predicate is merely to satisfy a set of very general, very intuitive a priori laws—a set of platitudes, which I have not tried to circumscribe in any rigorous

1. See Chapter 1, discussion note 1.

or putatively complete fashion, but which will certainly accord a central role to the connection between truth and assertion and its consequence, the Disquotational Schema; to derivable principles concerning negation and correspondence; and which we may wish to see augmented by considerations about stability and absoluteness.[2]

2. A comparison is interesting here with the overtly rather different list of constitutive characteristics—*marks* of truth, as he styles them—drawn up by David Wiggins in his "What Would Be a Substantial Theory of Truth?" in Zak van Straaten, ed., *Philosophical Subjects: Essays Presented to P. F. Strawson* (Oxford: Oxford University Press, 1980). Wiggins' list overlaps the above with respect to the fundamental connection between assertion and truth, and the implication of some notion of correspondence in the very idea of truth, but includes three more:

> that, at least in favourable circumstances, there should be a tendency
>     of agents to converge on the truth;
> that a statement's being true or not is independent of any particular
>     subject's means of appraising its truth value; and
> that a conjunction of statements is true just in case each of its con-
>     juncts is.

These additions are perfectly plausible. But Wiggins should have remarked that they are each implicit in the claim that the Disquotational Schema embodies an essential mark of truth. Reflect that convergence about the applicability of the truth predicate will, via the DS, be elicitable in all cases where there is convergence concerning the acceptability of statements featuring on its right-hand side. So since it is merely a consequence of the discipline to which any genuine range of assertoric contents will be intrinsically subject that, at least in favourable circumstances, there will be a tendency to convergence of the second sort, any minimally truth-apt discourse will satisfy Wiggins' convergence mark. This same discipline (the currency of acknowledged standards of warranted assertibility) will presumably be apt to ensure that, as Wiggins glosses the second requirement (the intersubjectivity mark), "[the truth] of a judgement cannot consist . . . in the bare fact that the judgement is judged" (*ibid.*, p. 210). Finally the Conjunction Equivalence

"P & Q" is true if and only if "P" is true and "Q" is true

is, of course imposed by the DS itself, granted only assumptions analogous to those which featured in the derivation of the Negation Equivalence from the same, viz. that to each pair of assertoric contents corresponds an assertoric content which is their conjunction, that the discourse in question, for which the DS is affirmed, is closed under conjunction, and that conjunction is subject to its standard introductory and eliminative rules of proof. Accordingly, someone in sympathy with Wiggins' characterisation should find the approach I am here pursuing broadly congenial.

(iii) However to call these principles "platitudes", while it may suggest it, does not of course ensure that a predicate which satisfies them can be, as I announced, metaphysically lightweight. That implication is made good by the third main thesis advanced: that *any assertoric* discourse will permit the definition upon it of a minimal truth predicate—a predicate satisfying the platitudinous constraints. Here it is vital that, for the purposes of the claim, assertoric discourses are demarcated not by any deep feature of their contents which might be simulated or masked by surface syntactic features, but merely by their statements' being subject to acknowledged conditions of acceptance and their possessing the appropriate surface syntactic features: to wit, primarily, their availability for embedding within negation, the conditional, and other connectives (identified as such by their inferential behaviour), and as objects of propositional attitude. If a discourse has these features, there can be no objection to laying down the Disquotational Schema as partially definitional of a truth predicate for it—a predicate which will thereby satisfy the core minimalist constraints.[3]

I have, I admit, presented no consideration which, strictly, imposes the minimalist way of looking at these matters. Rather, it seems to me that we are here concerned with issues which turn on theoretical advantage. And minimalism promises considerable advantages if it can be sustained. Expressivism has always had to contend, for example, with the headache of valid inferences which move among "mixed" statements—statements only some of which, according to the expressivist point of view, qualify as genuinely assertoric. What property is transmitted from the premises to the conclusion of a valid inference, only some of whose ingredients are

3. The DS is, remember, the parent platitude for those about correspondence, negation, and the distinction between truth and justification, and it generates Wiggins' three marks discussed in footnote 2. Of itself, it is, so far as I can see, neutral on the matters of absoluteness and stability; but that there is no provision for the predicate's being applicable to sentences to lesser and greater degree, and that it has no significant tense, can always be ensured by stipulation. The basic connection with assertion, for its part, may be ensured merely by so characterising the conditions of application of the truth predicate to propositions that a version of the Equivalence Schema—it is true that P iff P—goes in tandem with the DS.

genuinely truth-apt? For minimalism, by contrast, an answer can be given along perfectly conventional lines, since a notion of truth preservation across inference will now be uniformly available. But more generally, the minimalist proposal is conservative of our ordinary style of thought and talk about the comic, the revolting and the delightful, the good, and the valuable, which finds no solecism in the description of contents concerning such matters as "true", or in the applicability of ordinary notions of supposition and inference to them.

These advantages, comparable as they are to the related advantages of a corresponding minimalism about the notions of object and reference when applied to pure mathematics,[4] strike me as very great. But they would be entirely offset, in my opinion, if the minimalist proposal had to forgo all means for recovering and clarifying the intuitions which motivate realism and anti-realism about selected discourses. That's a matter to which we must shortly turn.

(iv) Finally, there is no reason to expect that the minimal platitudes will constrain their interpretation to within uniqueness. A *variety* of predicates may qualify as truth predicates, and we have to be receptive to the possibility that the truth predicates across different regions of discourse may differ in important respects. Two important potential satisfiers are Putnam's *assertibility under empirically ideal circumstances,* and the rather different idea (or range of ideas) I introduced of *superassertibility*—assertibility which would be durable under any possible improvement to one's state of information.

The latter is an especially important example, since, so I argued, it demonstrably satisfies the minimal platitudes for any discourse which sustains the general epistemic constraint

$$P \leftrightarrow P \text{ may be known,}$$

and it is plausible that this is a form of epistemic constraint imposed quite generally by Dummettian semantic anti-realism. The semantic anti-realist thesis can thus be interpreted as being that truth should be conceived globally as superassertibility. This

4. See Chapter 1, note 18.

thesis diverges from the detail of the internal realism which Putnam's more recent writings have defended. But it is, it seems to me, entirely in harmony with Putnam's core thought, that truth should be conceived non-metaphysically, as a projection of the standards of rational acceptability which actually inform our ordinary practices of enquiry and assertion.

## II. The Realism Debate: Whither Now?

I have now said more or less all I'm going to say about the first part of the task which I set myself:[5] an indication of notions of truth and truth aptitude which may be accepted as metaphysically neutral, and hence as available common ground in disputes between realism and anti-realism in different areas of discourse. It is a matter of recognising the legitimacy of a minimal notion of assertoric content, characteristic, naturally, of all the regions of discourse for which the realism debate arises, and of recognising that where sentences have that kind of content, there is no obstacle to defining upon them a predicate which will satisfy the minimal constraints on truth. Their aptitude for truth is thereby settled just in the precise sense that, on occasion, it will be justifiable to claim that they are true.

The consequent question, if all this is accepted, is: what, in that case, are such debates *about?* Haven't we merely surrendered the underpinnings for such debate, committing ourselves to the kind of bloodless *quietism* for which some writers find inspiration in the later Wittgenstein? Don't we simply have to settle for the bland perspective of a variety of assertoric "language games", each governed by its own internal standards of acceptability, each sustaining a metaphysically emasculated notion of truth, each unqualified for anything of more interest or importance? Don't we lack a basis, now, for any kind of unequal comparison between, say, claims about what is funny and claims about the primary qualities of material objects?

For some, such a quietism, if it could be shown to be principled, would come as a relief. But my own view, to repeat, is that

5. Though see the discussion note to this chapter.

the minimalist approach to truth and truth aptitude must be held hostage to the possibility of justifying negative answers to these questions.

In order to begin to see how matters may proceed, let us reflect once more on Michael Dummett's conception of realism—the suggestion that the distinctive thesis of a realist about a given area of discourse is that its semantics is truth-conditional, with the relevant notion of truth understood either as satisfying the principle of Bivalence, as in Dummett's original formulations, or anyway as evidentially unconstrained. Suppose we sustain this conception of the semantics of a particular discourse. Two consequences are immediately salient. First, a distinction is enforced between the truth predicate for the discourse and superassertibility. Superassertibility is, as we noted, essentially an evidentially constrained notion—if a statement is superassertible, it has to be possible to gather (defeasible) evidence that it is. Accordingly, any demonstration that a discourse's truth predicate is epistemically unconstrained—has no essential connection with the availability of evidence—is a demonstration that it has a feature which superassertibility essentially lacks, and hence that the latter is inadequate as an interpretation of it.

The second consequence is that since statements of the hypothesised discourse can be true without being superassertible, and since the superassertibility of a statement is a matter of its being enduringly sustained by the most refined application of the standards which actually inform our practice of the discourse in question, the thought is at least invited that the world's making such statements true is something conceptually quite independent of our standards of appraisal—something, as it were, which is wholly between the statement and its truth maker, and on which we impinge only in an (at most) detective role. And that is, of course, exactly the "modest" (contrast: the presumptuous) component in realism which I distinguished at the outset of Chapter 1.

The Dummettian debate, then—the debate about whether the truth predicate applicable within a given discourse may properly be taken as evidentially unconstrained—thus provides one very clear illustration of how, once a minimal conception of truth has been conceded as neutral, the issue between realist and anti-realist may nevertheless be joined. If the anti-realist wins the debate, it is open to him—so far—to contend that, for all that our practice dictates to the contrary, the truth predicate within the discourse may be construed in terms of superassertibility, and its applicability taken as nothing more than a reflection of the minimally assertoric character of the declarative sentences in question. By contrast, if the realist wins, it would appear to be impossible to take that view of the discourse's truth predicate. Rather, we shall be forced to think of the truth of its statements as conferred by factors other than those which determine proper practice within the discourse, and hence as being, in whatever sense is thereby imposed, not of our making but a matter of a substantial relationship between language, or thought, and independent states of affairs.

Well and good. But now I think we are in a position to see that there are a *number* of ways in which a relevant debate might proceed, and that the Dummettian debate provides only one possible direction. Effectively, we can represent Dummett's realist as believing

> (a) that the truth predicate applicable within a contested discourse has certain characteristics which importantly supplement those involved in satisfaction of the minimal platitudes;
> (b) that these characteristics enforce a distinction between the discourse's truth predicate and superassertibility.

The key realisation, it seems to me, is that these claims can be separated. We ought to be receptive to the possibility that a truth predicate may have certain more-than-minimal features, as it were, which in some way define and substantiate realist intuitions about the discourse in which it operates without entailing a lack of evidential constraint and enforcing a distinction from superassertibility for that reason. The crucial matter for debate, I want to suggest is, in all cases, *whether any of the properties of a local truth predicate additional to the essential minimal set may somehow justifiably inspire a realist perspective on the discourse concerned.* To show that the

predicate operative within a given discourse is evidentially unconstrained would be one but only one way of accomplishing a positive
answer.

Well then, what other ways of accomplishing that answer may
we envisage? There are two broad strategies to be distinguished,
and a variety of tactics falling under each.

The first strategy continues to focus on superassertibility, and
its relationship to the truth predicate. Dummett's realist insists
that, considerations of vagueness apart, we can be entitled to
regard certain statements as determinate in truth value even
though we may know, or reasonably assume, that we shall never
have the means to determine what truth value they have. Such a
view enforces a distinction in *extension* between truth and superassertibility: if we hold it, we consider ourselves in position to say
that there are truths which are not superassertible. But the *interest*
of that claim is that it imposes a recognition that truth and
superassertibility originate in different ways, from different
sources. And now the obvious question is: why should making
that out depend on reason to think that the two notions actually
extensionally diverge? Cannot extensionally coincident predicates
nevertheless express different properties?

There is a connection here with a well-known contrast expressed
in Plato's *Euthyphro*. It certainly looks as though a valid form of
debate is illustrated by the claims, respectively, that

> It is because certain acts are pious that they are
> loved by the gods

and

> It is because they are loved by the gods that cer-
> tain acts are pious.

The debate involves, presumably, that the two occurrences of "because" be construed differently. One who avers the first claim and
repudiates the second (the view taken by Socrates)[6] intends to
credit the gods with a certain ability of detection—an ability to

6. See Jowett, tr., *The Dialogues of Plato* (Oxford: Oxford University Press,
1892), vol. 2, pp. 84–86.

*track* piety. On this view, the gods are, by their natures, cognitively responsive to piety; and citation of the piety of an act can thus quite properly feature in the explanation of the gods' estimate of it. As we might say: the piety of an act is one thing, and the gods' estimate of it another, and it is merely that the gods are so fortunately endowed that the piety of an act need never elude them if they so choose. By contrast, one who avers the second claim at the expense of the first (the position taken by Euthyphro) intends to repudiate the thought that piety has sufficient, as it were, constitutive independence from the opinions of the best judges (gods) to feature in the explanation of the direction that those opinions take; rather, such opinions enter in some constitutive sense into the determination of which acts are pious. Thus, the "because" in the second claim adverts, on this view, to the *conceptual* ground of an act's being pious.[7]

Notably, it is open to each of the antagonists in this debate to acknowledge that pious acts extensionally coincide with those which, at least potentially, are loved by the gods. Socrates is contending that the piety of an action is, as it were, constituted independently of the gods' estimate of it, and Euthyphro is denying that, but each can agree that the two characteristics invariably accompany one another.

Now, if this is a significant form of debate, there will be provision for a debate of essentially similar structure about the relationship between truth and superassertibility even in the case of discourses for which it is acknowledged on all sides that the two predicates extensionally coincide. One side—the realist—will contend

> It is because certain statements (in the discourse
> in question) are true that they are superassertible,

while the other will contend

> It is because they are superassertible that such
> statements are true.

7. However, it is arguable that this gloss on the debate is in one respect potentially inaccurate—see note 36 to the appendix below.

The first claim will intend to advert to some constitutive independence of truth from superassertibility, while the second side claims that there is none. And to stress: constitutive independence is what is wanted for the realist basic thought—the idea that the *sources* of truth in the discourses in question somehow distance themselves from the matter of what meets our most refined standards of acceptability.

The suggestion, then, is that we may see the Dummettian debate and the *Euthyphro debate* as essentially complementary ways of attacking the more general, crucial question about the relationship between superassertibility and truth. Dummett's debate will be the natural focus in the case of discourses (such as pure number theory) where we at best lack any assurance that truth and superassertibility coincide in extension, or even—the view of a Dummettian realist about the past—have some assurance that they do not. The Euthyphro debate will arise for the case of discourses where we do have such an assurance, and where the issue concerns, rather, further aspects of the relation between the two concepts: for even if they are co-extensive, it can still be, crudely, that truth is one thing and superassertibility is another, provided the Socratic view is correct—provided, that is, a statement's being true *explains,* in some appropriate way, its being superassertible.

None of this, of course, is to indicate in the slightest how an instance of the Euthyphro debate might properly be conducted. A natural starting point would be the question whether the decidability of the statements in question was assured only as a matter of contingency, or—closely relatedly—whether the coincidence of truth with superassertibility within the discourse was something that could be known only a posteriori. There are connections here with one important strand in Locke's distinction between primary and secondary qualities in material objects, the suggestion being attractive—to me at least—that primary qualities might turn out to lend themselves to a broadly Socratic treatment, while the account of the secondaries would be Euthyphronic. But I do not think that the contingency, or a posteriority, of the connection between truth and superassertibility is the only possible crux on which to fit the distinction. Even in cases where decidability is guaranteed a priori—for instance, statements describing one's own sensations, or quantifier-free numerical statements—there ought to be space for a contrast between the thought that the truth-conferring states of affairs are necessarily *detectable* by an appropriate subject, and the thought that they are, rather, conceptually grounded in the judgements of such a subject. But I shall not now broach the question of how such a contrast might be drawn, or any of a number of fascinating questions to which the Euthyphro contrast gives rise.[8] My point is merely to indicate that there is conceptual space for a debate essentially complementary to the Dummettian debate, focussing on the same crux—the relation between truth and superassertibility—but proceeding precisely on the assumption that truth is *not* evidence-transcendent in the discourse in question. The possibility of such a debate is obviously highly germane when we remember one original source of dissatisfaction with Dummett's paradigm, viz. precisely its inapplicability to the issue between realist and anti-realist in the case of discourses, like comedy, or morals on a wide class of construals, where evidence transcendence is simply not in view.

## III. Truth and Correspondence

It is, however, on a second broad strategy or direction of debate on which I now want to concentrate. This is the strategy of simply looking for features of the truth predicate in a contested discourse which go beyond the minimal constraints and in some way, without necessarily having any direct bearing on the relationship between that predicate and superassertibility, serve to clarify and substantiate realist preconceptions.

Consider again the *Correspondence Platitude:*

> For a statement to be true is for it to correspond
> to the facts, "tell it like it is", etc.

It is undeniable that when this platitude, whether in the formulation

8. For further discussion, though still of a preliminary character, see the appendix to this chapter.

(CP)      "Snow is white" is true if and only if things are
              as "Snow is white" says they are

or in the Horwich version

(CP$^+$)    "Snow is white" is true *because* snow is white,

is generated in the way illustrated in Chapter 1, its content falls
way short of the *intent* of those who have made the complaint to
which Horwich wanted to respond. Nothing is accomplished to
make out the idea that the truth of a statement consists in its
representation of something external, in its holding up a mirror to
the world—the kind of idea which, as I suggested earlier, is naturally introduced by the separation of truth and superassertibility
insisted on by a Dummettian realist. The feeling will be that while
the minimalist can perhaps use such manipulations to entitle himself to the *phrase* "represents the facts", or "corresponds to reality",
as a permissible gloss on "is true", he does not thereby earn the
intended substance. This intended substance is what is gestured at
by the stress on "because" in Horwich's formulation; it is the idea
that, crudely, talk of "representation of the facts" is not just admissible phrasing, a harmless gloss on talk of truth, but incorporates
a philosophically correct—as we might say, *seriously dyadic*—
perspective on the truth predicate (at least for discourses where
realism is appropriate). And of course, no deflationist can or *should*
want to entitle herself to that perspective; her point ought to be
that it is additional metaphysical theory, foisted onto phrases
which, while characteristic of the idea of truth, can be saved by a
deflationary account and merit no such metaphysical interpretation.

Our interest, however, is different. It is in whether there is a
way, besides pursuit of the issues to do with truth and superassertibility which we have already reviewed, of giving debatable
content to this talk of additional substance, substance essayed but
not necessarily carried by the legitimate use of correspondence
phraseology. The foreseeable problem, of course, is that if such
phraseology is in the market *both* for minimal interpretation—as
bestowed by the derivability of the Correspondence Platitude from

more basic platitudes—*and* for some form of more substantial interpretation, when it takes on a content more consonant with realist intuition, then so, very likely, will be anything we say in the attempt to explicate the contrast between the interpretations. At any rate, it seems unlikely that we can nail down the intended contrast simply by italics, emphases, scare-quotes and yet more circuitous paraphrases. So how to proceed?

The way forward is to ask what, if any, considerations sometimes operate on the interpretation of correspondence phraseology besides the fact that it—and all the paraphrases we are likely to think of—are co-licensed, as it were, with talk of truth. Superficially viewed, the Correspondence Platitude takes us from a predicate, "true", to a relation, and lays it down as necessary and sufficient for the predicate to apply to a statement that the latter bears that relation to a suitably designated object-term. The question should be, I suggest, whether our understanding of what it is for this relation to obtain has, in the case of any particular discourse, *more* to it than can be derived from the co-permissibility of the claim that it obtains with the claim that a relevant statement is true, and the co-permissibility of the latter with the claim that that statement is assertible. *That* much understanding is what is bestowed by the derivability of the Correspondence Platitude from the minimal platitudes concerning the truth predicate. The additional substance, putatively inaccessible to deflationism, must thus be located in what further understanding, if any, we may, in suitable regions, possess of the claim that "P" corresponds to the facts.

Well, there are, naturally, only two places to look for such additional content. One is the *relational term*—the idea of representation, or correspondence. Here the quest will be for some additional aspect of our understanding of the relational term, exceeding anything imposed by its liaison with the minimal platitudes, which somehow gives a point to realist intuition in the area of discourse in question. The other course is to work on the object-term—*the facts*—and, once again, to try to show how we are committed, in that area, to a more robust conception of them that is entrained merely by the minimalist permission to gloss "is true" as "corresponds to the facts".

Each of these simple ideas is harnessed, as I shall try to bring out later in this chapter and in subsequent ones, to a widely perceived crux of traditional and contemporary debate about realism in ethics, and elsewhere.

## IV. Realism versus Anti-realism: Summary of Strategies for the Debate

Let me, then, briefly recapitulate the two broad strategies I have distinguished for the prosecution of realist and anti-realist debate between antagonists who are content to agree that the discourse in question sustains minimal notions of assertoric content and truth.

The first strategy focusses on the relationship between the discourse's truth predicate and the notion of superassertibility which may be defined upon the standards of assertoric warrant to which its statements will be subject. The realist will argue for, and the anti-realist will resist the suggestion that the notions are importantly distinct in source, with truth either (potentially) outrunning superassertibility in extension or, even if extensionally coincident, serving as the latter's explanatory base.

The second broad strategy, by contrast, involves scrutiny of the Correspondence Platitude and its defensible interpretation. Here, the key question is whether the relational term, and the object term, are, with respect to a particular discourse, properly understood in ways which exceed the content conferred upon them by the derivability of the Platitude from the minimal constraints, and whether they do so in a fashion which gives concrete shape to the imagery of mirroring by which realism pretheoretically defines itself.

So there are at least four kinds of debate to have: the Dummettian debate, the Euthyphro debate, a debate about "represents", and a debate about "the facts". Instances of the Dummettian debate have, of course, been quite vigorously prosecuted in recent years, and many of the moves are familiar. The same is not obviously true of the other three, though, as I suggested a moment ago, much contemporary debate about ethics is fruitfully interpreted as coming under the latter two heads. In any case, I hope this much is already plausible: that we do not, in going minimalist about assertoric content and truth, set ourselves on a fast track to quietism about traditional philosophical controversy concerning realism and objectivity. Plenty of avenues remain by which to try to give focus to those controversies, and even to pick the winners. And this holds good not just for discourses where we think of the truth predicate as evidentially unconstrained, but also for those, like comedy, where we incline to the contrary view.

However the issue of quietism will require more direct theoretical attention. I shall return to it in Chapter 6.

## V. Minimalism and Error-Theory

Before we take up issues to do with the Correspondence Platitude in earnest, there is an item of postponed business: the question whether all scope for the error-theoretic genre of anti-realism is closed off by minimalism.

The position, I think, is that error-theoretic proposals remain theoretically feasible but that their development is interestingly constrained. Suppose a philosopher denies that anything or much of what we say within a given discourse is true but grants that its truth predicate admits interpretation as superassertibility by its standards of assertoric warrant. Then he has to produce reason to deny that anything, or very much, of what we say is superassertible in the light of those standards. And that will be a commitment to denying that any, or very many, of the statements of the discourse are even assertible by those standards.[9]

So far as I can see, there are just two ways such a denial might be sustained. One is to contend that while the standards in question are perfectly coherent, little of what we accept really complies with them; our "error", on this view, will consist in a propensity to apply those standards erroneously. The other is to argue that the discourse is not governed by coherent standards of assertoric

9. Since, as observed in section V of Chapter 2, there is no such thing as holding warrant to assert a statement while simultaneously having warrant to believe that that warrant can be defeated—as the claim that the statement is not superassertible implies.

warrant, and consequently that nothing is genuinely warranted by those standards.

Now it's notable that most actual error-theorists do not tend to adopt either course. Neither Mackie nor Field, for instance, attempts any case that moral or pure mathematical discourse is governed by standards of warrant which are incoherent, and hence unsatisfiable, or so demanding that our ordinary practice hardly ever measures up to them. Rather, they proceed in ways which presuppose that the relevant truth predicates *cannot* satisfactorily be interpreted in terms of superassertibility—which presuppose, more specifically, that there is no entailment within the discourse from superassertibility to truth, so that to acknowledge that a good deal of what is asserted within the discourse may be superassertible by the proper standards is no commitment to its truth. Field, for instance, takes it for granted that the correct account of the truth conditions of pure mathematical statements has the effect—because of its implication of an objectionably abstract ontology—of putting them beyond establishment by ordinary proof methods. And Mackie takes it that the correct account of the truth conditions of moral judgements—because of its implication of metaphysically preposterous properties—puts such judgements beyond appraisal by ordinary moral reasoning and sentiment. Each thus implicitly contends that truth and superassertibility come apart in the discourses they respectively consider.

Well, no doubt such a claim must at least be coherent if it is ever to be possible to argue that the truth predicate operative within a discourse is not superassertibility by that discourse's actual standards. The great question, it seems to me, concerns not the coherence of error theory but its *motivation:* why insist on construing the discourse in terms of a notion of truth which has us in massive error when the alternative of superassertibility is prima facie available and would avoid the charge? This is a question which may have a good answer; it may be, for instance, that the purposes and importance which we feel the discourse to have cannot properly be recognised under the aegis of a superassertibilist construal of truth but demand some kind of external standard. It is another question, however, how well actual error theorists have answered it, or whether they have perceived its importance at all.

## VI. Convergence and Cognitive Command

David Wiggins[10] makes it a defining mark of an expression's functioning as a truth predicate within a discourse that there should be a tendency for competent practitioners to converge in opinions concerning its application. Certainly, the matter of convergence has often been regarded as a point of sensitivity for would-be realists about value, and has supplied a popular strategy of argument with relativistic opponents. But why should it be supposed that there is anti-realist capital to be made out of a (putative) lack of trans-cultural convergence about, say, sexual morality, or moral questions to do with punishment, or the moral status of suicide?

A straightforward answer would be that if, as proposed by Wiggins, a tendency to convergence about its applications is indeed, subject to certain conditions, an essential mark of any bona fide truth predicate, then a manifest lack of convergence in moral judgement, or other forms of evaluation, may allow manipulation into an effective argument that moral or other forms of evaluative discourse are not really in the business of truth and falsity at all.

Clearly, the conclusion of this simple strategy of argument will not be congenial to anyone in sympathy with the broad approach to these matters which I have been sketching. But might such a conclusion really be secured so simply? The crucial question is, evidently: what *exactly* is supposed to be the guiding connection between convergence and truth aptitude? An appealing but vague suggestion would be this:

> *Convergence 1:* A class of statements are apt to be true only if there would be a tendency, in suitable circumstances, for competent subjects to agree on the truth, or falsity, of members in that class.

This is certainly plausible enough. But it is also completely anodyne. In effect, it comes to no more than the claim that the possession of assertoric content is a necessary condition of truth. For we ought to expect that *any* class of statements which possess

10. See note 2 above.

determinate assertoric content will thereby be associated with standards of proper assertibility which their users will acknowledge and about whose satisfaction they will, in suitable circumstances, agree.[11] And an agreement that they are satisfied will naturally be convertible, via the Disquotational Schema, into an agreement about the application of the truth predicate. Convergence 1 is indeed a mark of anything worth regarding as a truth predicate. It is for instance, as it had better be, a characteristic of superassertibility. Just for that reason, though, it puts up too low a barrier to provide any real hope that a successful anti-realist argument might use it in the very simple way canvassed. Moral discourse is unquestionably possessed of minimally assertoric content—moral opinions are subjected to a high degree of discipline, and there is both an enormous degree of convergence about them within cultures, and a very considerable degree across cultures. Perhaps there are, on specific questions, major disagreements within or across cultures; and perhaps the prospects for the convergence of opinion on these specific questions are sometimes very slight. But if that's so, it is fine by Convergence 1, which is content to articulate a condition on the truth aptitude of a whole *class* of statements, with no explicit requirement on each and every member of the class.

In sum: Convergence 1 is indeed a correct test for truth aptitude; but—just for that reason—what it tests for is *minimal* truth aptitude. For the purposes of an anti-realist who wants to make capital out of what she takes to be an irremediable lack of convergence in opinions held in some area, it is therefore too easy a test to pass.

If there is anything to this strategy of anti-realist argument, then, a more strenuous condition needs to be involved. And it will not be a condition on truth aptitude *simpliciter,* since all minimally assertoric contents are truth-apt. Let us say that a discourse is apt for *substantial* truth just in case its truth predicate has certain further characteristics, over and above the minimal set, in virtue of which, at least to some extent, it becomes appropriate to think

---

11. But see discussion note 1 of this chapter.

of the discourse realistically.[12] Then our question becomes: is any convergence property plausibly to be viewed as a necessary condition of aptitude for substantial truth?

The hunch that convergence is somehow a crux between realist and anti-realist involves, it seems to me, the thought that— ignoring for a moment complications which will be generated by vagueness—it ought to be a *global* property of the statements at issue. The idea, for example, that something is shown about the (lack of) objectivity of comedy by the possibility of irreducibly divergent opinions about it is not assuaged at all by the reflection that there is, very probably, convergence in some—probably many—comic opinions. By contrast, and to stress: it is no part of a discourse's being minimally truth-apt that disagreements cannot occur in which, not for reasons of vagueness, neither disputant can be justly criticised. Minimal truth aptitude requires the operation of standards of proper assertibility and, consequently, the existence of criteria for the ascription of ignorance or error. There has to be, at least potentially, use for these notions in the description of disputes. But nothing need be involved which ensures that, in any disagreement, at least one party must be guilty of violation of those standards of proper assertibility, or of ignorance or error by those criteria.

Accordingly, the most immediately natural strengthening of Convergence 1 will simply involve requiring that the kind of irreproachable disagreements which are not precluded by minimal truth aptitude be precluded anyway; that the "tendency" of which Convergence 1 speaks be supplanted by a more exacting condition which eliminates such disagreements. The intentions of those who have felt that convergence is important might thus be better reflected by:

> *Convergence 2:* A class of statements are apt for substantial truth only if *each* of them will, under suitable circumstances, command a convergence of opinion about its truth or falsity.

12. I introduce the phrase "substantial truth" merely for ease of discussion, to register the presence of realism-relevant features within a discourse. Its use is not a commitment to the idea that truth itself divides into more and less substantial kinds.

Obviously this test would be applicable only to statements for which the possibility of evidence-transcendent truth could be excluded. The intuition it is trying to reflect is that in any region of discourse where we can't provide that excuse—can't explain how relevant aspects of the world might simply outstrip our cognitive powers—it's proper to think of ourselves as dealing in "genuine fact", as it were, only if we have an assurance that, at least in favourable circumstances, no intractable disagreements will arise.

But this is not much better. Convergence 2 is spoiled by its failure to impose any controls on the phrase "in suitable circumstances". There are, no doubt, empirical pre-conditions for an exceptionless convergence in senses of humour, or moral response. Why doesn't the satisfaction of such conditions amount to the obtaining of "suitable circumstances"? But of course, it mustn't be allowed to do so, or every minimally truth-apt discourse in which any particular disagreement is empirically explicable will allow of a specification of "suitable conditions" under which that disagreement would not have occurred, and hence will qualify as apt for substantial truth. The phrase "in suitable circumstances" clearly marks a place that has to be filled somehow or other; it would be futile to impose a condition of convergence *tout court*. But it mustn't be allowed simply to embrace any set of conditions actually conducive to the emergence of a consensus.

It is when we begin to reflect on what it ought to mean, if a substantial test is to be conveyed in keeping with the original intuition, that we can begin to see that the matter of convergence is actually beside the point and that those who have thought it important have somewhat misformulated their requirement.

The crucial thought here, I suggest, is yet another platitude—this time one connecting convergence with the idea of *representation*. Think of a device—a camera, or fax machine, or whatever—whose function is the production of representations. The following seems incontestable:

> *Convergence/Representation Platitude:* If two devices each function to produce representations, then if conditions are suitable, and they function properly, they will produce divergent output if and only if presented with divergent input.

The platitude is vague, but highly suggestive. It is a basic ingredient in intuitive realist thinking about a discourse (at any rate, of realist thinking of the "presumptuous" sort) that, by respecting that discourse's warrant-conferring standards, we do, as it were, put ourselves into "representational mode"—do put ourselves in position to produce mirrors, in thought or language, of the states of affairs with which the discourse distinctively deals. Realism, when it is not blighted by scepticism, is exactly the view that the opinions to which we are moved in the prosecution of a favoured discourse are the products of (successful or unsuccessful) representational function, and are thereby endowed with representational content. But now suppose someone maintains that, in forming views about comedy, we do indeed function representationally. Then, by the Convergence/Representation Platitude, disagreements in output—disagreements in which such opinions we accept—require less than suitable conditions, or less than proper function, or divergent input. And the fact is that we don't ordinarily think that disagreement about the comic has to be attributable to factors which may naturally be assigned to *any* of those three categories.

Isn't that the intuitive core of the instinct for anti-realism about comedy, so far as it is motivated by lack of convergence? If so, the key thought is nothing specifically to do with convergence. It is rather that it is only if intractable *divergences* in opinion have to be attributable to certain sorts of factors that their possibility will be consistent with a claim to representational function—only then will it be true that forming opinions in a manner respectful of the standards which govern assertibility within the discourse ranks as a species of representational activity, if "representational" is understood as constrained by the Convergence/Representation Platitude.

Generalisation of this idea in the direction of a definite constraint would result, as a first shot, in something like the following principle:

*Cognitive Command:*[13] A discourse exhibits Cognitive Command if and only if it is a priori that differences of opinion arising

13. Called "Rational Command" in my 1987 Gareth Evans Memorial Lecture, "Realism, Anti-realism, Irrealism, Quasi-realism", in French, Uehling and Wettstein, eds., *Mid-west Studies in Philosophy,* vol. 12 (Minneapolis: University of Minnesota Press, 1988), pp. 25–49.

> within it can be satisfactorily explained only in terms of "divergent input", that is, the disputants' working on the basis of different information (and hence guilty of ignorance or error, depending on the status of that information), or "unsuitable conditions" (resulting in inattention or distraction and so in inferential error, or oversight of data and so on), or "malfunction" (for example, prejudicial assessment of data, upwards or downwards, or dogma, or failings in other categories already listed).

Obviously, that's extremely rough. But the general drift is this. Thinking of the judgements to which we are moved in any particular discourse as constituting the output of, as it were, a seriously representational mode of intellectual function is justified only if we are justified in supposing that the discourse satisfies the Cognitive Command constraint, where satisfying that constraint means that any disagreement within the discourse involves something worth describing as a *cognitive shortcoming.* So much is merely imposed, so far as I can see, by the Convergence/Representation Platitude.

The emergent suggestion, then, is that the traditional disputes about convergence are best interpreted as pivoting on a Cognitive Command constraint, with (putative) divergence in basic moral views, for instance, being taken as prima facie evidence that ethical discourse fails the test, and hence does not qualify as seriously representational in the sense evinced in the Convergence/Representation Platitude. That conclusion, were it to be justified, would not (it should now be superfluous to say) call into question the permissibility of regarding moral truths, like all truths, as "representations of reality", "corresponding to the facts", "telling it like it is". For these ways of talking are licensed by the applicability of the truth predicate itself. What would follow, rather, would be only and precisely this: that the notion of representation, and its cognates, featuring in such phrases would not be able to draw the additional substance conferred upon it when a discourse satisfies Cognitive Command—the additional substance imposed by the analogy which may then be displayed, in the context of the Convergence/Representation Platitude, with the products of other everyday representational systems.

Cognitive Command will be the focus of attention in the next chapter. Let me close this one by emphasising two points about it. The first is to explain again (I hope not *ad nauseam*) why Cognitive Command is a significant additional constraint on minimally truth-apt discourses. Minimal truth aptitude results from the currency of standards of warranted assertion which doubtless will generate convergence in a significant class of circumstances. But it is consistent with the minimal truth aptitude of a discourse that the relevant standards are highly tolerant, or underdetermine a substantial class of potential disagreements, or otherwise allow a degree of idiosyncrasy in their application, and so permit divergences of opinion in which, judged purely by those standards, no shortcoming need be involved. Cognitive Command precisely tightens down on that slack.

Second (and this will be a point of some importance later) it seems essential that the constraint be formulated, as above, in terms of *apriority:* of its being a priori that disagreements are attributable to factors within the prescribed range. It wouldn't be of any interest if all relevant disagreements were, *merely as a matter of fact,* invariably attributable to such factors—as a matter of serendipity, as it were. It might have been, for instance, that we all shared a single sense of humour, and that disagreements about the comic were always in practice down to something worth describing as a cognitive shortcoming, of one of the kinds listed, in relation to *non-comic* factors. But if that were so, it would be something which could only be determined a posteriori, and would have no intuitive bearing on the objectivity of discourse about comedy. There would be no such intuitive bearing precisely because it would still be readily conceivable that senses of humour might substantially differ and be none the worse for it. If our interest is in the question whether comic discourse, *by virtue of its very content,* is fitted to express the products of a seriously representational mode of function, then any constraint designed to capture that idea must, it seems, be so formulated that satisfying it requires the possibility of a priori knowledge that the relevant conditions are met.

## DISCUSSION NOTE

*The thought has now surfaced more than once that the "discipline" imposed on the use of a range of statements just by their possession of assertoric content will ensure some degree of convergence about when they may be regarded as warranted. It featured, for example, in the argument given in footnote 2, that any minimally truth-apt discourse will allow the definition of a truth predicate satisfying Wiggins' convergence mark; and more recently in the explanation of what Cognitive Command adds to minimal truth aptitude. But is there not a crucial ambiguity here? It is plausible enough that, in order for a class of sentences to possess determinate assertoric content, there has to be some consensus about which conditions warrant their assertion. But "warrant" can mean "permit" or it can mean "mandate". It is, for example, permissible to opine that something is funny when one finds oneself amused by it; and it is generally acknowledged to be so. But nothing need <u>mandate</u> that opinion; others can quite permissibly disagree. Thus, a consensus about what conditions warrant a particular judgement—in the sense in which determinacy in assertoric content arguably presupposes such consensus—need have no implications about convergence in actual judgements.*

*This is important because it is convergence of the latter kind which is a mark of truth in Wiggins' view. Thus, a discourse may display the syntactic potentialities emphasised in the characterisation of minimal truth aptitude and the "discipline" associated with a consensus about when its statements are permissible, yet a truth predicate introduced over it via the Disquotational Schema may fail to display Wiggins' mark. Truth may thus be a rather more expensive commodity than minimalism allows.*

Just what is implicit in the idea of "discipline" here no doubt provides a natural focus for resistance by those with lingering expressivist and error-theoretic sympathies. Since the notion will be important in what follows, and especially for the discussion in Chapter 5, I shall take some trouble with it now.

Let me first try to sharpen the objection. The gap it is concerned with lies between subjects' agreeing that a statement is justified and their all endorsing it—precisely the gap opened if "justification" is merely *permission*.[14] A discourse all of whose statements had only permissive assertion conditions would still be disciplined by the relevant rules of permission; but one could not, without further assumption, expect its practitioners to agree in significant measure on which such statements they actually endorsed, any more than one would expect children given permission to go on just three rides at the funfair to want the same ones. Such a discourse, the objection continues, might still have the syntactic apparatus—negation, the conditional, and so on—characteristic of assertoric content. So one could still lay down the Disquotational Schema as stipulative of a "truth" predicate for it. But competent practice would not demand any significant degree of

14. I am setting on one side what I take it would be a misunderstanding of the intent of one for whom the objection as formulated strikes a chord. There is another gap—that between agreement about what *would* justify any of a range of statements and agreement about which statements in that range should actually be regarded as justified. This distinction is valid even if we restrict attention to statements with mandatory (in whatever is the intended sense) rather than permissive assertion conditions; and it is presumably only a consensus about the first component—about what it takes to justify the statements in a certain range—which is immediately implicit in a community's having assigned them a determinate meaning. There is therefore a *possible* line of objection to the effect that since consensus of that sort entails nothing about consensus in actual judgements—hence in applications of the truth predicate—the train of thought of note 2 concerning the convergence mark must be spurious. This line of objection, however, makes nothing of the contrast between permissive and mandatory. Moreover, it demands that it be intelligible in general how speakers' agreement in *meanings* (agreement in their conception of what ideally counts as justifying a particular kind of statement) may co-exist with the absence of any significant degree of agreement in their *use* (agreement about which such statements are actually justified). Philosophers of Wittgensteinian or Davidsonian sympathies will, of course, reject such a suggestion. But the decisive point in the present context is that if the motivation to include consensus among the essential marks of truth in the first place is just the thoughts (i) that truth is essentially normative of assertoric practice, and (ii) that the operation of a norm over a practice will tend to show in a consensus about which moves observe it (and if that isn't the motivation, then what is?), then what the objection really challenges is (ii), hence the appropriateness of including convergence among the essential marks of truth. And if that is under challenge, then even if the note 2 thought were to fall to the objection, it would not follow that "truth may thus be a rather more expensive commodity than minimalism allows".

consensus about which of its statements were "true", and "truth" so introduced would not be normative of its competent practice. This shows that the contention that any assertoric discourse—one satisfying the appropriate constraints of syntax and discipline— allows the definition of a minimal truth predicate is good only if the discipline is constituted by *mandatory* assertion conditions. And that is just what isn't true, plausibly, of talk about the comic, the boring, and so on. So such discourses are not truth-apt—not even minimally so.

Is this the way for the error-theorist or expressivist to build a bridgehead, even within the minimalist framework? Possibly. But I do not think, to begin with, that it is at all obvious that there are really any such things as *permissive* assertion conditions. Perhaps the clearest apparent example would be provided by vagueness. Are there not shades of colour, for instance, which it is permissible to describe as "red"—such a description would not be determinately wrong—but also permissible not to, since that description would not be determinately right either? Such a view of vague statements ought to be controversial. To describe such shades as permitting but not mandating the verdict "red" is to assign them a certain sort of *determinacy* in status. But of course the boundary between shades which permit description as "red" and those which mandate it will itself be vague. Do we wish to say, accordingly, that the verdict "permits description as vague" itself has both permissive and man- datory assertion conditions? Or should we conclude that it is wrong to think of "borderline cases" as things which determinately permit but do not mandate verdicts—that it is better to think that the vagueness of the contrast between "red" and "not red" consists not in the existence of an intermediate region of permissive shades but in the fact that, while either verdict can be justified only by being mandated, the contrast between what mandates "red" and what "not red" is not everywhere determinate? On this view, there is no region where it is determinate that neither "red" nor "not-red" is mandated but where both are permissible; it is merely that it is not everywhere determinate *which* is mandated.

Even if we think of borderline cases of "red" as, so to say, issuing permissions, it remains that such shades contrast with shades where the description as "red" or as "not red" is mandated: shades where assent, or dissent, from the verdict "red" is in no way discretionary. Is this essential? The above objection will be answered if every assertoric content with permissive assertion conditions also necessarily has mandatory ones. Could there be a contentful discourse—a *fully permissive* discourse—in which all statements, including negations, were associated *only* with permissive assertion conditions?

Clearly the contrast between conditions which permit an assertion and conditions which do not cannot itself be wholly permissive. If all statements are at least determinately *not* permitted under certain circumstances, then, under the assumption that it was made permissibly, one could infer from the correctness of such a statement that conditions of that sort did not obtain, even if one learned nothing else. But if none of the assertions in question is ever determinately not permitted, no one on receiving one of them, even if she presumed it had been made within the rules, could—without collateral information about the patterns of use displayed by her "informant"—derive any information from it at all. Nothing would be excluded by the "correctness" of such an assertion. So there would be nothing for its correctness to consist in, and no determinate assertoric content involved. At the least, assertoric content requires conditions which mandate *not* making a statement, and whose obtaining therefore defeats it. That much discipline is a precondition of saying anything at all.

That, though, doesn't answer the question. Could there be an assertoric discourse—one with all the syntax of assertoric content: negation, the conditional, and so on—in which each ingredient statement is associated just with two kinds of conditions: those under which it is permissible and those under which it is not? The obvious question concerns what the role of "assertion" would be in such a discourse. It is a basic feature of assertion that it transmits justification; specifically, if another makes an assertion which I am entitled to regard as justified in her situation, and if I have no other information bearing on the proposition asserted, then I acquire justification for that proposition. On the face of it, this feature—call it transmissiveness—could be conserved in a discourse in which all justification was permission: if I have reason to regard your verdict of "red" as permitted by the shade of the object presented to you, and if I have no other information bearing on the colour of that object, then your verdict ought to give me permission for the same verdict. But let's look closer. What content will assertions in the fully permissive discourse carry? *All* one could acquire sufficient reason to accept on receipt of the assertion that P, taking the assertion to be justified and having no other relevant information, would be that P is permissible. That P is permissible cannot, however, be taken to be the content of the statement that P, since—worries about impredicativity apart—the former will presumably be mandated when P's permission conditions are met, whereas P, by hypothesis, has *no* mandatory assertion conditions. It follows that there will be a contrast between the content of the conditionals "If P, then Q", and "If P is permissible, then Q". Now, in order to count as a conditional at all, the former must be at the service of inference by modus ponens. But since "P is permissible" does not, presumably, entail P, it cannot be that every kind of justification for "If P, then Q" is justification for "If P is permissible, then Q". Naturally, we do not yet know, at this skeletal level of description, what other kind of justification there might be for the former. But, whatever it is, suppose I have it; and suppose I am informed that P—that is, someone makes what I take to be a justified assertion that P and, having no other relevant information concerning P, I thereby acquire justification for P. Then I now apparently have justification for both premises of a modus ponens step. But plainly I have no justification for the conclusion—not even if justification is taken to be permission— since my justification for P consists in no more than a warrant to accept that P is permissible and I don't have justification for "If P is permissible, then Q". Conclusion: a fully permissive discourse could not sustain both the transmissiveness of assertion and a genuine conditional—one allowing the unrestricted validity of modus ponens. But that is to say that a fully permissive discourse could not really have all the trappings of *assertoric* content.

It may be rejoined that it does not follow that such a discourse could not be contentful at all. Content might accrue to its utterances by virtue of an agreed understanding of the consequences of their acceptance—of the practical commitments, for example, which someone would thereby incur, and the aspects of her mental and social career whose explanation could usefully appeal to her acceptance of such a statement. So the error theorist and expressivist could still follow the general strategy of trying to show that what superficially might pass for an assertoric discourse turns out not really to be so—that, perhaps in relatively unobvious ways, it falls short even of the constraints of syntax and discipline which minimalism emphasises. Indeed, does not the argument just given disclose, if successful, one such relatively unobvious way? Maybe, then, the real effect of the minimalist approach is not to show that truth is a relatively inexpensive commodity but that assertoric content, even by the minimalist's lights, is a relatively expensive one.

Clearly there are issues for further investigation here. But assume, for the sake of argument, that assertoric content as conceived by minimalism ought to be viewed as a rather less superficial characteristic than I have perhaps suggested—so that it is still possible, up to a point, for a discourse which seems to be subject to publicly understood rules of use and to display the syntactic resources characteristic of assertoric content, merely to masquerade as assertoric. The real question, even so, is of course whether discourses which have actually tended or are likely to inspire error-theoretic and expressivist accounts do actually so masquerade. Comedy—to continue with the same stalking-horse—is, of course, a very complex matter. But I think it is clear, even on a cursory inspection, that it is not a region where discipline is constituted by rules of permission nor, for that reason, one where there is cause to look askance at the assertion-related constructions, such as the conditional, which it apparently contains.

Let us carry out the cursory inspection. Basically, and obviously, the assertion condition for a comic statement is to experience amusement. But the warrants thereby conferred are open to defeat in a variety of ways—and this defeat frequently takes the form not merely of cancellation of warrant to assert but of a (defeasible) mandate for denial. To begin with, if a comic response is to justify a comic claim, then it has to be at least *intelligible,* even among those who do not share it. Avalanches, crying babies, drying paint, the sound of wind in the trees, the call of the curlew, a hunting lioness, a man pruning apple trees—none of these things could intelligibly be found funny without some very special stage setting. The comic is, in addition, a highly unstable companion of tragedy, evil, and suffering as well as excellence, nobility and beauty, and is largely constrained to subservience to them. The unintended spoonerisms and muffed anecdotes in an after-dinner speech by a pompous and unpopular administrator are not risible if you know that he is distracted by the serious illness of his child. Otters' clowning on thin ice is not funny if the river is dangerously contaminated. The stilted and exaggerated stage mannerisms of a prima donna are not funny if you appreciate the magnificence of the music. A small child laughs at the contorted expression and rolling gait of a marathon runner only because he has little conception of competitive sport in general or marathon running in particular. Then again, comic reactions can, of course, be merely badly informed and the claims they warrant correspondingly open to defeat by better information of no particular moral or aesthetic relevance. The politician's quip is not funny if you heard the heckler's question correctly, since the joke depended on an ambiguity which wasn't actually there. The incidental movements of the philosophy lecturer's eyebrows are not funny if you manage to understand what he is saying. Finally, considerations of all these sorts are themselves open to potential defeat, with reinstatement of the original claim as one possible consequence. An apparently unintelligible fit of the giggles may come to be only too intelligible. The "marathon" may turn out to have been staged by John Cleese.

This is already a lot of "discipline". It makes room for the ideas of being amused by what is not funny and of overlooking what is, and hence provides, in particular, a use for claims of the form, "I thought that was funny but it wasn't", and "I didn't realise that was funny, but it was"—the seems right / is right contrast that is pivotal, of course, for the ideas about private language mooted in *Philosophical Investigations* §§258–260. In addition, it apparently entrains a use for at least one kind of genuine conditional with a comic antecedent: if considerations of a certain kind can mandate denial of a comic claim, then a conditional will hold good whose antecedent puts up that claim and whose consequent denies those considerations. But it should be replied that a purely permissive discourse could be expected to appear to sustain such conditionals too, since the consequences of the correctness of any of its "statements" will certainly embrace everything implied by its being permissible. Likewise, use for the first half of the seems right / is right contrast demands only the possibility of mistaken belief that permission conditions are met. Comic discourse is not *fully* permissive if its statements do indeed have certain mandatory denial conditions. However, the argument above, that a fully permissive discourse could not be genuinely assertoric, involved no consideration of negations in any case. It will therefore still apply if we restrict attention to positive claims about comedy unless they too are mandatory in certain circumstances. But that is precisely what seems not to be so.

However, I think it is just a misrepresentation to suppose that someone who is tickled by some situation, and believes there is no reason why this reaction might be regarded as callous, or offensive, or deranged, and so on, is in a position when it is merely permissible—that is, optional—to opine that it is funny. Rather, that is the view which it is then *appropriate* for her to take, and failure to do so will be taken either as an indication of unsureness whether something about the situation, properly appreciated, would, for example, cause her to feel embarrassed or ashamed at her reaction or else as displaying a rudimentary ignorance of how discourse about comedy works.

What, then, if it is not that their satisfaction does not confer a mandate, sets up the *appearance* of permissiveness in the assertion conditions of comic statements? One suggestion would be that, in contrast with opinions of many other kinds, mandate for a comic opinion is not suspended *just* by the failure of others to experience the same affect. If something looks red to me but to no one else, I have a warrant for the claim that it is red only if I can appropriately explain away others' failure to be appropriately affected—my claim is guilty until proved innocent, as it were. It is otherwise with comedy. If something amuses you but no other bystander, that fact by itself does not provide a reason for you to suspend your view—though it may alert you to the presence of factors which should prompt a change of mind in any case, even without the stony-faced responses of the others. Comic claims are, in such circumstances, innocent until proved guilty, and your (eccentric) verdict is consequently permissible.

On this view, to think that the conditions which justify you in holding a comic opinion are merely permissive is to locate the permission in the wrong place: your verdict is no less mandated than the verdict that something is red is mandated by its red appearance. What is merely permissible is sticking to that verdict when apprised of the unsympathetic response of others. But can this be quite right? One might of course stick to one's view out of confidence that the others could be brought around—because they have missed certain features of the situation, for example. But in *that* kind of case it is also permissible to stick to the claim that an object is red. Suppose you are confident that no defeating considerations of any of the kinds reviewed could be marshalled against either opinion in a disagreement about comedy, which is therefore down to a difference in sense of humour. Is not our "intuition" that there would then be *some* kind of impropriety in sticking to the unqualified claim: that is funny? But if so, what kind of impropriety?

Let that matter ride for a moment. First, I want to suggest, as in effect I did in Chapter 3, that the idea that there is something permissive about warrant for comic opinions comes to nothing other than the preconception that the comedy fails of Cognitive Command. When a discourse exhibits Cognitive Command, any difference of opinion will be such that there are considerations quite independent of the conflict which, if known about, would mandate withdrawal of one (or both) of the conflicting views. That is what seems not to be true of comedy. In the scenario described, the conflict gives you some kind of reason not to lay down the law, as it were. But there need be nothing about the processes whereby you and the others came to your respective views, nor any other consideration independent of the fact of disagreement, such that to know it would have been for one side or the other to have reason to respond differently. If this is right, then there is no reason to think that a fully satisfactory account of the practice of comic discourse has need of the idea of permissive "assertion" conditions at all. The original objection, at least as applied to comedy, is therefore misconceived.

But the objector is likely to be unsatisfied. A truth predicate, he will charge—even a minimal truth predicate—is definable over comic discourse only if there can be the kind of convergence in its applications which is proper to its functioning normatively in the way any truth predicate must; and this can be so only if there is convergence in what are considered warranted comic claims—or at least the degree of convergence proper to the idea that some shared set of standards determines the acceptability of such claims. Let it have been mistaken to suppose that acceptability here means permissibility, and therefore mistaken to suppose on that account that there can be no expectation of such convergence. The fact remains that if warrant is to connect with convergence, we are no nearer to understanding what warrant for comic claims *is*. If comic discourse is disciplined only in the ways so far reviewed, then what, for each of us, regulates its practice is the ideal of an *irreproachable comic response:* the positive opinions about comedy I ought to hold are just those to which I am moved by my sense of humour and which are not open to defeat in any of the ways reviewed. This is a kind of superassertibility. But since the base—the sense of humour—may blamelessly vary from person to person, there can be no assumption that the opinions which pass the test will not vary from person to person also. Of course we could, at this point, go "relative" and save comic discourse for minimal truth aptitude by localising it to senses of humour: in claiming that something was funny, I would be claiming the irreproachability of that opinion relative to *my* sense of humour; and that notion of irreproachability would then function as a truth predicate for *my* claims about the comic. But the challenge concerned *our* comic discourse and the contention that it is subject to a single truth predicate normative for all its practitioners, in the applications of which we may expect to converge.

This line of objection forgets the matter we shelved: that there *is* an impropriety in persisting with an intrinsically irreproachable comic claim against the current of an irreproachable lack of sympathy with it. So a lack of convergence is *some* sort of defeating consideration for such claims. And if that is so, there will naturally be a tendency to convergence in opinions about which among them are not open to any sort of defeat! If, for example, "x is funny" just meant "x can be irreproachably agreed to be funny", then, even if our views are intrinsically irreproachable, x isn't funny if we cannot agree; and we *can* be expected at least to come to an agreement about that. I do not suggest that agreement so features in the truth conditions of comic claims. But any account which recognises a lack of agreement among otherwise irreproachable views as providing cause for an eccentric to withdraw has the same resource. The question is *how* precisely that fact should be recognised, if not by some consensual or dispositional account of comic claims' truth conditions.

Why do we not express our opinions about comedy in an explicitly personal form—say, "I (irreproachably) find x funny", rather than the objectified mode: "x is funny"? What function does the latter have? Either it is idle or its proper use must, for each of us, be disciplined by some objective by which the personal form would not be. The correct account is surely obvious enough, though its precise slant is somewhat subtle. It is useful to have the objectified form because we can often successfully assume some community of comic response. If I wish to decide whether to watch a TV comedy show, there is no point in my asking you whether it is any good unless I think I can learn something about myself from your reaction. But this presupposition of community does not involve that claims about comedy are answerable to a community of response as part of their *content*. The presupposition enters not at the level of a correctness condition for the objectified claims but at the level of the *constitution* of the norm—roughly: irreproachability in the light of *our* sense of humour—at whose satisfaction comic discourse aims as an optimum. The relation between community in humour and the content of objectified comic claims is thus to be compared to the relation, on a Wittgensteinian view, between community in the most basic applications of the concepts involved in doing arithmetic[15]—those too simple to argue about—and the content of ordinary arithmetical claims. "$57 + 65 = 122$" does not state or entail anything about consensus; but there would be no standard of correctness for it to meet if there were no consensus at that basic level. The difference is that failure of the presupposition is consistent, in the comic case but not in the arithmetical, with continued mutual understanding of the claim at issue (if not with the fullest reciprocal *Verstehen* of the claimants).

As a first approximation, then, comic discourse is disciplined by the objective of irreproachability in the light of a community of comic sensibility. And warrant for comic claims is warrant to think that they can meet that objective. The impropriety of persisting with irreproachable but eccentric comic claims is thus traceable not to failure to meet a standard but to the lapsing of the standard which one aimed to meet. It is not so much a matter of losing as of failing to respond to the manifest abrogation of the conditions for play. "Community" of sensibility, here, does not of course mean "speech community", but will be variable with the context and purposes of the comic claim. And the comic sensibility—sense of humour—does not need to be thought of as something static but may be supposed educable and capable of greater and lesser refinement, like any aesthetic sense. Those are complexities with which a less than cursory inspection would have to reckon.

Whether or not these proposals are on the right lines as far as comedy is concerned, the discussion at least indicates one possible form of discipline which could operate on a discourse on which a minimal truth predicate was definable but which failed of Cognitive Command—though of course the latter notion stands, at this point, in need of further work, some of which will be undertaken in the next chapter. The general *practicability* of this form of discipline will depend, to be sure, on the general satisfaction of its presupposition—the existence of a relevant community of sentiment. That, in the case of any particular discourse, such a presup-

15. Not all of which are arithmetical, of course—think, for example, of the plethora of concepts of shape exercised in scanning a written calculation.

position is sufficiently generally satisfied is not guaranteed just by the determinacy of the assertoric contents—comic or otherwise—in which it deals. But where—as the very survival of the discourse suggests it is—the presupposition is met, there determinacy of assertoric content will connect with convergence in the way I claimed in footnote 2 and which the objection contested.

# Appendix. The Euthyphro Contrast: Order of Determination and Response-Dependence

## I. Basic Equations

If we suppose that all and only pious acts are loved by the gods, the biconditional

> For any act x: x is pious if and only if it is loved by the gods

is common ground between Socrates and Euthyphro. And a natural enough way of gesturing at the difference between them is to say that Socrates accords a certain priority to the left-hand side of the biconditional, while Euthyphro accords priority to its right-hand side. Style the first view *detectivism* about piety; and the second, *projectivism*. Call a *basic equation* a quantified biconditional of the form

> For all S, P: P if and only if (if CS then RS),

where S is any agent, "P" ranges over all of some wide class of judgements (judgements of colour or shape, or moral judgements, or mathematical judgements, for instance), "RS" expresses S's having of some germane response (judging that P, for instance, or having a visual impression of colour, or of shape, or being smitten with moral sentiment of a certain kind, or amused) and "CS" expresses the satisfaction of certain conditions of optimality on that particular response. If the response is a judgement, then S's satisfaction of conditions C will ensure that no other circumstances could have given the judgement formed a greater credibility.

That is in essentials (a modest generalization of) an idea deployed by Mark Johnston.[16] Johnston proposed as instances of true such basic equations the familiar formulations:

> x is square if and only if x would look square to standard observers under standard conditions,

and

> x is red if and only if x would look red to standard observers under standard conditions,[17]

and suggested that one central distinction between shape and colour was that the former might be read in a detectivist, the latter in a projectivist direction; and that this difference reflected one central form of distinction between primary and secondary qualities generally. He further suggested that ethical discourse would sustain basic equations comparable to those for colour in this crucial respect; and indeed that the proper cast to give projectivist intuition in general is not the traditional expressivist line, whereby the assertoric surface appearance conceals the true function of, say, moral discourse, but, in the way prefigured by the idea of right-to-left priority, to write human responses into the account of a substantial truth condition.[18]

16. In a seminar given jointly with Bas van Fraassen in Princeton in 1986. Subsequently Johnston has moved away from this idea. An impression of his present views can be gathered *ob iter* from his "Objectivity Refigured: Pragmatism without Verificationism", in J. Haldane and C. Wright, eds., *Reality: Representation and Projection* (New York: Oxford University Press, 1992); see especially his Appendix 3, "On Two Distinctions".

17. In what follows I ask the reader temporarily to overlook the fact that these formulations for "red" and "square" are, fairly obviously, false. Some of the reasons for this will contribute towards fashioning the general proposal that follows in section II.

18. A development and criticism of this proposal is contained in my "Moral Values, Projection and Secondary Qualities", inaugural address to the 1988 Joint Session of the Mind Association and Aristotelian Society, *Proceedings of the Aristotelian Society*, suppl. vol. 62 (1988), pp. 1–26.

This suggestion struck me as a useful way of attempting to sharpen a proposal which Wiggins and McDowell [19] have made: that a proper acknowledgement of the genuine elements of subjectivity in judgements of value may be reconciled with their being robustly true or false, proper objects of knowledge, as objective as anyone could wish who wanted to fend off any kind of disadvantageous comparison between, for example, morals and "hard" science. But the trouble, of course, is that, at the level of characterisation offered, we have merely gestured at a distinction which it would be good to be able to draw but which we have not yet explained *how* to draw. Nothing has been said about how to determine the classification of controversial cases—how to debate, for instance, with someone who reckoned that shape, colour and moral value are all on a par in sustaining a detective reading of the appropriate basic equations.

The distinction between *extension-determining* and *extension-reflecting* judgements developed in my "Notes on Basic Equations, etc." [20] represented one way of trying to remedy this lack. In what

19. See for instance McDowell's "Non-Cognitivism and Rule-Following", in Holtzman and Leich, eds., *Wittgenstein: To Follow a Rule* (London: Routledge and Kegan Paul, 1981); and idem, "Values and Secondary Qualities", in Honderich, ed., *Morality and Objectivity: A Tribute to John Mackie* (London: Routledge and Kegan Paul, 1985). Wiggins' complementary ideas may be found in his "Truth, Invention and the Meaning of Life"; esp. section 6, and "A Sensible Subjectivism", esp. section 5; both papers are reprinted in his *Needs, Values, Truth* (Oxford: Basil Blackwell, 1987).

20. Private circulation, written in 1987. The idea has figured in a number of other papers of mine. See "Further Reflections on the Sorites Paradox", in *Philosophical Topics* 15, no. 1 (1987), section VII, esp. pp. 274–279; "On Making Up One's Mind: Wittgenstein on Intention", in *Logic, Philosophy of Science and Epistemology, Proceedings of the Eleventh International Wittgenstein Symposium*, ed. P. Weingartner and Gerhard Schurz (Vienna: Holder-Pickler-Tempsky, 1987), pp. 391–404, esp. 401–403; "Realism, Anti-Realism, Irrealism, Quasi-Realism", pp. 42–46; "Moral Values, Projection and Secondary Qualities", pp. 14–25; and "Wittgenstein's Rule-Following Considerations and the Central Project of Theoretical Linguistics", in Alexander George, ed., *Reflections on Chomsky* (Oxford: Basil Blackwell, 1989), pp. 233–264, esp. 244–256. The issue is also raised in my "Anti-realism: The Contemporary Debate—W(h)ither Now?", the paper I originally presented at the St. Andrews 1988 conference on Realism, to which Appendix 3 of Mark Johnston's paper referred to responds, and which appears alongside his in *Reality: Representation and Projection*.

follows, I will rehearse, in section II, some of the steps which led me to propose it as one possible step in the direction that we want to be able to take. Section III will consider certain quite general objections to the resulting form of account. Section IV will briefly canvass a contrasting way of developing the Euthyphro contrast proposed by Johnston and Philip Pettit.

## II. Order of Determination

The train of thought followed in the "Notes on Basic Equations, etc." can be summarised in seven stages.

### i. What Kind of Responses?

Reflect that while many regions of discourse about which we might want to raise the Euthyphro question are associated with distinctive forms of affective, non-judgemental response (nausea, amusement, certain forms of aesthetic response, having things look red, or square to one, and so on), many others do not. In particular, and crucially, the phenomenology of judgements of modality, and especially of conceptual or logical necessity, is *not* comprehensively pervaded by the impressions of unassailable conviction, unimaginability of the opposite, and so on which the prosecution of the more traditional kind of projectivist account would seem to demand. And a corresponding claim, so I have suggested, should be allowed for ethics.[21] What there *does* have to be, for all discourses about which we may want to raise the Euthyphro question, is the response of *judgement:* of endorsing what is affirmed by a tokening of an assertoric sentence of the discourse. So, at least as an initial position, I took "RS" in the general form of basic equation delineated above to be:

$$S \text{ judges that } P,$$

and the Euthyphronic thesis becomes, correspondingly, that, for the discourse in question, optimally conceived judgement—*best opinion*—is the conceptual ground of truth.

21. See "Moral Values, Projection and Secondary Qualities", section III, pp. 11–13.

## ii. The Substantiality Condition

Claims about conceptual grounding ought to have implications for modality: if best opinion is a conceptual ground for truth within some discourse, it ought to be necessary that the deliverances of best opinion are true; and if it is *the* conceptual ground for truth, it ought to be necessary that any truth is accessible to a best opinion. So, it is natural to suggest, the Euthyphronist is committed to the *necessity* of the relevant basic equation.[22] By contrast, if, as according to Socrates' detectivist view, best opinion is merely *responsive* to truth, then it seems that it ought to be a possibility that the causal order be so constituted that opinions formed under the conditions which, as things are, ensure that they track the facts, might not have done so. That suggests—modulo further refinements—that it is at least a potentially sufficient condition for the propriety of a detectivist view of a discourse that all the true basic equations which it sustains be at best contingently true.

So formulated, however, the requirement is evidently unsatisfiable. Suppose we characterise "standard conditions" as ones supplying everything necessary (whatever-it-takes) to enable a standard observer to apprehend shapes correctly—*mutatis mutandis* for "standard observer". Then the basic equation for "square" above is, trivially, dignified as a necessary truth. There is therefore no hope of capturing the distinction we want by reference to contrasts in the modality of true basic equations unless we stipulate that the C-conditions imposed on the subject be specified *substantially:* they must be specified in sufficient detail to incorporate a constructive account of the epistemology of the judgements in question, so that not merely does a subject's satisfaction of them ensure that the conditions under which she is operating have "whatever-it-takes" to bring it about that her opinion is true, but a concrete conception is conveyed of what it actually does take. Of course there is much more to say about what, for these purposes, substantiality in a specification should be taken to require.

22. Cf. Colin McGinn, *The Subjective View* (Oxford: Oxford University Press, 1983), p. 6, n. 2.

*iii. Rigidification*

We have something of a delicate balancing act to perform. We are after a sharp, operationally applicable account of the—or at least a—Euthyphro distinction. But we cannot *ab initio* foreclose on the possibility that, when we have gained it, colours and shapes may fall out on the same side. Nevertheless, we have to be driven, in attempting to construct the account, by the assumption that they will not; for one hope we have is precisely to provide something which sustains and explains that assumption.

We are therefore obliged to pay attention to the following intuition about colour: that had the typical visual equipment of human beings been very different, or had the lighting (by day) on the earth typically been of a quite different character—perhaps resembling the illumination generated by sodium street lighting—that need have made no difference to the colours things actually are. The extensions of "red" and "green" would not have been different if all human beings had been colour blind, and would not change if they were to become so.[23]

The intuition is, effectively, that the colour of an object supervenes on its intrinsic physical character. It appears to dictate that a would-be Euthyphronist about judgements of colour is not going to be able to construe the idealising C-conditions which an appropriate basic equation will impose on judging subjects—crudely gestured at by the use of "standard" in the formulations above—in any broadly *statistical* sense. "Standard" must not mean, broadly, "usual", if we want an appropriate basic equation to hold necessarily true, but recognize that changes in what is usual for observers and conditions of observation would not necessarily be associated with changes in colour.

On the other hand, if a non-statistical account is to be given, there is a clear risk of running afoul of the Substantiality condition. If it is to be a matter of specifying *ideal* conditions of observers and observation, "ideal" must not reduce to: whatever conditions are conducive to the reliable appraisal of colour. Of course, we can attempt to specify in substantial physical and physiological terms

23. McGinn is oddly cavalier about this; see pp. 9ff. of *The Subjective View*.

what those conditions are, but the price of achieving substantiality by such means, it appears, is likely to be that the *necessity* of the basic equation is jeopardised. For there seems to be no difficulty in conceiving, for instance, of alterations of the laws of nature of such a kind that objects whose surfaces we perceive as coloured thus-and-such would, without undergoing any intrinsic alteration, induce dramatically different visual effects in us, and would appear as they now appear to us only to creatures with a radically different visual physiology. Insisting, in the teeth of this possibility, that basic equations for colours, formulated as proposed, were necessarily true would amount, once again, to repudiating the above intuition—to insisting that intrinsically unaltered objects would, in certain possible circumstances, rightly be regarded as having changed in colour.

An attractive strategy of response to this dilemma, of some independent plausibility, is to *rigidify* the original statistical construal. Thus, the Euthyphronic proposal can be: it is the judgements of those who are *actually* statistically standard observers, in what are *actually* statistically standard conditions of observation, which count.[24] Were we all to become colour blind, our judgements would, *ex hypothesi,* no longer be in line with those which, constituted as we actually are, we are disposed to make. Means are thus recovered to sustain the intuition that, in that counterfactual situation, colours need not have changed; they need not have changed because the judgements which we *would* have made, had we still been visually constituted as we actually are, need not have changed.

*iv. Dropping Modality: The Apriority Condition*

There may be other ways of coping with the difficulty. And of course, it would be necessary in any case to be much more specific about the character of the conditions, broadly statistically specified, which we were proposing to rigidify.[25] But we can

24. Cf. Wiggins, "A Sensible Subjectivism", section 13. The idea goes back, of course, to M. Davies and L. Humberstone, "Two Notions of Necessity", *Philosophical Studies* 38 (1980), esp. pp. 22–25.

25. For the beginnings of an attempt to be so, see my "Wittgenstein's Rule-Following Considerations and the Central Project of Theoretical Linguistics", pp. 247–248.

already foresee a new difficulty. Rigidification is apt to change modal status. Whether P is true may be a contingency; but if it is true, the proposition that P is *actually* true will be necessary—at any rate on all conceptions of necessity similar, at least in their rudiments, to the standard conception deriving from Leibniz. Possible worlds are individuated by what holds true in them; hence if P is true in any particular possible world, including the actual world, then it will be true in all possible worlds—and hence necessary—that P is true in that world. The worry is therefore that, by introducing rigidifiers into a basic equation for colour, we may *overdetermine* its necessity in such a way that the corresponding pattern of basic equation for shape, similarly rigidified, would also turn out as necessary. The prospective contrast in point of modality would then be lost.

Does there really have to be this problem? Let S be an actually typically visually equipped subject, and let "CS" stipulate that S satisfies that condition and that her judgements are formed under actually typical (daylit) conditions, and that she satisfies further, substantially specified conditions in such a way that

(i)     P if and only if (if CS, then S would judge that P)

is true, where P ascribes some shape—say, squareness—to a visually presented object. Then, as noted,

(ii)     Actually: P if and only if (if CS, then S would judge the P)

would be, on standard accounts, necessarily true. But it will occur to the alert reader that, in order to assess whether the described threat materialises, the above is not what we need to consider. For the scope of the rigidifier needed should not be the whole proposition but merely the statistical elements in the specification of the C-conditions; what we want is thus

(iii)     P if and only if (if S were in the same condition as one who is actually C, then S would judge that P).

And it cannot be assumed without further ado that a rigidifier occurring, in this way, within the antecedent of an embedded conditional will have the same effect on the modal status of the whole as an occurrence of "actually" whose scope is the whole sentence.

That is, of course, correct. But it is doubtful whether the reflection helps in the present case. For what we "export" to nearby possible worlds when we stipulate that S operates under the same conditions as one who is actually C will be a complex of conditions—on S, on the background circumstances, and on the prevailing laws—which, on the hypothesis that (i) is indeed true, suffice to ensure that in the actual world S's judgements of shape track shape facts. And with *so* much retained, in the counterfactual worlds to be considered, it is quite obscure how the equation could be anything but true in them too—and hence how its truth conditions, which embrace only relevantly "close" worlds in any case, could be anything but necessarily satisfied.

There are various possible responses. We might seek a more fine-grained way of rigidifying a broadly statistical account of the appropriate conditions of observation without thereby rigidifying the physical laws which actually sustain or are somehow implicated in those conditions. And in that case counterexamples might yet be forthcoming for (iii): worlds in which, owing to the operation of different physical laws, observers having actually typical visual equipment would not, under conditions of observation like those which actually typically obtain, in general receive faithful impressions of shape. Alternatively, one might accept that (iii) is indeed necessary, but attempt to argue that the *kind* of necessity imposed by its containing a rigidifier can be distinguished from a further (more interesting) necessity which characterises the corresponding basic equation for colour.

These approaches raise questions which it might be interesting to pursue for their own sake. In the "Notes on Basic Equations", however, I followed a simpler line. Whether or not the kind of necessity generated by actualisation can be interestingly contrasted with that which, one might have hoped, would characterise basic equations sustained by a discourse for which Euthyphronism was correct, it is certain that no proposition whose necessity is owing entirely to actualisations can be known *a priori*. By contrast, the truth, if it is true, that the extensions of colour concepts are constrained by idealised human response—best opinion—ought to be accessible purely by analytic reflection on those concepts, and hence available as knowledge a priori.

I therefore imposed an *Apriority condition:* roughly, it will *suffice* to classify a class of judgements on the detectivist side of the Euthyphro contrast if, while they do sustain true basic equations, complying with the Substantiality condition, none of these basic equations can be known to be true a priori. Correspondingly, one might now suggest, it will be a *necessary* condition for the propriety of Euthyphronic viewpoint that appropriate, substantially specified basic equations can be known to be true a priori.

### v. Dropping the Basic Equation: Provisional Equations

But these suggestions confront a further, major difficulty. Analyses taking the form of subjunctive conditionals have hardly been conspicuously successful in the history of philosophy. One very basic form of difficulty which they encounter is raised by the possibility that, where the kind of state of affairs conferring truth on P is causally active and acted upon, the proposal

> P if and only if were it the case that Q, it would
> be the case that R

is always liable to be confounded by the possibility—where it is not actually the case that Q—that realising Q might causally interfere with a state of affairs that actually has an effect on the truth value of P. This is the possibility illustrated by Johnston's Chameleon.[26] If the Chameleon sits on a green baize in the dark at t, then bringing about "standard" conditions of observation—that is, inter alia, irradiating the creature with something like normal daylight—may bring about a *change,* we conceive, in the Chameleon's skin colour. But if the truth conditions of P, = "The

---

26. See appendix 2 of "Objectivity Refigured". I have changed the example to have the actual observation, rather than the presentiment of it, generate the Chameleon's change in colour.

Chameleon is green at t", were correctly captured by the subjunctive conditional that figures in the appropriate basic equation, then we should have to say that the Chameleon is green before the lights go on.

When first noticed, this general form of problem—which Johnston calls "altering"—is likely to strike one as something of a dead hand on the prospects of interesting conditional analyses quite generally. Indeed, it prompted Robert Shope[27] to stigmatise the very idea of successful subjunctive conditional analyses as incorporating a fallacy—the "Conditional Fallacy". If the class of judgements in which we are interested participate—or supervene upon participants—in the causal order, and if realising the antecedent of the purported conditional analysans would perforce involve changes in states of affairs so participating, then, it seems, however unlikely interference might actually be, it at least cannot be *a priori* that the changes involved would not impinge on the truth value of P. Nor, therefore, can it be a priori that P's truth conditions are captured by the purported analysans. So, as an attempt at a true *conceptual* claim, the analysis must fail.

I believe this pessimistic first impression is sustained by further reflection. But there is a natural objection. Surely, in appraising a counterfactual conditional, we only have to consider relevantly *non-remote* possible situations in which its antecedent is true. The problem dwells on the *mere possibility* that implementing the antecedent of a purported analysans in conditional form might causally impinge on the states of affairs which actually determine the truth value of the analysandum. But in order for this possibility to jeopardise the capacity of the conditional to capture the truth conditions of the analysandum, it has to be realised in some relevantly non-remote counterfactual circumstances. Why suppose that has to be so?

Well, it *is* so in the case of the Chameleon, and other similar examples. But the objection is in any case missing the nature of the difficulty. To stress: the sort of equivalence in which we are interested has to be a candidate for holding *a priori*. That is to

27. Robert K. Shope, "The Conditional Fallacy in Contemporary Philosophy", *Journal of Philosophy* 75 (1978), pp. 397–413.

say, it has to be possible to know a priori, independently of knowledge of the detail of the actual world, and whatever P's truth value in it, that implementation of the antecedent of the conditional analysans will not materially affect matters which bear on the actual truth value of the analysandum. And how could one possibly know that without collateral empirical information about the character of the world one is actually in?

The moral is quite clear: a priori correct subjunctive-conditional characterisations of the truth conditions of the kinds of statements in which we are interested are not to be had. The Basic Equation has to go.

My response to the difficulty in the "Notes on Basic Equations" was to shift the focus to what I there called "provisoed biconditionals", and elsewhere "provisional equations". Obviously, there could not be this kind of problem about alteration in the Chameleon's colour if we had stipulated that it is its very colour under "standard" conditions which a "standard" observer is to review. More generally, "altering" in the truth value of P which would or might occur were conditions C cannot be a problem if it is P's truth value under C-conditions which, under C-conditions, S is to appraise.

The general form of the provisional equation is thus

> If CS, then (it would be the case that P if and
> only if S would judge that p).

We focus not on biconditionals with conditional right-hand sides, but on conditionals with biconditional consequents.

Naturally, though, this reshuffle of the scope of "CS" is not without cost. We may still plausibly assert that if all the true, substantially formulated provisional equations sustained by a given discourse are at best a posteriori true, then it is proper to think of our knowledge of the states of affairs therein described as purely a "tracking" accomplishment, and of the states of affairs themselves as constituted quite independently of human response. As before, if a discourse sustains substantially formulated true provisional equations which can be known a priori to be true, then that makes the beginnings of a case for regarding the discourse as dealing in states of affairs whose details are conceptually dependent upon our best opinions. But the shift from basic to provisional equations carries in train the penalty of a loss of generality. Provisional equations say nothing about the constraints on P's truth or falsity under *non*-C-circumstances. Yet, we conceive, things are, for example, determinately coloured under lighting conditions of whatever sort.

In sum, whereas basic equations, when they meet the right conditions, purport to exhibit a way in which truth values in the discourse in question are *everywhere* bounded by the deliverances of best opinion, the corresponding provisional equations can at most yield the result that what it is true to say in the discourse in question is so bounded *under the conditions in which a best opinion is enabled.* They say nothing about what, if any, conclusions are warranted about the role of our judgements under other, less than best circumstances. It is for this reason that I have usually said elsewhere that what is in prospect here is a framework for making a case that truth within a particular discourse is *partially* determined by best opinion.

## *vi. The Independence Condition*

As matters developed in the "Notes on Basic Equations", the Euthyphro contrast thus crystallised as that between judgements the extension of the truth predicate among which is determined in conceptual independence from the verdicts of best opinion, and judgements among which the extension of the truth predicate is, at least in part, conceptually constrained by what the verdicts of best opinion would be. However, if this is the target distinction, then an issue now arises about the terms in which it is appropriate to formulate the C-conditions.

So far, we have merely required that the formulation be "substantial", and have suggested no very definite account of this beyond its exclusion of offerings of the "whatever-it-takes" line of goods. But what kind of formulations should count as substantial? Well, because we are not in the business of trying to provide reductive *analyses* of the truth conditions of the judgements in the substitution class for "P", there may seem no immediate barrier to characterising the C-conditions, or the relevant response, in ways involving the very concepts which distinctively feature in those judgements. At least, there is no barrier erected by the threat of circularity, as that philosophical vice is usually conceived. If the project is not to analyse the concepts in question but to exhibit the implication, in the truth conditions of judgements involving those concepts, of facts about idealised human response, circularity of that kind need surely be no objection to what we produce.

However, it does not follow from the fact that there is no objection from circularity that there is no objection at all—that we run no risks of spoiling things if we make unfettered use of the concepts in question in the specifications of the C-conditions and the appropriate response. On the present proposal, the Euthyphronic thesis about a class of judgements is to the effect that the extension of the truth predicate among at least a proper subclass of them is determined as a function of best opinion. Suppose this thesis advanced for judgements of colour. Then using colour concepts in the specification of the C-conditions—of what makes an opinion "best"—raises a (somewhat subtle) worry not about circularity but about making implicit demands on the extension of colour concepts which are inconsistent with the very Euthyphronism which we would be trying sharply to formulate. If what it needs to make the relevant opinions "best" under certain circumstances is represented as depending on facts about the actual extension of colour concepts in those same circumstances, how do we answer a critic who questions whether, in presupposing that those facts are fully determinate, we are implicitly presupposing some mode of constitution of colour facts which is conceptually unconstrained by best opinion and hence potentially at odds with the Euthyphronist's central claim?

In a particular case, depending on the exact mode of involvement of the concepts in question in specifying the C-conditions, it might be possible to answer this doubt head on. For example: once having shifted to provisional equations, the Euthyphronic thesis must in any case be confined in the first instance to a claim about the truth conditions of judgements about colour made under a restricted class of (best) circumstances. There is therefore the formal possibility that colour concepts might be implicated in specifying these conditions only in ways which, though presupposing determinate colour facts, presuppose nothing about the distribution of truth values among this partial class of judgements. Maybe. Even so, there would be some discomfort in that situation for a Euthyphronist who wanted to regard the best-opinion constrained class as in some way fundamental.

We might try to develop the worry like this. Suppose x is a solid and P is "x is red all over". And suppose, not implausibly, that, in an attempt to construct a true provisional equation for P, we find ourselves including among the C-conditions a stipulation that x be stable in colour throughout some relevant period.[28] Since this stipulation occurs precisely as part of a specification of more comprehensive conditions under which, we hope to be able to show, facts about colour are best-opinion constrained, we have to be able to conceive of this fact—x's stability in colour—as likewise so constrained. But to say that x is stable in colour throughout some period is just to say that there is some colour predicate, F, which characterises x throughout. And now, manifestly, we cannot explicate *this* fact—x's being F through the specified period—in terms of a congruence of best opinions about x's colour in that period, if we need the notion of stability independently to characterise what makes an opinion best.

The reply is available, of course, that just as the Euthyphronist about colour is not in the business of analysis of colour predicates, so he is not in the business of the analysis of the concept of colour stability. But clearly a much more careful investigation is needed here. To stress: a Euthyphronist who is content to implicate the distinctive concepts of a discourse in his formulation of the C-conditions, in such a way that satisfaction of the C-condition turns on details of the actual extension of those concepts, has to expect the challenge: "Show that the way that you have implicated those concepts is consistent with your overall thesis, that their extension is, at least partially, constrained by best opinion."

The "Notes on Basic Equations, etc." offered a somewhat conservative response to this difficult matter. Evidently there can be no well-founded worry along the lines described, provided an *Indepen-*

28. Since S is presumably going to have to conduct a series of observations of x, from different points of view.

*dence condition* is satisfied: the relevant concepts are to be involved in the formulation of the C-conditions only in ways which allow the satisfaction of those conditions to be logically independent of the details of the extension of those concepts. There are, roughly, two ways in which that might be accomplished. One is, obviously, to avoid the use of the targeted concepts altogether. The other is to allow the concepts to feature within the specification of the C-conditions only *inside the scope of intensional operators*—as, of course, already occurs in the description of the relevant response, since "S judges that P" places the vocabulary figuring in P in *oratio obliqua*. Provided one or the other course is followed, the Euthyphronist should be safe from the sort of concern outlined.

The motivation for the condition is thus that it *suffices* to preempt a certain kind of complaint. That is not to say that respecting it is necessary if the complaint is not to arise.[29]

*vii. The Extremal Condition*

Suppose, finally, that we construct, for some region of discourse recognisably a priori true, substantially specified provisional equations whose C-conditions avoid all use of the distinctive concepts of the discourse. Will we have vindicated the thought that, in at least a central class of cases, best opinion has a determinative rather than a merely representational role to play?

Well, there ought to be a distinction, so far unaddressed, between extension-determination and *infallibility*. May there not be states of affairs in whose determination facts about the deliverances of best opinions are in no way implicated although there is, a priori, no possibility of their *misrepresentation* by best opinion? A plausible example is provided by pain, conceived—as we naturally conceive it—as something whose occurrence requires no capacity of judgement on the part of the subject.[30] There seems every reason

29. Mark Johnston, in particular, regards it as unnecessarily strong. He is followed in this by Philip Pettit; see section 2 of his "Realism and Response-Dependence", *Mind* 100 (1991), pp. 597–626.

30. This natural conception is implausibly challenged by John McDowell in his "One Strand in the Private Language Argument", *Grazer Philosophische Studien* 33–34 (1989), pp. 285–303.

to think that a provisional equation meeting the conditions described so far might be given along the lines:

> If S has the concepts requisite in order to entertain the judgement that she is in pain, then (S is at pain at t if and only if S judges that she is in pain at t).

Yet it is not, one might feel, that the extension of the concept pain is determined, at least in part, by the judgements of those who have the appropriate concepts. Rather, such judges are, precisely, infallible about their pains.

A distinction seems called for, then, between discourses within which the extension of the truth predicate is (in part) determined by the deliverances of best opinion and discourses within which best opinion is merely guaranteed, a priori, to track the facts. The final condition imposed in the "Notes on Basic Equations, etc." suggested that the distinction should be captured along the following lines. Where it is possible, without mention of human judgement or the conditions under which, in the case in question, such judgement would be best, either fully to analyse, or at least to draw attention to very general characteristics of the truth-conferring states of affairs in such a way that it is a *consequence* that there is an a priori guarantee that best opinion will be on track, then it is appropriate to think in terms of infallibility. Where it is not, where no further characterisation of the type of states of affairs is possible in terms of which we can explain why it is possible to construct provisional equations meeting the other conditions, then the notion of (partial) extension-determination has its proper place.

## III. Three Objections

I want to claim for the foregoing only that it describes the shape of *one* coherent distinction, close enough in spirit to the Euthyphro contrast to constitute a sharpening of it, and sufficiently definite to set up the possibility of investigating which, if any, types of judgement fall on one side of it or the other, and to subserve the interest of such an investigation. For instance, I believe, though

I shall not argue here, that there is indeed a distinction between judgements of colour and judgements of shape to be elicited along these lines—though the formulation of what counts as a best opinion about colour has to engage an extensive variety of complications.[31] I also think that there is no way of so constructing provisional equations for moral discourse that all the conditions described can be met.[32] That, of course, need do no damage to the (now rather hackneyed) comparison between secondary quality judgement and moral evaluation if some other interesting analogy can be sustained. But I would regard it as a benefit of the approach described that it brings questions like these into sharp focus.

There are, however, certain quite general objections which it is worth responding to briefly (even if, unavoidably in an appendix, not in detail).

*First Objection:* The first contends that, in any case where it proved possible to construct provisional equations meeting the conditions imposed, but where the claim of the corresponding basic equations to capture the relevant truth conditions would fall foul of the Conditional Fallacy, a question would have to arise about the *univocity* of the distinctive concepts of the discourse concerned—a question which, according to a powerful intuition, ought not to arise.

Consider the case of colour. Plausibly, the claim of any basic equation to capture, a priori, the truth conditions of a colour judgement is indeed going to be confounded by the Conditional Fallacy. But suppose that, as I suggested, true provisional equations meeting each of the four conditions stipulated—Apriority, Substantiality, Independence and Extremal—can be written for simple colour judgements, say "x is red". Then will we not have

31. Apart from the matter of explaining in substantial terms, but in such a way as to serve the apriority of the eventual formulation, what should count as standard conditions of observation and standard observers, there are factors to write in, such as the effect on an object's apparent colour of its being in rapid motion, and of variation in the colour of the background against which it is perceived. I have discussed the issue a little more fully, though not in the detail it needs, in "Wittgenstein's Rule-Following Considerations and the Central Project of Theoretical Linguistics".

32. See section V of "Moral Values, Projection and Secondary Qualities".

to recognise two quite different types of truth condition for such judgements, depending on whether or not the conditions under which they are envisaged as being made are "best"? If best conditions obtain, then x's colour is a function of our judgement; if they do not, then—at least for all that has been said—x's colour is determined by factors of a quite different sort. Such a distinction, the objection runs, must impose a kind of ambiguity on "red". And the strong intuition that there is no such ambiguity thus becomes a reason to doubt that true provisional equations meeting the relevant conditions can be written.

The objection, generalised and in short, is that, if the Euthyphro contrast is drawn by way of the distinction outlined in the previous section, then in none of the likely areas of discourse, where a Euthyphronic point might initially seem attractive, will it be possible to make that point—since in no case will there be the kind of ambiguity which that way of drawing the contrast implicitly requires.

When the objection is put at this level of generality, the correct and short reply should be that it underestimates what it takes to generate something worth regarding as an ambiguity. An ambiguous term is one with two or more quite different kinds of meaning, for which two or more quite different kinds of explanation are appropriate. But in recognising that the extension of "red" is partially constrained by best opinion, we suffer no commitment to any such explanatory multiplicity. Quite the contrary—precisely because "red" features on both sides of the biconditional consequent of the relevant provisional equation, such a formulation is *explanatorily useless,* even under presumed best conditions. Univocity is under no threat, since the provisional equation is offered neither as an *introductory explanation* nor as a reductive *analysis* of "red", even for a restricted class of cases, but merely as disclosing one a priori feature of the concept—something recoverable by analytic reflection on the meaning of "red" when explained as it normally, univocally, is.

There is a more specific point to be made in the particular case of colour, however. Earlier, I gave sympathetic mention to the thought that it is an a priori feature of the colour of an object that it supervene on its other physical characteristics. Supervenience relations come, of course, in a variety of forms and strengths. The relevant notion here is, roughly, that an object cannot change colour without ulterior physical change; and that a replication of an object in all physical respects except its colour is, perforce, a replication of its colour too. The claim that colours so supervene on other physical characteristics is, of course, quite consistent with holding that there is a chaotic multiplicity of physical states exemplified by, for example, scarlet things, and is accordingly a weaker contention than that colour words have the semantics of natural-kind terms.[33] But it is a commitment to the idea that physically alike objects—whether numerically distinct or the same object at different times—share colour, even if one inhabits "best" conditions for an appraisal of its colour and the other does not. This supervenience is thus, as it were, a force for univocity in colour concepts as applied under best and less than best conditions: in company with the claim that the extensions of colour terms are partially determined by best opinion, it imposes certain uses of them under non-best conditions in a way which would be quite unintelligible if any genuine ambiguity of the kind claimed by the objection were involved.[34]

33. A fortiori, it is a weaker contention than the claim that they *successfully* discharge that semantic role, i.e., that colour characteristics really are natural kinds.

34. In order to be entitled to make this point, it might seem that I ought first to offer some assurance of the *consistency* of a view which both holds that the extension of colour-words is (partially) determined by best opinion and acknowledges the relevant kind of supervenience of colour on the physical. And someone might think there is an evident tension. What a priori barrier is there to divergence between best opinions about the colours of physically indistinguishable objects? Why, for instance, may it not happen that contrary verdicts be given at distinct times on the colour of a physically unchanged object, even though each verdict is formed under best conditions?

Whether it is possible to give a good direct answer to the question depends, obviously, on how the detail of a substantial account of *best* conditions for colour appraisal should run—detail not to be attempted here. But the right response, I think, is not to attempt a direct answer, but to point out that the worst the question adverts to is a philosophically very familiar phenomenon, of great generality: the association of a concept with potentially, though not actually, diver-

*Second Objection:* The second objection is strategically similar to the first. Like the first, it contends that in a wide class of likely cases the claim that the relevant class of judgements are extension-determining will be at odds with entrenched intuitions about their content, and hence that drawing the Euthyphro contrast in the way I have proposed will put us out of reach of the kind of point for which we want the contrast in the first place. The putatively offended intuitions relevant to the first objection concerned univocity. The second objection, for its part, has it that certain entrenched *explanatory* intuitions will be seriously compromised.[35]

Colour again provides an apt illustration. The fact is, so the objection runs, that we think of the actual colour of an object as (potentially) *causally explaining* the impression we form of its colour, even when the impression is formed under the very best conditions of judgement and judge. How can that be reconciled with the thesis that an appropriate provisional equation holds a priori? Let a Euthyphronist contend that, where C is a substantial specification of best conditions for colour appraisal, and P a particular judgement of colour, it is a priori that

---

gent criteria of application. Someone who contends that our ordinary understanding of colour implicates both the feature that best colour judgements are extension-determining and the feature that colours supervene on intrinsic physical characteristics is making a *descriptive* claim. His point, recall, is that if it is felt—which is in any case contestable—that the first feature introduces an implausible ambiguity, the second works in favour of univocity. It is no objection to this, as a reflection about our ordinary understanding, to point out that the two features might conceivably clash. For one thing, it is not clear that we would count anything as a clash; rather it is very plausible that, in any apparent conflict, we would insist that the object *must* have changed, or that the two sets of conditions of judgement *cannot* both have been best. And it is not clear how such claims might be defeated. But the more basic point is that, even if we could somehow be forced, in certain special circumstances, to acknowledge a clash, the descriptive claim, that our ordinary understanding of colour incorporates both features, would be quite unimpugned. Concepts which incorporate potentially conflicting criteria of application are no news to philosophy.

35. What follows is an adaptation of the "missing explanation" objection which Mark Johnston ("Objectivity Refigured", appendix 1) believes he finds in Plato's own text. Johnston, however, uses the objection to cast doubt not on one particular way of drawing the Euthyphro contrast but on the whole idea that the contrast has any significant work to do in descriptive philosophy.

If conditions are C, then (P if and only if S
judges that P).

Then the explanatory intuition has it that

(Even) if conditions are C: if S correctly judges
that P, the fact that P will contribute to the causal
explanation of her doing so.

And if the relation between the colour of an object and S's judgemental response is causal, it surely cannot be a priori that there is
the kind of co-variation between them which the provisional equation postulates. No genuinely causal relation can be divined a
priori, merely by conceptual reflection. So if, even under C-conditions, the redness of a poppy is *causally* sufficient for our judging
it to be so, it cannot also be *a priori* that it is so sufficient. It
follows that if P is a judgement of colour and C is a substantial
specification,[36] it cannot in general be a priori that

If conditions are C, then if P, then S judges that P.

So the provisional equation cannot be a priori either.

This line of objection is natural but, I think, mistaken. The
principle which drives it—in effect, that if A is among the causes
of B, it cannot be known a priori that it is so—obviously has some
pull. But, mindful that apriority generally is an artifact of description, or mode of presentation, one would not expect the principle
to be exceptionless. The truth in it, it seems to me, is roughly
that if under circumstances C the obtaining of state of affairs A is
causally explanatory of the obtaining of state of affairs B, then
there must be modes of presentation of the two types of states of
affairs, $M^A$ and $M^B$ respectively—modes of presentation which are
in some sense *basic* or *identifying,* though I shall not now try to say
what that means—such that the proposition that under C, a state
of affairs of type $M^A$ is causally explanatory of one of type $M^B$ is not

36. Of course, no such conclusion would be licensed if the C-conditions
were not substantially specified; apriority in a "whatever-it-takes" provisional
equation is quite consistent with conceiving of subjects' judgements of the
relevant kind as causally responsive to states of affairs determined quite independently of best opinion.

knowable a priori. But that, of course, is quite consistent with the existence of another mode of presentation, $M^{A*}$, say, of the type of state of affairs presented by $M^A$, such that the sufficiency, under C, for a state of affairs of type $M^B$ of an instance of $M^{A*}$, so specified, *may* be known a priori.

That indicates a space which a response to the objection might try to occupy. But it does not yet explain how it is occupied. Here a comparison may help with the kind of *reference fixing* that figures in the standard informal semantics of natural-kind terms. The reference of a natural-kind term—"gold" or "water", for instance—is fixed, according to the picture familiar from the writings of Putnam and Kripke, by what, in an earlier style of philosophical thought, would have been regarded as *criteria* for the applicability of the term. According to the earlier style of thought, the criteria for a sample's being of gold (its possession of features such as being made of a heavy, yellow metal, having a certain distinctive lustrousness, being resistant to corrosion, and so on—features associated with "gold" by the common knowledge of ordinary users of the term) entered into the meaning of "gold" rather as the elements of the appropriate "cluster" of definite descriptions would, according to the "cluster" theory of names, enter into the meaning of an ordinary proper name. Against this, the now orthodox view is that it is indeed part of the meaning of a term such as "gold" that it stands, if for anything, then for that kind of stuff, identified in physically fundamental terms, which is *dominantly causally responsible* for the co-instantiations of the sorts of features noted. But the role of those features is only, in this way, to fix the reference (if any) of "gold"; they do not somehow cluster together to determine a sense.

It is notable that, on such an account, an a priori connection is forged nonetheless between the typical manifestations of gold—the criteria—and the substance itself; specifically, nothing will *count* as being gold unless it is identified, by some successful physical theory, as being of a kind of stuff which features, by the lights of that theory, in the usual causal explanation of co-instantiations of the criteria. It will thus be a priori that an item's being made of gold is a (potential) cause of its satisfying some significant proportion of the criteria. And this a priori connection is quite comfortable alongside a proper understanding of the principle which drives the objection. What we are committed to, in treating "gold" as a natural-kind term, is that there is some (microphysical) level of description of gold, $M^G$, such that it is true but knowable only a posteriori that a sample's satisfying $M^G$ is potentially causally explanatory of its satisfying some significant proportion of the criteria.

My suggestion is that an accommodation with the objection may build on an analogy between, for example, colour predicates and natural-kind terms. But I do not go so far as to suggest that colour predicates are, semantically, natural-kind terms. On the contrary, I think that would be a definite error; and it would in any case be inconsistent with the thesis that the extension of such predicates is partially determined by best opinion. For in the case of natural-kind terms, the connection, forged a priori if it is forged at all, between satisfaction of the reference fixers and instantiation of the substance, may *not* in fact have been forged at all: there may simply fail to be any interesting physical essence underlying the manifestations which have a salient similarity for us. We hold out a hostage to fortune in attempting reference fixing of this kind, and the hostage may not be redeemed. Developments in physical theory might force us to acknowledge that there is no such thing as gold—or so, at any rate, we have to allow if we think that "gold" is a natural-kind term and has the kind of semantics outlined. By contrast, if our ordinary understanding of (at least kindergarten) colour words is such that appropriate a priori true provisional equations can indeed be constructed for them, there is no comparable hostage: our judgements about redness, formed under the relevant C-conditions—or indeed any others—will not be defeasible by the discovery that there is no interesting physical unity in the class of objects to which they are applied. Rather, we shall treat the discovery as teaching us that the class of, say, red things is not in fact a natural kind while holding on to the ordinary belief that there are, after all, no end of red things; and we shall thereby have responded in a way inconsistent with the claim that "red" is semantically a natural-kind term.

This point about the semantics of colour predicates is, however, quite consistent with the belief that, *as it happens,* there are interesting underlying physical characteristics in common among the objects which best opinions determine as, say, red; characteristics which are involved in the aetiology of, inter alia, those very opinions, and which, by—as it happens—being common to and distinctive of red things, have a case to be regarded as physically constitutive of redness. In short: the explanatory intuition which sets up the objection need come to no more than an epiphenomenon of the presumed correctness of the belief that here is something which redness physically is and which features among the causes of best judgements about what is red.

It is, of course, a consequence of this way with the objection that, were we to become convinced that there is only a multiple physical *heterogeneity* among, say, same-coloured things, it ought to cease to seem sensible to ordinary thought to view colours as causally explanatory of best opinions about them.[37] But so I think it would.[38]

*Third Objection:* The Third objection questions the very coherence of the idea that a concept might have its extension determined as

37. Naturally, intermediate cases are possible. The physics might so work out as to make it useful to think not in terms of there being *no* physical kind constituting redness, but in terms of there being several.

38. It is also a consequence of this way with the objection that the original gloss placed, in section II of the main chapter, on the Euthyphro contrast—that the protagonists are distinguished by rejection of each other's "because" claims—needs qualifying. The Euthyphronist about piety is not committed straight off to denying that

> It is because certain acts are pious that they are loved
> by the gods,

even when—implausibly, of course, in the context of the particular example—the claim is understood causally. The claim can be saved for Euthyphronism if it so happens that best opinion about piety hits on a causally efficacious kind. But the Euthyphronist is, of course, committed to denying that the whole truth about the relation between best opinion and piety is captured in that causal claim; and the detectivist remains committed to rejecting

> It is because they are loved by the gods that certain
> acts are pious.

a function of best opinion—or any other appropriately constrained response. It is (an analogue of) one raised by Johnston against the exposition of the distinction between extension-determining and extension-reflecting judgements which figured in a previous discussion of mine.[39] That exposition proceeded, for simplicity's sake, in terms of basic rather than provisional equations. But so far as I can see, Johnston's objection, if sustained against its intended target, would do equal damage to the distinction as explained above. He writes:

> Wright's distinction turns on the directional idea of determination. But how can the extension of the proposition P be determined by anyone's belief under specified circumstances that P? Surely only if the belief that P already has some extension already associated with it. For if the belief that P has no extension and so no mode of determining an extension associated with it, then the belief that P will be devoid of content and so will not constrain anything at all.
>
> As far as extension determining goes, there seem to be just two live options. Either P and "believes that P" have their extensions determined together, in which case talk of *order* of determination is out of place, or talk of order is in place and the order in question is the order exhibited in a standard compositional semantics.

The objection naturally read into this passage goes like this. In order for best opinion to determine—whether wholly or in part—the extension of a concept, there have already to be facts about how best opinions appropriately involving the concept would go; and these are, perforce, facts in whose constitution the very concept in question is implicated. So the concept must already exist fully fledged, as it were; wherefore, must it not already have an extension, *prior* to the putative determination by the directions taken by best opinions?

Is there a problem here? I think we will be inclined to think so if, but only if, we read the terms "order" and "determination" as

39. In my "Whither Now?"; Johnston presents the objection in appendix 3 of "Objectivity Refigured".

if they were meant to have connotations of *temporal* priority. It will then seem as if someone who contends that the extensions of, say, colour concepts are (partially) best-opinion determined is inviting us to picture a world in which they have, as yet, no fully determinate extension, and will get one only when God creates facts about the deliverances of best colour judgements. Against this picture it would indeed be natural to protest that even God cannot bring into being facts of the latter sort unless there are already the conceptual resources to hand to feature in the content of the judgements in question. Bringing facts into being about how best judges would appraise colours requires, as part of the process, the existence of colour concepts and hence—prescinding from vagueness—of determinate extensions for them.

But there is no real problem—only a bad picture. It is true that in order for there to be best judgements about colour—or better, facts about how best judgements would go—there have to be the concepts, including concepts of colour, necessary to specify the content of those judgements. And where there is a concept there has to be a (perhaps vaguely bounded) extension. But nothing at all follows *about the principles whereby such an extension is determined or constrained.* The Euthyphronist may cheerfully admit that he is committed, by the role he assigns to best judgement, to crediting the concepts that figure in these judgements with determinate extensions; his point is then precisely that those extensions are constrained, inter alia, by the deliverances of best judgement.

The objection is, in effect, a version, directed at the formulation of the R-response, of the sort of worry to which, when directed at the formulation of the C-conditions, I responded conservatively by proposing the Independence condition.[40] "If the relevant concepts figure in the specification of the response," the objection says, "then there must already be facts about their extension—and hence those facts cannot be constrained by best response." Well, the reply to this should be merely that its final claim is just a *non sequitur.*

On the other hand, the objection can be formulated more cau-

---

40. And to which, Johnston puzzlingly contends *(ibid.),* that was an unnecessary and needlessly demanding response.

tiously, in line with the way it was presented above in connection with the C-conditions: we replace the final claim by something like

> ". . . and hence there must be a question about whether demands are being made on the way their extension is determined which cannot be made to square with the Euthyphronist's central thesis."

And now the reply is, in effect, the one prefigured above: that in contrast with the ways in which, were we simply to drop the Independence condition and replace it with nothing else, such concepts would be likely to feature in specifications of the C-conditions, their mode of occurrence in the description of a judgemental response is *intensional,* and thus makes no demands on the actual details of their extensions. Of course they have to *have* extensions; but the character of the principles whereby these are determined is an issue which, merely by involving those concepts in the characterisation of the responses adverted to by appropriate provisional equations, we have left entirely open.

I therefore think that the objection is misplaced. The substantive point is that to make a case for thinking that a class of provisional equations satisfies each of the four main conditions (Apriority, Substantiality, Independence and Extremal) which were described is to make a case for thinking that best opinions about the class of statements they concern *are not merely responsive to* matters determined independently of best opinion—that their a priori rightness is not a matter of infallibility, not a matter merely of guaranteed reflection of the extension of the truth predicate in the discourse in question. Once the substance of the distinction is grasped, the rhetoric— "order of determination", or whatever—doesn't matter very much.

## IV. Response-Dependence and Dispositions

Recently Johnston and, following him, Philip Pettit[41] have canvassed a rather different account of the Euthyphro contrast. The

41. In addition to "Objectivity Refigured", see Johnston's "Dispositional Theories of Value", in *Proceedings of the Aristotelian Society,* suppl. vol. 63 (1989), pp. 139–174; and Philip Pettit, "Realism and Response-Dependence".

suggestion is, in effect, that the basic equation should only ever have seemed attractive as a starting point insofar as it represents a standard but crude attempt to capture the notion of a *disposition;* the problems of "Conditional Fallacy", typified by the example of the Chameleon, are problems for this crude account, not for an underlying conception of Euthyphronism which proposes that the characteristic concepts of whatever discourse is in question are concepts of *response-dispositional* properties—properties identified, a priori, as dispositions to elicit specified cognitive or affective responses under suitable (substantially specified) circumstances in suitable (substantially specified) subjects. The Euthyphronist's central thesis about, for instance, the property of being red should be cast along the lines that it may be known a priori that

> The property of being red is the disposition to
> look red to standard observers under standard con-
> ditions

(where both occurrences of "standard" are to be replaced by substantial specifications); and that the concept expressed by "the property of being red" is consequently disclosed to be a *response-dependent* concept.[42] The characteristic Euthyphronic thesis, according to this proposal, will thus be, locally or globally, the response dependence of concepts, to be disclosed by construction of appropriate a priori truths of the illustrated kind.

This line demands, of course, a new account, better than the basic equation provided, of response dispositions and dispositions in general. Johnston recognises this, of course, and has some interesting initial suggestions on the matter.[43] In his view, the simple conditional construal of dispositional properties offered by the basic equation goes wrong in general because it fails to take sufficiently seriously the point that, in ascribing dispositional properties, we are ascribing *intrinsic* characteristics by which, when the relevant kind of conditional is true, its truth is sustained. This is why, in so many cases, simple conditional formulations are beset by the problems of *altering, mimicking* and *masking* which his

42. I here simplify Johnston's own account somewhat.
43. See "Objectivity Refigured", appendix 2.

various examples—chameleons, mysterious rays, interceding angels, and so on—are intended to bring out.

In ascribing to an object a disposition to F under C, we do not intend, in Johnston's—surely correct—view, to claim that it will or would F under all C-circumstances. Rather, the claim is, roughly, a *ceteris paribus* claim. We have to allow for the possibility that an object which has the disposition might be *altered,* under certain background conditions, by the coming about of C-circumstances in such a way as to lose it. That possibility does not justify withholding ascription of the disposition as things actually are. Conversely, while actually lacking the appropriate disposition, it might be that the object, under certain conditions, would be so altered by the implementation of C-circumstances that it acquired it; and that would not vindicate ascribing the disposition to it in actual, non-C-circumstances. A third kind of case is when the wider conditions under which C-circumstances are realized *mask*— that is, prevent—the characteristic manifestation of the disposition. Thus, an Angel prevents what is actually a fragile cup from breaking when it is dropped; or—to give a more prosaic example—a powerful electrical current nearby prevents a compass needle from aligning itself with magnetic north. Finally, although an object lacks the appropriate disposition and the coming about of C-circumstances does not bestow the disposition upon it, the wider conditions under which they are implemented may happen to be such that the characteristic manifestation is caused anyway— a case of *mimicking.* A gold chalice has nothing of the microstructure of fragility but when it is dropped, the Angel breaks it anyway, by an act of will. A spark plug is defective and lacks the disposition to ignite the fuel/air mixture when properly fitted and in receipt of the appropriate electrical imput; but a volatile substance happens to be present in the air in the spark gap which will explode chemically when subjected to the small difference in electrical potential generated across the gap of the defective plug by the normal firing stimulus—so that were those conditions to obtain, the mixture would ignite anyway.[44]

44. It is actually rather difficult to think of plausible (non-supernatural) examples of mimicking. This nice case is due to Jim Edwards.

These are agreeable reflections and surely do respond to elements in our intuitive thinking about dispositions. The question is whether to expect that they can be developed with enough precision to give *effective* guidance in the drawing of the Euthyphro contrast, conceived as proposed. No less is demanded than a general account of what a dispositional characteristic is; and the account must be formulated in such a way that means are provided to adjudicate controversial cases—properties which, like colour or ethical value, do not wear their response-dispositionality on their sleeves. It is too early for confidence that such an account can be provided; nor is it clear, if it is possible to give such an account, what relation to expect to obtain between properties classified as Euthyphronic by its lights and those so classified in accordance with my own proposal.

I am in no doubt, nevertheless, that there are modes of judgement dependence or response dependence which the apparatus of provisional equations I have outlined will not capture. In particular, while I remain convinced that it will be via proposals in this general spirit that we finally come to command a clear perspective on the phenomenon of first-person authority for intentional psychological states, I have written elsewhere[45] of some of the obstacles in the way of applying the apparatus of provisional equations to the intentional—in particular, those to do with the prospects of complying with the Substantiality and Independence conditions.[46] And in this case we have, in addition, the problem that best *opinions* are themselves instances of precisely the kind of state of affairs with which we are concerned.[47] So the more proposals about these mat-

45. See "Wittgenstein's Rule-Following Considerations and the Central Project of Theoretical Linguistics", section IV, pp. 250–254.

46. See Alex Miller, "An Objection to Wright's Treatment of Intention", *Analysis* 49 (1989), pp. 169–173. A sophisticated discussion of the issues may be found in Jim Edwards, "Best Opinions and Intentional States", *Philosophical Quarterly* 42 (1992), pp. 21–33.

47. As Paul Boghossian has noted; see pages 54–57 of his essay "The Rule-Following Considerations", *Mind* 98 (1989), pp. 507–549. But it is not as clear as Boghossian takes it to be that the point is fatal to the prospects of Euthyphronist claims about mental and linguistic content parallel to those which I have mooted about colour; as in the formulation of the C-conditions, so

ters that are on the table, the better. The problems in the way of giving enough of an account of the notion of a disposition to enable the Johnston/Pettit proposal to be applied in actual philosophical debate stand so far largely unaddressed, and their difficulty is not to be underestimated. But open-mindedness remains the wisest council. We should expect that a multiplicity of distinctions cluster around the Euthyphro contrast. Most of the work of exploring them and rendering them serviceable for use in debates about realism and objectivity is still to be done.

---

in the description of the response itself, the undeniable constraint is only that we avoid using the concepts in question in any way inconsistent with the supposition that their extension is *partially* determined by best opinion. It is not obvious that the sort of mention of (counterfactual) facts about opinions which provisional equations, by their very nature, make, has to violate this constraint—is inconsistent with the claim that the range of truths about intentional states, including opinions, is partially determined by best opinions. (Though this much, of course, is clear: there is no space here for any analogue of the conservative response, embodied in the Independence condition, which I imposed in response to the corresponding worry about the formulation of the C-conditions.)

My own instinct is that we do better, in the case of intentional states, to look for a *holistic* mode of dependence: roughly, that the details of a subject's intentional states are, a priori, determined in such a way as to maximise harmony with her self-conception, as manifest in her own elicitable self-ascriptions (or, at least, to minimise inexplicable discord with it). But fuller discussion must await another occasion.

# 4. Cognitive Command
## and the Theoreticity
## of Observation

## I. Résumé

I have been urging the merits of a conception of assertoric content which views it as something ensured by a discourse's satisfying constraints of internal discipline and surface syntax. (Roughly, the discipline ensures that we have bona fide *contents,* and the syntax ensures that they are *assertoric.*) Any of the areas of discourse which historically has provoked, or is likely to provoke, a realist/anti-realist debate is also likely to satisfy these constraints. And assertoric content, so ensured, suffices for the definability upon the discourse of a predicate which, by dint of its satisfaction of certain basic platitudes, qualifies, so I have contended, as a truth predicate.

It is worth emphasising that even from this minimalist perspective, there is yet scope for argued criticism of the idea that a class of utterances which are taken to be truth-apt really are so. Such criticism will properly focus on the question whether the (putative) discourse really does satisfy the constraints of syntax and discipline which ensure the applicability of a truth predicate. One line of attack, connected with the idea that the discipline involved in a particular case might be constituted merely by rules of *permission,* was explored in the discussion note to Chapter 3. But the most illustrious example of such a critique is, of course, the argument against "Private Language" surrounding §258 of the *Philosophical Investigations*. Effectively, Wittgenstein's thought there is precisely that a private language (specifically, a language for the recording of sensations, construed as Cartesian objects) could not possess the requisite discipline, since, famously, there would be no distinction between seeming to be right and being so—even if, we might add, its user were to attempt to embed its sentences in the connectives of an ordinary public language in such a way to ensure that, were these sentences genuinely contentful, their content would be assertoric. So Wittgenstein's point—if you believe him[1]—may be represented as being that even minimal notions of truth and assertoric content cannot grip in circumstances of Cartesian privacy; and hence that since they do characterise our everyday discourse of sensations, a misunderstanding of the meaning of such talk is involved in the conception that its subject matter is epistemically private.

But private language and "purely permissive" discourse are very special cases. Typically, once the legitimacy of the minimalist perspective is granted, there should be no issue about the truth aptitude of a contested discourse, or—at least for those philosophers for whom error theory does not remain a standing temptation—about the justifiability of claiming that many of its sentences are true. In the previous chapter we began to review the question: what, in that case, might still be in dispute? What could yet be missing which might be sensed as a deficiency and incline us away from an intuitive realism? What, additionally, might be present and incline us to the familiar kinds of realist thought about autonomy, objectivity, independence and so on?

The answer counselled here is pluralistic. There are a *variety* of features that may be possessed by minimally truth-apt discourses, any of which may contribute in some measure towards clarifying and substantiating realist preconceptions about it. As matters were described in Chapter 3, such features may be classed under two

1. As I think you ought—see my essay "Does *Philosophical Investigations* 1, 258–60 Suggest a Cogent Argument against Private Language?", in P. Pettit and J. McDowell, eds., *Subject, Thought and Context* (Oxford: Oxford University Press, 1986), pp. 209–266.

broad heads—about which a reminder in a moment. But I acknowledge, of course, that other ways of conceiving the taxonomy may be possible, and other kinds of realism-relevant features besides those I am focussing on may deserve recognition.

A basic anti-realism about a discourse (of course the epithets "realism" and "anti-realism" come to seem less and less happy from a pluralistic perspective) would be the view that it is qualified by *no* interesting feature serving to give point to an intuitive realism about it—that it deploys minimally truth-apt contents, and that's the whole of the matter. But local debates will typically concern specific realism-relevant features, and a victory for the "anti-realist" may consequently have a much more qualified significance than actual protagonists have tended to realise. For instance, to anticipate the agenda for Chapter 5, it may be that when the dust settles, moral states of affairs turn out *not* to feature in the best explanations of our moral beliefs. That finding need not upset the entire moral-realist applecart if we can accomplish an overview according to which the "best explanation" test, however exactly it should be formulated, is merely one among several realism-relevant considerations, and moral discourse's failure to pass it is consistent with its possession of other features which independently substantiate a drive away from the basic anti-realist position.

The two broad headings under which I have suggested we can distinguish a number of realism-relevant features which a discourse—more specifically its truth predicate—may have concern, respectively, superassertibility and the Correspondence Platitude. If nothing bars the interpretation of a discourse's truth predicate as superassertibility, then it is open to us to think of the truth of its statements as consisting merely in their durably meeting its standards of warranted assertion—a property for which all minimally assertoric sentences are eligible. But if truth and superassertibility can be prised apart—if it can be shown that superassertibility is a bad interpretation of the truth predicate in question—then the thought is at least strongly suggested that what confers truth on a statement is not a matter of its meeting standards internal to the language game, as it were, but its fit with an external reality.

One very obvious way of showing that superassertibility is a bad interpretation of a truth predicate is to show that their extensions diverge—or at least to show that we have, and perhaps can have, no reason to think that they do not. Someone who believes that the relevant truth predicate is evidentially unconstrained thinks exactly that. But that is only one way. Another is to show that, even if we have reason to think that there is no extensional divergence, this is reason a posteriori, and we can conceive of circumstances under which divergence would be possible. Yet a third line of attack would be to show that, even though extensional divergence is excluded a priori, it is proper to think of the truth of a statement of the discourse in question as the *explanatory ground* of its superassertibility, perhaps after the fashion in which a categorical base stands as the explanatory ground of a disposition. These latter two approaches belong to what, in honour of Plato's anticipation of the issue, I called the Euthyphro debate.

The second broad heading covers features whose significance devolves from their bearing on the interpretation of the Correspondence Platitude. As we have seen, the permissibility of correspondence phraseology as paraphrase of "true" is the merest by-product of the minimal platitudes. But too many philosophers have tried to express their realism in the form of correspondence theories of truth for it to be likely that there is nothing more substantial there, struggling for an outlet. The thought has to be that there is, at least in selected areas, more that may be legitimately conveyed by the phraseology of correspondence than merely the content bestowed on the Platitude by its links with the minimal constraints. And if that is so, there are only two places to look for such additional content: we can look at what else, besides the links with the minimal constraints, conditions the interpretation of the idea of "correspondence"; and at what, in a particular case, is the proper way of thinking about "the facts".

So much, then, by way of résumé of the framework I want to recommend. Chapter 3 introduced the idea of *Cognitive Command*.  It is a notion whose interest belongs with the attempt to explore features under the second general heading just distinguished. More specifically, it bears on the interpretation of the relation of correspondence. Qualifying and simplifying the formulation previously offered, we may say that a discourse exerts Cognitive Command if and only if

> It is a priori that differences of opinion formulated within the discourse, unless excusable as a result of vagueness in a disputed statement, or in the standards of acceptability, or variation in per-nal evidence thresholds, so to speak, will involve something which may properly be regarded as a cognitive shortcoming.

The qualifications deserve some comment, though it will have been obvious to the alert reader as soon as the idea was mooted that any fully satisfactory version of the Cognitive Command constraint would have somehow to be fashioned to allow for vagueness. Even in the most robustly objective area of enquiry, vagueness— whether in the content of a statement at issue, or in the standards for appraising it,[2] or in what one might style permissible thresholds of evidence—may set up the possibility of disagreements in which nothing worth regarding as a cognitive shortcoming is involved. It's tempting to say, indeed, that a statement's possessing (one kind of) vagueness just *consists* in the fact that, under certain cir-cumstances, cognitively lucid, fully informed and properly func-tioning subjects may faultlessly differ about it. Some measure of vagueness in the standards of assessment of a statement, even one relatively precise in content, may have the same effect—most obvi-ously, if *inference* from vague statements may be involved in its justification. And the notion of what counts as a *sufficient* justifica-tion for a particular appraisal of a statement may also be vague. This is especially clear with probabilistic evidence. The incidence of childhood leukaemias at Sellafield in Cumbria is many times the national British average. Most people who know the facts agree that it's reasonable to believe that the proximity of the nuclear fuels reprocessing plant is responsible. But, manifestly, there is no specific real number, n, such that an incidence n-times the national average justifies that belief, while anything smaller does not. Rather, there is a vaguely bounded range of values for n where, as

---

2. There is an ambiguity in this phrase as between vagueness about what the standards in question are and vagueness about whether agreed standards are, in particular cases, satisfied. It is, of course the second which is meant.

we might put it, suspicion about the effects of the reprocessing plant would not be unreasonable but where someone who took a more sanguine view would not be determinately irrational either. The thresholds of probability which determine commitment and action are, in some measure, a personal matter.

An immediate concern would be that, once so qualified to allow for vagueness of these various kinds, the Cognitive Command constraint may no longer add significantly to the conditions for minimal truth aptitude. But I think we can be sanguine that that is not so. In the kind of disagreement about comedy where we intuitively feel that nothing worth regarding as a cognitive shortcoming need be involved—the kind of case where, in terms of the conception of the norms governing comic discourse outlined in the discussion note to the previous chapter, the presupposition of a rough community of comic sensibility breaks down—no vagueness in the disputed statement, or in the question whether some acknowledged standard has been properly applied, or in personal thresholds of evidence, need be active. The contrast of view may purely and simply concern whether something is funny. There need be no relevant analogy with, say, a conflict in the description of a borderline case of red, where, as the shade edges towards another determinate colour, one party "shuts off", as it were, before the other. There need be no disagreement about any other relevant matter. And standards and evidence may simply not come into the question. Alternatively, it may be—as with certain kinds of moral disagreement—that a conflict of standards does lie at the root of the disagreement. But there need be no operative vagueness in the matter of what complies with the respective sets of standards. If it can be argued that such a divergence of standards can, in certain circumstances, involve nothing deserving to be viewed as a cognitive failing, and that it is consistent with a shared understanding of the disputed judgement, then a case will have been made that moral judgements do not—as a group—exert Cognitive Command, even when the constraint incorporates the needed qualifications about vagueness.[3]

3. I am not at this point suggesting a view on either proviso. My concern is just with one possible structure for a dispute about minimally truth-apt contents which would imply that they failed the Cognitive Command constraint as reformulated.

I made a case that it is Cognitive Command which is really at stake in the long-standing debates about realism which have centred on *convergence*—with seemingly intractable divergences (for instance, certain cross-cultural moral disagreements) constituting prima facie evidence of a failure of Cognitive Command; and a propensity to convergence, by contrast, being prima facie evidence that the constraint is satisfied. The formulation offered is an attempt to begin to crystallise a very basic idea we have about objectivity: that where we deal in a purely cognitive way with objective matters, the opinions which we form are in no sense optional or variable as a function of permissible idiosyncrasy, but are *commanded* of us—that there will be a robust sense in which a particular point of view *ought* to be held, and a failure to hold which can be understood only as a rational/cognitive failure.

It is tempting to say that this just is, primitively, what is involved in thinking of a subject matter as purely objective, and of our mode of interaction with it as purely cognitive; and that the Cognitive Command constraint, as formulated, is merely what results when the basic idea is qualified to accommodate various germane kinds of vagueness. Certainly, Cognitive Command is precisely what is or ought to be at issue in those debates in which philosophers have distinguished *cognitivist* and *non-cognitivist* protagonists. But if what was said in the preceding chapter is right, the truth is that the constraint does not reflect a wholly primitive characteristic of the notions of objectivity and cognitive engagement but derives its appeal, at least in part, from a truism to do with the idea of *representation*. For to think of oneself as functioning in purely cognitive mode, as it were, is, when the products of that function are to be beliefs, to think of oneself as functioning in representational mode; and that idea is then subject to a truism connecting representation and convergence—that representationally functioning systems, targeted on the same subject matter, can produce divergent output only if working on divergent input or if they function less than perfectly. The nerve of the Cognitive Command constraint is a specialisation of that idea to the case where the representational system is a thinking subject engaged in the formation of belief.

Any discourse over which a truth predicate operates will, to repeat, sustain the Correspondence Platitude. But if the discourse exerts Cognitive Command, then an important analogy is established between the idea of representation, or its cognates, as it features in the Correspondence Platitude, and the, as I should like to say, more full-blooded use of the notion evinced in the truism about convergence and representation. Showing that a discourse exerts Cognitive Command thus has the effect of "beefing up" the Correspondence Platitude in just the kind of realism-relevant way I advertised. One shows precisely that the idea of representation featured therein has a characteristic which minimal truth aptitude does not impose, but which it had better have if there is to be real substance in the idea that, in using the discourse in ways which respect the standards of assertoric warrant by which it is informed, we function as representational systems, responsive to states of affairs which, when we are successful, our beliefs and statements serve to map.

Cognitive Command is, as I stressed, a substantial increment over minimal truth aptitude, since the discipline presupposed by the latter need require no more than the operation of a core of generally acknowledged standards of warranted (that is, mandated) assertion. A conflict of opinion in which one party fails to respond to the satisfaction of such a standard, or erroneously takes it to be satisfied, will thereby involve cognitive shortcoming. But conflicts may also be possible in which, for instance, the competing views are mandated by, as it were, cognitively optional standards, lying outside the acknowledged core, or in which—as suggested for comedy in Chapter 3's discussion note—the very disagreement, in the circumstances prevailing, marks the lapsing of a presumed standard. In such cases there need, intuitively, be no facts, leaving on one side the fact of disagreement itself, such that knowledge of them would require a retreat by either antagonist; no element of ignorance, error, or prejudicial over- or under-rating of data need be at work. By contrast, when Cognitive Command is present, then—vagueness apart—cognitive shortcoming *always* has to be at work in the generation of conflicting views.

However, I do not think that if a discourse exerts Cognitive

Command, that immediately takes us all the way to a vindication of an intuitive realism. One can readily envisage the rules of assessment for a particular class of statements being so tightly circumscribed that Cognitive Command was ensured and yet reason remaining to doubt that the statements in question were genuinely representational. Any non-realist about, say, elementary arithmetical statements is implicitly taking just such a view, since it seems impossible to understand how a disagreement about the status or result of an elementary calculation might be sustained without some cognitive shortcoming featuring in its explanation. That suggests that Cognitive Command merely marks one step on the road towards vindication of a broadly realist conception of a discourse, and cannot unsupplemented carry one all the way. But one might wonder whether, conversely, all roads to realism have to go *through* Cognitive Command—whether it is a necessary feature of any discourse about which the basic anti-realist view is to be exceeded, and is hence implicated in any sufficient case for going beyond that view. I suspect that it is. But we do not at this point have in place the apparatus necessary to motivate a firm view on the matter. If I am right, then of course Cognitive Command becomes a point of great strategic importance for the opponent of realism: show that a discourse lacks it and you will blow away with one stroke all conceivable forms of realist resistance.

## II. Resisting Trivialisation

But, the reader may want to protest, it is, for all that has so far been said, totally unclear *how* that might be shown. Cognitive Command as so far elucidated is a *formal* constraint. If what has been suggested is right, then the realist thought that a particular discourse is harnessed to the production of representations of independent, objective states of affairs is a commitment to the claim that the discourse satisfies the constraint. But that much can be agreed on by all parties without there being any agreement about what would count as a demonstration that the constraint is not satisfied. To elicit a *criterion,* applicable to controversial regions of discourse, we need, it appears, to put some independent controls on what is to count as a *cognitive shortcoming.* How is that to be done without begging the substantial question in any particular case?

Let me continue to take it that if any minimally assertoric discourse fails the Cognitive Command constraint, it is discourse about comedy. And now, to make the problem vivid, consider a would-be trivialising theorist, who responds like this:

> But it *is* a priori that any difference of opinion concerning the comic, when not attributable to vagueness and so on, must involve cognitive shortcoming, since, if all else fails, ignorance or error will at least be involved *concerning the truth value of the disputed statement.*

How can this trivialising response be tackled? Naturally, it simply presupposes that we may think of comic statements as recording "facts of the matter", which the opinions of the disputants merely reflect or misrepresent. And that is just the idea on which the Cognitive Command constraint is meant to exercise control. But how can it be made to do so unless we tackle head-on the hard question: what makes an opinion-forming faculty genuinely *cognitive,* and then argue a case that the responses involved in comedy do not fit the bill?

The situation looks like a bind. But in fact it makes all the difference here how we conceive of the rules of debate. If the trivialising response may, as it were, be presumed innocent until proved guilty, then its critic has to make the running, and the hard question may well be impossible to avoid—and maybe to answer as well. But matters look different if the theorist who offers the trivialising response is held to owe a defence. That will seem plausible in the present instance, in which instinct—"common sense"—already recoils from realism about comedy. But I would suggest that the *general* rule should be that realism must be earned. It is the view that the truth predicate operative in a given discourse has realism-substantiating features which needs to be made out. The prephilosophical or "default" stance about a discourse should be one of parsimony: the basic anti-realism adverted to earlier which allows that the discourse operates with minimally truth-apt contents, but—pending evidence to the contrary—takes it that no other features belong to its truth predicate to give point to a realist conception of its subject matter.

If these are the ground rules for the debate, then the trivialising theorist may be force marched, as it were, through a space of alternatives in which every path terminates in substantial philosophical obligation. Let me outline its map.

It seems right to assume that a dispute about the comic quality of a situation need at least not involve any cognitive shortcoming in relation to any of its *non-comic* aspects—aspects for whose description no recourse to the distinctive vocabulary of comedy would be needed. When we disagree about whether a joke was funny or not, neither of us need be deprived of any material information about the context or ancestry of the situation, about the characters referred to, or anything else that might conceivably affect one's comic reaction. Rather, the difference may purely and simply concern whether or not the joke was funny. So it seems that in such a case the cognitive shortcoming whose existence is claimed by the trivialising theorist must specifically and irreducibly concern comic quality. There is then an obvious question: can an *intuitional* epistemology of comedy be avoided—can the theorist avoid invoking the idea of a *sui generis* cognitive sense or faculty of comedy, sensitive to *sui generis* states of affairs? And if not, will not difficulties ensue?

Let us go carefully. Consider a dispute about comedy in which the disputants are agreed about all non-comic aspects. The trivialising theorist insists that cognitive shortcoming must nevertheless be involved. The first question to press is whether she regards comedy as something which properly functioning human subjects are invariably equipped to appraise, or whether it may be undetectable. (The latter option seems, of course, entirely bizarre in the present example, but our concern is with the map of the options in general.) If she is prepared to regard the comic quality of a situation as something which may lie beyond human detection, then she is of course quite right to insist that, assuming that the disputed situation is comically determinate, as it were, at least one of the disputants must be in ignorance of or in error about it.

That is just to say that someone who accepts the potential evidence-transcendence of truth in a particular discourse is committed to its satisfying the Cognitive Command constraint. So that's an option. But if the theorist wants to take it, she has to stop trivialising and take on the serious work of explaining how comedy—or whatever subject matter is distinctively described by the discourse in question—can transcend all possibility of human knowledge.

But suppose the theorist finds the idea of evidence-transcendent truth simply too *outré* in the case of comedy and declines that path. Then she commits herself to allowing that the claimed cognitive shortcoming has to consist in someone's having failed fully and properly to exercise capacities which do put us in effective position to track comedy. The crucial issue now is whether the theorist proposes, in basic cases, to regard opinions about comedy as inferentially or as non-inferentially justified. Here I mean the notion of inferential justification to be understood in what is, I hope, a very straightforward way: a subject's opinion on some matter is *inferentially justified* just in case he has independently justified beliefs from which it follows and no other justification for it but to cite that relationship; his opinion is *non-inferentially justified* just in case it is somehow justified, but not inferentially. We now press the question whether our comedy-detective cognitive capacities should be seen as enabling the construction of justifying inferences to comic conclusions, or whether what they enable us to do, at least in basic cases, is to arrive at non-inferentially justified comic beliefs.

Suppose the theorist opts for the latter possibility—that the basic epistemology of comedy is non-inferential. Then she must presumably think of it as *intuitional*—in the way in which we normally think of perception, and at least some operations of memory and of a priori knowledge, as intuitional.

Let that ride for a moment, and consider the other possibility: that the basic epistemology of comedy is conceived as inferential—with justification invariably flowing, when it is possessed at all, via inference from other independently justified beliefs. (Again, this is of course highly implausible in the case of the actual example.) It will be circular, or viciously regressive, to suppose that such inferentially justifying beliefs can themselves invariably concern comedy. Rather, the inferential option must, at some point, break out of comic discourse and view justification as flowing, via linking principles of inference, from justified beliefs about non-comic matters. But our hypothesis was that the disputants are *agreed* about non-comic matters; so the explanation of their disagreement, if it is not to be inferential error, will have to be that they disagree about which such linking principles—principles conditionally linking non-comic with comic claims—are acceptable.

Think of such principles as conditionals of the form $N \to C$. The theorist who has gone for the inferential option must now make a case, if the original claim to Cognitive Command is not to fall, that such principles themselves exert Cognitive Command. And now the same options arise as before: exit into evidence-transcendence, or face the dilemma whether to construe the basic epistemology of such principles as intuitional or inferential. As before, the first option requires serious work:[4] one has to explain how the truth of such a principle can be beyond human ken, what it is about its subject matter that potentially makes it so. But if the theorist chooses instead to take the dilemma, she had better recognise that taking the inferential option can only be a stalling tactic, since another set of principles—think of them as being of the form $N' \to [N \to C]$—will immediately arise for consideration, which in turn will have to exert Cognitive Command if her original claim is not to lapse. So in effect the options reduce to two: evidence-transcendence, or the invocation, sooner or later, of an intuitional epistemology—sooner if at the basic level of simple ascriptions of comic quality, later if at the level of principles of inference embedding comic vocabulary essentially in their consequents.

Remember here that we are not trying to work towards a refinement of the Cognitive Command constraint so sharp that it will be possible to apply it more or less mindlessly to an arbitrary

4. And is any way foreclosed if the theorist rejects the evidence-transcendence option for basic statements about comedy, since they *would* be potentially evidence-transcendent if principles of inference needed to justify their assertion were.

region of discourse. What I am arguing is merely that the constraint is not open to trivialisation in the way which threatened—that claiming Cognitive Command for a discourse is a commitment to serious philosophy, and is defeasible by a failure to discharge that commitment. And now we're close to seeing that. For there are constraints on the responsible invocation of the idea of an intuitional epistemology. Postulating such an epistemology involves crediting the knowing subjects with a certain appropriate cognitive endowment, and crediting the states of affairs known about with certain appropriate characteristics to which that endowment is able to be appropriately non-inferentially responsive. And these are matters of which it should in principle be possible to give an account in some detail. For instance, if a theorist goes for an intuitional account of the epistemology of comedy itself, then a story should be forthcoming about what having a sense of humour most fundamentally consists in, and what the comic quality of a situation must fundamentally consist in, and of how a subject with the former is *thereby* fitted to appreciate the latter. It cannot be the last word on the matter just to say that there is comedy in the world and that we are, fortunately, so endowed that we are able to be directly receptive to its presence.

More generally, I suggest that the invocation of an intuitional epistemology has to respect the following constraint:

> We ought not to associate a special faculty with a particular region of discourse, a faculty, that is, apt for the production of non-inferentially justified beliefs essentially involving its distinctive vocabulary, unless the best explanation of our practice of the discourse, and especially the phenomenon of non-collusive assent about opinions expressed therein, has to invoke the idea that such a faculty is at work.

Here, the involvement of the idea of *best* explanation is crucial. An explanation doesn't count as best if it doesn't contain any *detail;* rather, it doesn't count as an explanation at all. If there is to be any content to the thought that beliefs of ours are formed via non-inferential response, courtesy of a special faculty, to the states of affairs that determine their truth value, then it is mortgaged to the possibility of some kind of account of how the alleged faculty works.

I mean this to be a very non-specific requirement, not to be equated, for instance, with the claim that we require some *naturalistic* or scientifically reductive account of what the states of affairs in question consist in, and a causal story of the interaction with them that the operations of the alleged faculty involve. Of course, an account of that kind would certainly discharge the obligation. But the philosophical point here is not an expression of naturalistic preference. The merchant of the *sui generis* epistemology is making a claim about the *shape* assumed by the right explanation of instances of non-collusive assent in comic judgements, or whatever the target class happens to be. But there is no a priori presumption in favour of an account of the claimed— interactive—shape. It is readily conceivable that the cognitive psychology of such assent should assume a different form. It is only via the acquisition of detail that the *sui generis* account can take on credibility.

Even if detail is added, such an explanation will not, moreover, count as best if another *equally good* explanation fails to make any play with the idea of a special cognitive sensitivity to the states of affairs in question. If such an explanation really is equally good, then it will explain how a defective—someone who lacked the alleged *sui generis* cognitive capacity—could mingle unnoticed in the linguistic community, classifying off his own bat comedy, morals, logical necessity, or whatever, as well as his neighbour. And once we can explain that, a version of Ockham's razor comes into play: nothing stands in the way of the thought that we might as well regard the *whole community* as "defectives"—the special cognitive capacity becomes a fifth wheel.[5]

5. These considerations have some grip in the context of a simple but influential point advanced in the course of Grice and Strawson's response ("In Defence of a Dogma", *Philosophical Review* 65 [1956], pp. 141–158) to Quine's "Two Dogmas of Empiricism" (reprinted in his collection *From a Logical Point of View* [New York: Harper and Row, 1953]). Grice and Strawson urge, against Quine's perceived denial of the reality of the analytic–synthetic distinction, that

Can it be claimed that the lessons of this discussion apply generally? It has depended on the hypothesis of a special feature of discourse about comedy, namely that differences of opinion about what is funny need not ramify into differences of opinion about anything else—or, more accurately, into differences whose expression needs no use of the distinctive vocabulary of comedy. Say that one discourse *disputationally supervenes* on another just in case the rational intelligibility of differences of opinion expressible in the former will depend on the existence of differences expressible in the latter. (Plausibly there is such a relation between, say, opinions about the significance and status of written calculations and empirical beliefs about the detail of the written patterns involved.) Our hypothesis was thus in effect that comedy is *disputationally pure*—that it is disputationally supervenient on no other discourse. How special a feature is that?

Disputational supervenience contrasts with the kind of supervenience often alleged to characterise, for instance, the relation between the moral and non-moral (natural). That notion alleges that, however the moral facts are, they could not have been different unless the non-moral facts had been different too. It does not follow that differences in moral opinion have to involve differences in non-moral belief, but merely that anyone who takes a moral view of some matter has to acknowledge that, had that view been wrong, the non-moral facts—possibly in respects about which

---

it is futile to deny that a distinction exists when it is manifestly applied in a non-collusive but mutually agreeable way within a linguistic practice. It is open to the Quinean to reply that that consideration, as far as it goes, is quite consistent with a cognitive psychology of the practice of the distinction which, in the explanations it offers of non-collusive but agreeable applications of it, makes no use of the idea that we respond to exemplifications of distinction, still less attempts any detail about how we are enabled so to respond. In short: Grice and Strawson make the beginnings of a case for supposing that ordinary talk of analyticity has, as a matter of sociological fact, sufficient discipline to qualify as minimally apt for truth; the Quinean riposte can then be that that falls a long way short of showing that it deserves anything amounting to an intuitive realism, and that the most formidable barrier to a further advance remains the provision of an epistemology, whether *sui generis* or somehow reductive, explaining how modal judgements generally possess Cognitive Command.

he has no opinion—could not have been entirely unaltered. The standardly acknowledged kind of supervenience of the moral on the non-moral is thus quite consistent with moral discourse's being disputationally pure. So the shape of the discussion of the trivialising response in the case of comedy may very well apply, for all ordinary supervenience has to say to the contrary, to morals too.

What would have happened if we had picked an example which lacked this feature—a discourse such that rationally sustaining a disagreement about one of its statements would necessitate differences of opinion lying elsewhere? Well, the claim of Cognitive Command for such a discourse would have to be extended to any discourse disputationally supervened upon; for if a difference of opinion expressed in the latter would not have to involve cognitive shortcoming, neither would a dispute expressed in the former which turned on that difference. Grant two plausible assumptions: that disputational supervenience is transitive, and that chains of disputational supervenience must finitely terminate in a disputationally pure discourse. Then a defence of Cognitive Command for any discourse in such a chain will involve a defence for the discourse at the terminus, for which the options will then be as discussed for the case of comedy.

Conclusion: an effective defence of the claim to Cognitive Command of a discourse must involve either maintaining semantic realism for it, or postulating an intuitional epistemology either for statements formulated in the distinctive vocabulary of the discourse or for statements which do not involve that vocabulary but are such that they must come into dispute if a disagreement in the original discourse is to be rationally sustained. So substantial philosophy has to be involved. A defence of semantic realism for the discourse must be provided; or a case must be made that the invocation of an intuitional epistemology, at whatever stage it is invoked, respects the requirement that doing so contributes to the best explanation of speakers' ability to practice the discourse in an agreeable, mutually intelligible way.

That's almost all I want to say about how the Cognitive Command constraint bears, in a fashion consonant with the general approach which I want to recommend, on realist/anti-realist disputes, and why it would be a mistake to think that, in the absence of any precise account of what should rank as a "cognitive shortcoming", the constraint will be unable to resist trivialisation. But before turning to an application of the idea, let me pause to note a distinction. A well-known debate in moral philosophy— Harman, Wiggins and the so-called Cornell realists have been the main protagonists—focusses on the question whether citation of moral states of affairs features ineliminably in the best explanations of our moral opinions. Participants in the debate agree that the question raises an important issue for moral realism, with moral anti-realism as perhaps the inevitable upshot if moral states of affairs fail to meet the implied constraint. Now, the idea that questions concerning the best explanation of the beliefs expressed in a particular discourse have an important bearing on the defensibility of realism about it is certainly something which someone attracted to the general framework I've been advocating ought to want to develop and locate. I shall offer some thoughts about the matter in the next chapter. Here I merely want to remark that I do not think we have already broached it in the play I just made with the idea of best explanation in the context of the invocation of *sui generis* epistemologies. It is one thing to propose such a constraint as operating on the justified invocation of *sui generis* epistemology; it is quite another to see it as a *general* constraint on the justification of realism. What I proposed is a constraint on the success of one particular form of defence of a claim to Cognitive Command. By contrast, what seems to be shared in the debate I alluded to is a perception of an independent watershed—a "Best Explanation" constraint—something which, like the issue of Cognitive Command, can be raised in connection with any discourse for which the question of realism arises. It is the nature of this (putative) watershed which will occupy us in Chapter 5.

## III. The Theoreticity of Observation

The Cognitive Command constraint is at the centre of a good debate about modality, in particular about logical necessity and contingency, in which the challenge to the realist is to locate the cognitive shortcomings of characters who betray no abnormalities in their non-modal judgements, but go variously eccentric when these judgements are embedded in modal operators, either refusing, for instance, to endorse any statements as necessarily true or applying the notions of necessity and contingency in ways which, while not committing them to any actual disagreement with us about the truth values of the embedded statements, strike us as bizarre and unmotivated.[6] In addition, I have suggested that it is the issue of Cognitive Command on which the interest, in the context of moral realism, of questions to do with convergence in moral opinions and basic moral outlook—the extent of such convergence, and the conditions for its existence—should be seen as depending. But the application which I now want rapidly to review concerns neither morals nor modality. It concerns an awkwardness for what might otherwise be an attractive general standpoint in the philosophy of science—an awkwardness which, in my judgement at least, calls into question whether we yet have the Cognitive Command constraint in fully operational form. But a different assessment of the significance of the situation will be possible.

The problem arises when we put together two quite natural thoughts, or at least one natural one and one fashionable one. The natural thought is that nothing in an intuitive scientific realism requires semantic realism—realism in Dummett's sense. What a scientific realist essentially wants to maintain is that there are aspects of reality for the description and cognition of which we are dependent upon the vocabulary and methods of scientific theory: aspects of the natural world which we can't understand or know

6. Contributions include chapter 23 of my *Wittgenstein on the Foundations of Mathematics* (Cambridge, Mass.: Harvard University Press, 1980); Edward Craig, "Arithmetic and Fact", in I. Hacking, ed., *Exercises in Analysis* (Cambridge: Cambridge University Press, 1985), pp. 89–112; my "Inventing Logical Necessity", in J. Butterfield, ed., *Language, Mind and Logic* (Cambridge: Cambridge University Press, 1986), pp. 187–209; Simon Blackburn, "Morals and Modals", in G. Macdonald and C. Wright, eds., *Fact, Science and Morality* (Oxford: Basil Blackwell, 1987), pp. 119–141; and Bob Hale's and my contributions to the symposium "Necessity, Caution and Scepticism", in *Proceedings of the Aristotelian Society* 63 (1989), pp. 175–238.

about without relying upon the techniques of concept formation and statement testing used by theoretical science. The important ingredients in the view are thus, first, against reductionism, the belief that scientific theoretical vocabulary is no dispensable *ersatz* for a vocabulary of some epistemologically more basic kind; and, second, the belief that statements formulated in scientific theoretical vocabulary are apt to be true or false in a substantial way, one associated with *representation* of or fit with objective worldly states of affairs.

These highly intuitive ideas seem prima facie quite consistent with semantic anti-realism's strictures against evidentially unconstrained truth. Those strictures need not entail, as is so often assumed, a thesis about the bounds of reality—the thought that, as it were, the totality of facts is conveniently (but mysteriously) trimmed to ensure that there is nothing there that outreaches human inquisitiveness. They are motivated by arguments to the effect that it is a condition on the full intelligibility of a representational content that its faithfulness—things being as it represents them as being—be in principle detectable; so it is quite consistent with acknowledging the force of such arguments to concede that it is unjustified to suppose that all aspects of reality allow of humanly intelligible representation. When matters are viewed like that, there is nothing to predispose against the intuitive scientific realist world-view—nothing to foreclose on the thought that scientific theory deals in genuinely representational but irreducible contents, rendered true or false by a real external source. And this may be a congenial reflection for anyone disposed to recognise the power of the global case against semantic realism. Unquestionably, scientific realism is the most attractive philosophy of science: cognitive adventure is a much more appealing project than utilitarian fiction.

The other component in the problem—the fashionable one—is the idea that the data of observation on which the credibility of any natural scientific theory ultimately depends are invariably theoretically conditioned—that observation is "theory-laden", as the matter is standardly unhelpfully expressed; and that the kind of clear distinction between theory and data which was dear to the

Logical Positivists, and a central plank in the instrumentalism which some of them adopted, is mythical. A number of distinct notions need disentangling here. Some at least of these notions—I shall mention three—pose no threat, it seems to me, to the traditional theory/observation distinction. But there is a fourth which, whether or not some version of that distinction might accommodate it, does create an awkwardness for a scientific realist who wants to work with an epistemic conception of truth. That will be the notion on which we shall concentrate.

Here are the three, as it seems to me, harmless senses in which observation might be claimed to be "theory-laden".

First, observing is perceiving, and perception is distinguished from mere sensation—*pace* John McDowell[7]—by being conceptually informed. What a subject will be inclined to report on the basis of a certain episode of sensory stimulation will be a function, naturally, of the concepts which they possess. There is therefore provision for the idea that subjects whose conceptual equipment differs may, for that reason, offer different reports on the basis of presumptively similar sensory episodes.

Second, any statement about the material world, including all those that we would not hesitate, prephilosophically, to regard as observably true or false, will outrun experience in indefinitely many respects. There are countless ways in which an experiential episode which prompts a particular observation statement might be augmented so as to confound it instead. The experiential content of an observational report thus invariably exceeds whatever experience actually motivates it.

Third, to grasp concepts is not merely to possess certain classificatory skills, but essentially imports the possession of certain general *beliefs*. I can, in any ordinary sense of the term, observe the presence of a zebra and correctly report as much. But possession of the concept *zebra* involves, more than such an ability of classification, some grip on the notion of an *animal,* and of a *species* of

7. See John McDowell, "One Strand in the Private Language Argument", *Grazer Philosophische Studien* 33–34 (1989), pp. 285–303. A rejection of the possibility of non-conceptual modes of experience also loomed large in McDowell's John Locke lectures delivered at Oxford during Trinity Term 1991.

animal, and the belief that zebras comprise such a species. Even concepts as apparently—but only apparently—simple as those of colour are properly understood only if the subject has grasped that they apply to enduring material objects, among other things, and can characterise such an object when it is not being perceived, or while placed in a darkened room.

All this is probably sound, and certainly familiar. But if the point of the idea that observation is ineliminably theoretical is to challenge the opposition between data and empirical theory, then no challenge has so far been made. To offer such a challenge, you have at the least to make a case that reports of observation do not count as acceptable, or unacceptable, independently of one's empirical-theoretical beliefs—that what it is proper to report oneself as having observed is a function of, inter alia, elements of empirical theory which one carries into the observational situation. Hence, the claims that concepts are involved in all perception, or—as illustrated in the cases of *zebra* and colour concepts—that grasping them may presuppose possession of certain *a priori* beliefs, are simply not to the purpose. Similarly, the seemingly indefinite experiential content of ordinary empirical beliefs seems to pose no immediate obstacle to their constituting pretheoretical data in at least this sense: it may still be that, provided one has the appropriate concepts, one's experience may assume such a pattern that one *ought,* irrespective of one's background empirical beliefs, to assent to such a statement, even though such assent is invariably in principle defeasible by untoward subsequent experience. The kind of theory-ladenness needed to make trouble for the traditional opposition between theory and data is, rather, of a fourth kind, in effect already noted. It has to be made out that the conditions of warranted assertion and denial of anything that might pass for a report of a publicly observable matter are invariably a function not just of the content of the report and the quality of input experiences, but also of collateral empirical beliefs concerning the circumstances in which observation takes place.

That something of this sort is true is, however, extremely plausible. Surely, the reports which subjects are prepared to offer on the basis of their experience will and ought to depend on their beliefs concerning the circumstances in which an observation is made. An experience which prompts subjects to assent to a certain description of colour, or shape, in certain circumstances may, quite properly, no longer do so if they come to believe that the conditions of observation are deceptive or non-standard in some way—or that their own perceptual function is abnormal. It is true that in any ordinary observational situation we may presumptively take the normality, or the conduciveness, of the conditions of observation and the competence of the observer for granted. But we could hardly maintain that such assumptions hold true a priori. On the contrary: they are liable to be confounded by experience and, indeed, by empirical theory of great sophistication. A hackneyed but vivid example is that of the Doppler effect on light passing between bodies of high relative velocity, so that the light reaching us from certain rapidly receding stars is preponderantly of frequencies towards the red end of the spectrum. As a result, an untutored observer will, perfectly properly but wrongly, be disposed to assent to "That star has a yellowish hue" in circumstances in which someone who knows enough about the physics of light and the relative velocities of the stars will not.

Suppose that all observation is indeed theory-laden in the sense gestured at. There are thus no statements of which it can be said that, in any particular context, any rational subject who understands them and whose experience in that context assumes a certain course is obliged to assent to them—no *synthetic* statements in the sense of the concluding section of "Two Dogmas". Rather, warranted acceptability of observation statements is a four-term relation holding between the statement, a subject, a course of experience, and a set of background empirical theoretical beliefs. What's the problem?

Our semantically anti-realist scientific realist wants to think of truth for scientific theories in a full-bloodedly representational way, notwithstanding epistemic constraint. And the thought is looming large in our reflections that at least a necessary condition for the propriety of doing so will be that (at least suitably selected) scientific theories exert Cognitive Command. So any differences of opinion concerning them, when no material vagueness is involved, must be attributable to something worth regarding as a cognitive shortcoming. But it cannot be, under the assumptions now in play, that such a shortcoming may be indefinitely unidentifiable. For if that were so—if a situation were possible where we could definitely say that one of a pair of disputing theorists was guilty of cognitive shortcoming, but there was no way of saying who—then there would be no identifying the *winner* (if any) in the dispute either; and that would be as much as to allow that a true theory might be unrecognisable after all. When truth is regarded as essentially epistemically constrained, Cognitive Command requires the *identifiability* of cognitive shortcoming wherever it occurs. The difficulty is going to be whether this requirement can be satisfiable if theory and observation are globally intertwined in the sense of our supposition.

Suppose theorist A accepts a certain theory $H_0$ on the basis on certain observations, $O_0$. But theorist B considers there is no reason to accept $H_0$. It is not, though, that he is merely ignorant of the observations. Rather, B assesses the experiences which motivate A's acceptance of $O_0$ in terms of a theory $H_1$ which A doesn't accept and which justifies B in not assenting to $O_0$ in those circumstances. So A and B are disagreed about the status of $H_0$. Must their disagreement, if not attributable to vagueness, involve some specific cognitive shortcoming? Naturally it may. But *must* it do so?

Let's tighten up the description of the case so as to preempt certain possible modes of involvement of vagueness and certain possible types of shortcoming. Let A agree that if $H_1$ is accepted, his experience does not provide sufficient grounds for accepting $O_0$. So the problem is not, for instance, to do with vagueness in $O_0$, nor with ignorance or error concerning the implications of accepting $H_1$. Rather, it concerns the status of $H_1$, accepted by B but not by A. If either vagueness or cognitive failings have to be involved in the original dispute, then one or other must be involved in the dispute about $H_1$. And again, that may be so. But it seems straightforward to continue the story in such a way that it is not yet made clear *how* it is so. Suppose for instance that B accepts $H_1$ on the basis of observations $O_1$; but A, unlike B, holds a theory $H_2$ which so conditions his assessment of the relevant experiences that he concludes that there is no reason to accept $O_1$. B, in contrast, does not hold $H_2$ but agrees that *if* $H_2$ is held, then A's response is perfectly appropriate. Clearly we are now embarked on a potential regress, in which each theorist disputes the acceptability of each theory, and each relevant set of observation statements, accepted by his opponent; but in which there is complete agreement about the *conditional* acceptability of each of his opponent's theories relative to the relevant disputed observations.[8]

Where is the cognitive shortcoming? At the most general level, it seems that there are only three kinds of shortcoming that might be involved. *Either* A or B has accumulated faulty evidence—some of the cited observation statements are mistaken; *or* A or B has accumulated sound evidence which the other lacks—either A or B is wrongly rejecting true observation statements; *or* one or the other is over- or underestimating the evidential force of the observations which he has made. But we may perfectly properly stipulate the third possibility away. Just as A and B are agreed, rightly as we may suppose, about what observations it is proper to record in response to their experience *if* certain relevant background theories are accepted, so we may suppose them rightly agreed about the character of the impact on relevant theories which those observations would have if allowed to stand. And we have also stipulated that A's and B's respective observation reports are correct *relative* to the background theories which condition them and the theorists' respective experiences. So if either is working with faulty data, that's going to require that he is conditioning his observation reports with a *false* background theory. And if either is working with materially incomplete data, that's going to require that his opponent is working with a *true* background theory to

8. Pictorially:

   A:  $H_0 \leftarrow O_0$; $\not{H}_1$; $\varnothing_1 \leftarrow H_2 \leftarrow O_2$; $\not{H}_3$; $\varnothing_3 \leftarrow H_4 \ldots$
   B:  $\not{H}_0$; $\varnothing_0 \leftarrow H_1 \leftarrow O_1$; $\not{H}_2$; $\varnothing_2 \leftarrow H_3 \leftarrow O_3$; $\ldots$

where "$\leftarrow$" indicates direction of justification, and "$H_n$", "$\not{H}_n$", "$O_n$", "$\varnothing_n$" indicate that $H_n$, $O_n$ respectively are or are not endorsed by A, B.

which he does not subscribe. In other words: the first two types of material cognitive shortcoming—accepting incorrect data or failing to accept correct data—are going to require analogous shortcomings with respect to the accompanying theoretical commitments.

The crux of the matter is accordingly: can it be guaranteed a priori that if a dispute originates, in a fashion we have illustrated, purely on the basis of competing background theory, and no other cognitive shortcoming or material vagueness is operative, there nevertheless will *be* cognitive shortcoming in the background theoretical commitments of the protagonists? Such a shortcoming can only consist, obviously, in one party or the other accepting a mistaken theory, or being in ignorance of a sound theory accepted by their opponent. But recall now that our reflections on the matter are, as it were, lumbered with evidential constraint: such a theory's being mistaken or sound has to be *recognisable,* at least in principle. And that can mean only that the correctness or incorrectness of such a theory has to be certifiable, if only defeasibly, by proper application of scientific method.

Such a certification, however, could consist, ultimately, only in the assembly of *independently credible* data which confer or tell against the theory in question. The predicament is therefore that, on the governing assumption of theory-ladenness, the independent credibility of such data is always hostage to that of any theory which is apt to condition their acceptability. So it seems we can't exclude the possibility of an intractable dispute on the matter, in the fashion of A and B. As long as the notion of truth appropriate to scientific theories is held to be essentially epistemically constrained, there can be no guarantee that, in the original dispute, either A or B must be guilty of cognitive shortcoming.

Someone may be bursting with the following objection. Consider any point in the regress where one theorist, by virtue of accepting some theory $H_N$, discounts observations, $O_{N-1}$, accepted by the other. Now reflect that, plausibly, the relationship between experience and reports of observation will be, as we might say, *positive presumptive.* That is, it is not as if it is *only* in the context of appropriate background empirical beliefs that experience has any tendency either to confirm or to disconfirm an observational report; rather, there are default relations of confirmation between experience and observational statements—the experience which prompts the report "That star is yellowish in hue" is a default justifier of that claim, insofar as it concerns colour. Suitable experiential justification is defeasible in the context of suitable background beliefs, but otherwise it stands presumptively. That being so, cannot we drive home a charge of cognitive shortcoming as follows? Do the theorists have between them any presumptive, so far undefeated observational support for $H_N$? If so, then the theorist who accepts $O_{N-1}$ must do so either on the basis of ignorance of this support for $H_N$, or on a prejudicial refusal to acknowledge its force. But if not—if there is no presumptive, so far undefeated observational support for $H_N$—then the first theorist's acceptance of $H_N$ is unjustified, and his opponent is quite right presumptively to accept $O_{N-1}$. Either way, we have found what we wanted.

But this objection overlooks the possibility that the regress of theories and observations may dovetail back, as it were—that the first theorist's observational support for $H_N$ may be provided by observation statements, $O_I \ldots O_J$, which have already featured at earlier stages in his personal system. In that case, his acceptance of $H_N$ is not without observational support; but the observations by which he supports it will be discounted by his opponent, by virtue of his differing theoretical commitments. Once the possibility of dovetailing is recognised, we can no longer affirm that, if nothing else has gone wrong, the theorists between them must at least be guilty either of deployment of unsupported theories or a failure to acknowledge the undefeated support afforded certain observational reports by available experience.

So there is the problem. If truth is evidentially constrained, and all observation is theory-laden, scientific-theoretical disagreeements cannot be guaranteed to involve cognitive shortcoming. None of this, of course, need provoke anything but glee in the scientific realist who is also a Dummettian realist. He will consider himself entitled to a conception of the truth conferrers for scientific-theoretical statements such that the most that the foregoing discloses are certain ways in which it might in principle be impossible to *decide* whose was the shortcoming in a scientific-theoretical dispute. But there would be a fact of the matter: so much is ensured by the idea, to which this realist considers himself entitled, that scientific theories can be determinately true or false in ways that transcend all available evidence. (And if, in a particular case, there is no fact of the matter, then that will be spoken to by the explicit proviso of vagueness built into the Cognitive Command constraint.)

To be sure, the possibility presented is highly abstract, even abstruse. It is unclear how even the beginnings of a concrete example might be constructed. But it would be completely misconceived to complain about that. For recall that the Cognitive Command constraint, as formulated, demands satisfaction *a priori;* so a discourse should be presumed to fail if no a priori reason is evident that the constraint is satisfied—and the abstract possibility described constitutes a presumptive case that there is no such reason.

For anyone out of sympathy with evidentially unconstrained truth, the threatened consequences of the situation seem to be dire indeed. First, all space for a moderate realism, intermediate between Dummettian realism and minimalist anti-realism, threatens to be closed off in the case of scientific theory. Second, and worse still, reports of observation are dragged down into the mire too, failing the Cognitive Command constraint in tandem with the theories that condition their acceptability. And then, third—the ultimate calamity—it is unclear how Cognitive Command can be exerted by *any* class of statements about which dispute may always originate in a difference of opinion about observable features of nature. So all statements are implicated whose epistemology at least partially involves ordinary observation—therefore all statements, I suppose, whose cognition is other than purely a priori.

Let me stress: none of this discloses any difficulty for the semantic realist. For the rest of us, the hope must be either that we can yet win through to some purified notion of an observation statement, one that does not involve "theory-ladenness" of the sort which is giving the trouble, or—more likely—that the Cognitive Command constraint can and must be refined in some way while remaining faithful to its motivation in the idea of representational function. I have no easy solution to suggest. But my main purpose has been to publicise the problem, and I shall not address it further in the remaining part of this study, deferring it to a sequel.

## DISCUSSION NOTES

*1. Now that we have seen the trouble that its inclusion leads to, is it not time to look askance at the occurrence of "a priori" in the formulation of Cognitive Command? The motivating thought, offered at the end of Chapter 3, was that*

> *It wouldn't be of any interest if all relevant disagreements were, merely as a matter of fact, invariably attributable to such factors—as a matter of serendipity, as it were. It might have been, for instance, that we all shared a single sense of humour, and that disagreements about the comic were always in practice down to something worth describing as a cognitive shortcoming, of one of the kinds listed, in relation to non-comic factors. But if that were so, it would be something which could only be determined a posteriori, and would have no intuitive bearing on the objectivity of discourse about comedy.*

*We may grant that this is compelling to the extent that some operator is clearly needed in the place where "a priori" occurs in the existing formulation of the constraint—the mere truth of what follows won't get at the intended intuitions. But why "a priori"? Wouldn't some nomic operator— say, "It is no accident that . . ." or "It is ensured by the Laws of Nature that . . ."—enable a reformulated constraint to capture what Cognitive Command is after? If so, then the mere a priori conceivability of a dispute of the structure illustrated would offer no compelling reason to think that scientific-theoretical discourse failed of Cognitive Command—one would need reason in addition to think that such a situation was a real practical risk. And there is no evidence for that.*

It would certainly be welcome if some such proposal could be sustained, and foolish, of course, to discount any role for nomic considerations in the formulation of debates about realism. But it is difficult to see that this could be the right way to approach the matter of Cognitive Command. For one thing, it would very likely be no accident but a consequence of natural law if there always *were* cognitive shortcomings involved in comic disputes—and that doesn't seem to engage any idea we have about objectivity: nothing speaks for the thought that, in such a situation, comic responses would have to have acquired an objectivity which they presently lack. Suppose a dominant gene gradually promotes a co-incidence in senses of humour and other psychological character-istics; consequently the human race eventually so develops that cognitive shortcoming about non-comic matters is always involved in comic disputes. That would have to be viewed—if Cognitive Command is to connect with representational content in a full-blooded sense—as taking comedy towards the sphere of repre-sentational judgement; and that seems implausible, at least if rep-resentationality is to supervene on *content,* since there is no evident reason why the content of comic claims would thereby have to have changed in any way at all. Even after such a development it would remain readily intelligible how senses of humour might irreducibly diverge, and no easier to argue than before that hypothetical such divergences would have to betray deficiency. By contrast, the representationality of judgements about, say, the shapes of the pieces in a child's puzzle involves just this: that no matter how differently we might be constituted biophysically, or what laws of nature might be in operation, differences in such judgements would have to be taken as an indication of less than perfect cognitive function. That is an idea which any formulation of Cognitive Command which is content merely to lay emphasis on the actual nomic constitution of the world seems essentially ill-fitted to capture.

In any case, there seems no doubt that the connection between representational function and divergences of output articulated in the parent principle—the Convergence/Representation Platitude—is an a priori one. So any constraint which is specialised to the representational activities of thinking subjects but is well moti-vated by that principle can likewise only impose an a priori requirement. If apriority is to be jettisoned from the formulation of Cognitive Command, that motivation must be jettisoned too.

2. *Surely* <u>*some*</u> *sort of shortcoming is involved in the dispute, under the circumstances described, between the theorists, A and B. For ought not each of them, recognising the equally good pedigree of his opponent's view, to withdraw commitment from his own? Indeed, the point does not require that there be any actual difference of opinion at all. If a theory can be devised conflicting, in the manner described, with mine at every point but no less well attested in the light of the evidence which that very theory allows one to recognise, is that not a fact which, were I to know of it, would rationally oblige me to suspend acceptance of my own theory? If so, then* <u>*both*</u> *A and B are guilty of cognitive shortcoming in the case presented. For* <u>*both*</u> *are unresponsive to considerations which, if accorded proper weight, would oblige them to back away from their favoured theories.*

Again, it would certainly be welcome if the awkward case could be disposed of so easily. Unfortunately, unless somehow restricted, the suggestion would merely have the effect of emasculating the Cognitive Command constraint altogether. Its implicit principle is that the holding of any opinion which can be matched by a conflicting but no worse opinion should be regarded, just on that account, as a relevant kind of cognitive shortcoming—either ignorance, if the competition is not known about, or a kind of hubris, I suppose, if it is. If this is allowed, then the kind of putatively irreproachable disagreements whose possibility was to mark the contrast between merely minimally truth-apt discourses and those exerting Cognitive Command will always involve cognitive shortcoming after all, and Cognitive Command will impose no additional hurdle.

Is there, however, some restriction of that principle which would enable us to square the situation of A and B with the Cognitive Command of their competing opinions? Sometimes, no doubt, a stand-off is *per se* a reason to withdraw. There is, for example, reason to suspend judgement between conflicting but equally well-corroborated explanations of the traces at the scene of a crime. But that is so because it is then reasonable to suppose that, within the limitations of the existing evidence, there is no getting at the *real facts of the matter*. And the transposition of that thought to the case of the A/B dispute will merely introduce a radically non-epistemic conception of truth for their competing views: a conception of truth which we had already set aside in developing and locating the problem. A different kind of example is illustrated by the discomfort we find in the objectified form of comic opinion—"x is funny"—after it has become clear that there is insufficient community of comic sensibility within the circle one wishes to engage to give any point to such a claim, in contrast to something more autobiographical. It is open to examination, of course, whether that discomfort properly attaches to the opinion rather than to its public expression. But if it does, persisting in such an opinion in the teeth of a stand-off had still better not count as a "cognitive shortcoming"—not anyway in the sense germane to Cognitive Command—if we want the constraint to help us mark a contrast between comedy and discourses of intuitively more objective subject matter.

In any case, epistemological "ought" implies epistemological "can": a stand-off can provide a reason to withdraw only in cases where withdrawal is a real option. It ought not too readily to be assumed that that will generally be so. Sometimes there may be no practical option of withdrawal without exit from the whole institution of judgement of the relevant kind. Recognition, for instance, that a particular moral conviction has no disputational supremacy—that someone who holds a conflicting view may be able to defend it no less well, at least from the point of view of a neutral—must not in general be sufficient cause to abandon one's view, or one may be debarred altogether from taking a moral stand on the matter concerned. It is, indeed, a constitutive feature of a conviction's being *moral* that it is not a reason for tolerating conflicting views that they are, from a neutral standpoint, equally well maintained.

It is arguable that there is, similarly, no practical option of withdrawal for the theorists, A and B, in the scenario depicted. Clearly if either of their theories ceases to be credible in those circumstances, then both do; so if there is an obligation to withdraw, it is, in effect, an obligation to "trash" all they have by way of explanatory empirical theory over the region of the dispute. That may simply not be a practical course. It might be suggested that A and B could still find a practical solution to their problem by withdrawing *belief* in their respective theories while retaining them as mere predictive *instruments*. But that is a rum idea under governing assumptions whereby, unlike those under which an instrumentalist view of scientific theories once flourished, there is no longer any theory-neutral field of observations whose successful prediction is the measure of instrumental success. Whatever form of withdrawal from their theories is supposedly mandated by the stand-off, it goes for A's and B's respective observations as well, and so for the entire corpus of their commitments within the disputed region. And the obvious thought in that case is that the supposedly mandated withdrawal, if it is to be consistent with *some* form of retention, if only for practical purposes, of A's and B's respective theoretical and observational views, can come to little other than a retreat from an intuitive *realism* about those views. Yet the whole point of the objector's proposal was to *save* an intuitive realism about those views, to the extent implicated in their exhibition of Cognitive Command. The proposal thus emerges as dialectically unstable.

These reflections are doubtless not decisive. But it is hard to see how to take the proposal further.

*3. The A/B problem would have been exploded by the objection that readers were "bursting" to make if it had not been for the (claimed) possibility of "dovetailing": the possibility that the observational support for one of the theorist's hypotheses, $H_N$, may be provided by observation statements, $O_I \ldots O_J$, which have already featured at "earlier" stages in his personal system in support of other hypotheses. But if dovetailing occurred, then, granted that an observation's confirming a hypothesis is the converse of its being best explained by it, wouldn't there have to be explanatory slack in the total theory in whose defence the dovetailing point is made? If we already have in other hypotheses, $H_I \ldots H_J$, the best explanation of the observations which provide dovetail support for $H_N$, then $H_N$ is de trop; if not, then $H_I \ldots H_J$ will be de trop once $H_N$ is hit on, and* *the system may no longer have the resources to explain away the prima facie recalcitrant experiences ratified by the opposing system. Either way, ordinary methodological criteria would yet resolve the dispute, and the proponent of the inferior theory could be convicted of an appropriate shortcoming.*

Well, it is not, I think, at all clear that the assumption of this objection—that confirmation is simply the converse of best explanation—is quite right. But the objection fails in any case to reckon with the possibility that $H_N$ is of *greater explanatory depth* than $H_I \ldots H_J$ and plays a theoretically unifying role, with $H_I \ldots H_J$ as integral consequences within the theory it helps to unify.

# 5. Realism and the Best Explanation of Belief

## I. Résumé

A truth predicate, I have argued, is one which satisfies a small set of basic principles—most centrally, certain platitudes linking truth with assertion and negation. The characteristics possessed by any satisfier of these principles are the only characteristics *essential* to truth. Moreover they are insufficient to motivate an intuitive realism about a discourse in which such a predicate applies. But a particular satisfier may, of course, have other characteristics as well. A basic anti-realism—minimalism—about a discourse contends that nothing further is true of the local truth predicate which can serve somehow to fill out and substantiate an intuitively realist view of its subject matter. Because of its unassuming character, this minimalism, I suggested, should always be viewed as the "default" stance, from which we have to be shown that we ought to move. This deprives it of the air of dangerous iconoclasm which has always been one of anti-realism's principal attractions (for those who like that sort of thing). But it also, of course, greatly increases its dialectical strength. It is realism which must try to make good its case, by showing that minimalism about the relevant discourse is wrong—showing that the minimal platitudes leave out features of the local truth predicate which substantially justify the rhetoric of independence, autonomy and full-fledged cognitive interaction by which realism pretheoretically defines itself.

174

Cognitive Command: the characteristic possessed by a discourse when differences of opinion formulated within it have to be attributable to something worth describing as cognitive short-coming—unless excusable by vagueness—is exactly such a feature. It is a truism that divergences in the output of systems whose function it is to produce *representations* of states of affairs, of whatever sort, have to be attributable either to divergences in input or to less than perfect function. Making out that a discourse exerts Cognitive Command is of interest, I suggested, because it is thereby shown that the relation of which the Correspondence Platitude speaks is importantly analogous to the concept of representation that features in that truism. That a discourse should exert Cognitive Command is a precondition of the propriety of thinking of *our* function, in the appropriately constrained acceptance of statements which it gives us the resources to make, as representational in that full-blooded sense—a sense going beyond anything implied merely by the permissibility of paraphrasing the characterisation of such statements as "true" in the way the Correspondence Platitude provides. In such a discourse, the idea of *correspondence,* as it features in "corresponds to the facts", has an additional characteristic, not demanded by the general permissibility of glossing any truth predicate as "corresponds to the facts"; and a characteristic, crucially, which is consonant with the basic realist idea that, in our practice of the discourse, we interact in a cognitive-representational manner with matters that are independent of us.

May we take it, now, that *any* significant move in the direction of realism about a discourse must involve regarding it as representational in a more full-blooded sense than anything involved in the Correspondence Platitude? And may we take it that any such more full-blooded sense must sustain the truism about divergence and representational function? Finally, may we take it that Cognitive Command is indeed, as I introduced it, merely the specialisation of that truism to the case where the "output" of the "system" is the formation of a belief? If "yes" on all three counts, then, as I conjectured, Cognitive Command is a necessary condition for the defensibility of *any* worthwhile form of realism. But that hard issue must wait for a definitive resolution until we have a fully satisfactory formulation of the Cognitive Command constraint. In this chapter

I want to consider a rather different set of considerations which, like Cognitive Command, also bear on the project of "beefing up" the Correspondence Platitude, as it were, but whose focus, rather than on the relation adverted to in the Platitude, is on its second term: "the facts".

## II. The Best Explanation Test

The considerations I have in mind are very familiar in contemporary moral philosophy. A well-known expression of them is provided in the first chapter of Gilbert Harman's book on morals.[1] Here, though, is not Harman but David Wiggins expanding on one of Harman's ideas:

> The scientist sees a vapour trail in a Wilson cloud chamber, and he says "there goes a proton". The scientist counts as observing a proton because the best explanation of his visual state is that there is a vapour trail, and the best theoretical explanation of the vapour trail itself is a proton.[2]

We can take the matter a stage further, and say that the scientist forms the belief "There goes a proton" because of his visual condition; that he is in that visual condition because there is a vapour trail observable in the Wilson cloud chamber in front of him; and that there is that vapour trail because of the passage of the proton. Thus, the event—the passage of the proton—may be claimed itself to feature in the best explanation of the scientist's true belief about it. This, in Harman's view, is in contrast with the situation in the moral case. There, the best explanation of a subject's moral judgement of an act—Harman's example is that of a group of hooligans who set fire to a cat—can

---

1. Gilbert Harman, *The Nature of Morality* (New York: Oxford University Press, 1977). Chapter 1 is reprinted as "Ethics and Observation", in G. Sayre-McCord, ed., *Essays on Moral Realism* (Ithaca, N.Y.: Cornell University Press, 1988), pp. 119–124.

2. David Wiggins, *Needs, Values, Truth* (Oxford: Basil Blackwell, 1987), p. 156.

> dispense altogether with the claim that the act was wrong . . .
> for . . . [his] reaction . . . is to be explained by [the subject's]
> "psychological set". The [act] had some non-evaluative property
> F, say, and F is a property that observers like you and me have
> been schooled to abhor. So the putative moral qualities of the
> [act] are simply irrelevant to why [he views the act as he does].[3]

Consider the belief that the act in question was one of hateful and
contemptible barbarity. We may accept that this belief is harmlessly and correctly described as "true". But even so, the best explanation of someone's holding it will not, in Harman's view, make
any specific mention of the putative truth-conferring state of
affairs—the actual hateful and contemptible barbarity of the act.
Rather, it can proceed entirely in terms of *non-evaluative* characteristics of the situation to which the subject is presumed sensitive
and certain background features of his psychology, specifically
those features of his psychology that are the product of his moral
schooling.

Wiggins describes Harman's thought, that there is here a test
for the applicability of truth within a discourse which moral discourse presumptively fails, as posing a "challenging line of objection" to moral realism. Fashioned so as to square with the outlook
on these matters which we have been developing, Harman's test
will be a test, if it can be well motivated, for a discourse's being
more than minimally truth-apt—for its truth predicate having a
feature which merits a move away from the basic anti-realist
stance. A simple-minded shot at the constraint which Harman
wants to impose would be this:

> *Best Explanation:* A discourse is more than minimally truth-apt
> only if mention must be made of the states of affairs which
> they concern in any best explanation of those of our beliefs
> expressed within it which are true.

So formulated, the test expresses a *necessary* condition for the justifiability of a more than minimalist stance. But Wiggins, who
believes that morality passes the test (when it is properly conceived), organises his discussion in a way which suggests he regards

3. *Ibid.,* pp. 156–157.

meeting the condition as *sufficient* for a commonsensical form of realism. I shall come to Wiggins' interpretation of the test shortly, but first we will do well to consider why it should be thought to have any intuitive pull at all, whether as a necessary or as a sufficient condition.

One can envisage a philosopher who, inclined to various causalist ideas about meaning and reference, maintained that only if a class of beliefs passed the Best Explanation test could it be appropriate to regard them as having any genuinely truth-evaluable content. Similarly, certain forms of causal theory of knowledge might have the effect that the propriety of regarding any of the statements of a discourse as known would turn on the Best Explanation test. But from the standpoint defended in the present study, the issue of truth aptitude is carried by the syntax and internal discipline of the discourse; and a correspondingly minimalist conception of knowledge will be borne in train with the idea that some such truth-apt contents may, by the standards of the discourse, be justifiably claimed as true. What then, from such a standpoint, can be at stake in Harman's test? How, if it does, does it gesture at a characteristic which can be regarded as relevant to realism *after* we have agreed that a particular discourse deals in minimally truth-apt contents which, moreover, in appropriate circumstances, it is perfectly proper to view as known?

It is illuminating here to make a comparison with a claim of Michael Dummett's about abstract objects—more specifically, about *pure* abstract objects (what Frege would have called "logical objects"). Dummett remarks, in the context of a discussion of Frege's platonism, that

> pure abstract objects are no more than reflections of certain linguistic expressions, expressions which behave, by simple formal criteria, in a manner analogous to proper names of objects, but whose sense cannot be represented as consisting in our capacity to identify objects as their bearers.[4]

4. M. Dummett, *Frege: Philosophy of Language* (London: Duckworth, 1973), ch. 14, "Abstract Objects", p. 505.

Taken in isolation, this passage could excusably be read as an expression of nominalism—of the view that there are no abstract objects and that singular terms purportedly standing for them actually have no such reference. But, as readers of Dummett's text will be aware, that is not the right interpretation of the passage in its context. Dummett, crucially, is *not* denying that singular terms purporting to refer to abstract objects do have reference. Nor, presumably, in conceding them a reference, does he mean or ought he to mean to be conceding merely a semantic role. (There are, for instance, empty numerical singular terms—say, "the largest prime"—whose mere significance ensures that they have a semantic role.) Rather, the way to take the passage, I suggest, is, in company with much of the surrounding discussion in that chapter, to see it as trying to get at a sense in which the notion of singular reference, as applied to pure abstract singular terms, is somehow thin and minimal, and consequently insufficient to warrant the kind of realism about mathematical objects typically associated with platonistic philosophies of mathematics, and certainly espoused by Frege.

In that discussion, I want to suggest, Dummett is best seen as taking a view which involves rejecting the idea that the whole issue about the reality of abstract objects is just the issue whether or not platonism or nominalism is the better line, so that once a view has been taken on that (Are there or are there not abstract objects?), no further questions remain to be confronted. This corresponds nicely to the more general view we have been taking about the issues to do with realism—that the matter of moral realism, for instance, is not effectively exhausted by the question whether or not to grant that moral discourse is truth-apt (compare: whether abstract singular terms really are in the market for singular reference), or if so, whether to grant that much of moral discourse is true (compare: whether many abstract singular terms do indeed refer). The whole thrust of our discussion has been that someone who takes a positive view on those issues about moral discourse still has further, realism-relevant philosophical questions to confront.

To pursue the comparison a little: Dummett claims, in the quoted passage, that a crucial disanalogy between pure abstract objects and other, especially concrete objects is opened up by the consideration that grasping the senses of pure abstract singular terms cannot be taken as consisting in a capacity to *identify* objects as their referents. That claim is liable to provoke a protest: that it is simply unclear what "identifying" an object should be taken to mean if recognising the truth of an identity statement featuring a term standing for it does not count as accomplishing it, at least when one of the related terms exemplifies a canonical mode of reference to such objects—and moreover that it is not, or better not be, in dispute that we have the ability comprehendingly to manage identity statements which feature abstract singular terms. I myself would not have expressed in the way Dummett chose what I take the crucial point to be. Its basis is that there is no *linguistically unmediated* cognitive contact with abstract objects: abstract objects can, in general, impinge upon us only as the referents of understood abstract singular terms. There is no question of such an object influencing the thought of someone who does not know what it is, or producing other kinds of effect on our consciousness, or on our bodies, or on non-human objects of any kind. By contrast with the ordinary, "robust" objects with which Dummett is making a disadvantageous comparison, abstract objects discharge a decidedly limited worldly role. The Fregean Platonist—in effect, a minimalist about singular reference—quite rightly finds no reason in such reflections to doubt the *reality* of reference to abstract objects. But after that is agreed, considerations still remain which force us to think of concrete objects as playing a role in the world quite independent of our thought and talk about them—considerations which underlie, I think, Dummett's invocation of the idea of a "realistic conception of reference" for concrete singular terms, and which simply have no counterpart for abstract objects. If "realistic" in Dummett's phrase is understood to contrast with "anti-realistic" or "nominalistic", then the phrase is unhappy. But I am suggesting that a much better contrast would be with "minimalistic", and that Dummett's contention, at the level of objects and singular reference, is entirely of a piece with the ideas which I have been presenting, at the level of statements and truth aptitude, about realism and truth.

In order to bring the comparison out more sharply, let us transpose the quoted passage as follows:

> The states of affairs which (merely) minimally true sentences represent are no more than reflections of those sentences, sentences which behave, by simple formal criteria, in a manner analogous to sentences which are apt to depict real states of affairs, but whose senses cannot be represented as consisting in our capacity to identify states of affairs necessary and sufficient for their truth.

Once again, the concluding part of the thought might naturally be taken as an expression of (one kind of) *irrealism* (compare: nominalism)—the suggestion that understanding such a sentence does not really consist in grasping truth conditions for it but should be characterised in some other way. But, again, that is not the only possible meaning. The thought can be that understanding such a sentence should not be seen as consisting in a capacity appropriately to *respond to* the relevant type of truth-conferring states of affairs. For, in parallel to the situation with abstract objects, there seems to be no question of such a state of affairs— say, something's being funny—directly influencing the thought of  someone who lacks the conceptual wherewithal to characterise it, or directly producing any other kind of effect on our consciousness, or on our bodies or on non-human objects of any kind. These claims may be contested, or may need qualifying in the case of the particular example.[5] But the general parallel is striking. Like pure abstract objects, the states of affairs purportedly depicted by merely minimally true sentences do not seem to *do* anything except answer to the demands of our minimally true thoughts. The irresistible metaphor is that pure abstract objects, conceived as by Fregean platonism, and the states of affairs to which, in accordance with the Correspondence Platitude, merely minimally true sentences correspond, are no more than *shadows* cast by the syntax

5. My own experience makes it irresistible to view some very young (three- to four-month-old) babies as manifesting *some* sort of sense of humour. How rich a conceptual repertoire do we implicitly ascribe to them by so doing?

of our discourse. And the aptness of the metaphor is merely enhanced by the reflection that shadows are, after their own fashion, real.

The intuitive appeal of the Harman test should now be clear. Once it is satisfied, once citation of truth-conferring states of affairs has to feature in any best explanation of the true beliefs which we register in a discourse, such deflating metaphors—"shadows cast by syntax" and so on—cease to be appropriate. When such a metaphor is appropriate, it is because what it is legitimate to think and say about the facts to which a class of merely minimally true statements corresponds is entirely driven by the bare propriety of thinking of such statements as apt for truth and falsity at all, and by truistic connections, like that articulated in the Correspondence Platitude, between claims about truth and claims about corresponding facts or states of affairs. And the legitimate uses of singular terms purportedly standing for such states of affairs will be restricted accordingly. But when the Best Explanation constraint is satisfied, matters are turned about. Now we are forced to think of such states of affairs as lying at the *source* of acceptable practice within the discourse and as having the autonomy which that role demands. Rather than constituting a class of items to which we are committed purely and simply by the assertoric cast of our thought in the area, so to speak, they are needed fully to explain the direction taken by that thought. And they are thereby fitted for comparison with the ordinary, robust, concrete objects for whose names Dummett claims our entitlement to a "realistic" conception of reference. Such robust objects are not, like pure abstract objects, items to which we are committed purely by the singular-referential cast of our thought in some area. Rather, a best explanation of the course assumed by that part of our thought will make ineliminable mention of them. In brief: Harman's test should be seen as an attempt to get at a condition whose satisfaction by a discourse will forestall, for its sentences and the facts which determine their truth values, any analogue of Dummett's complaint about purely abstract singular terms and the ghostly items for which they stand.

## III. Wiggins' Response

If the foregoing diagnostic remarks are right, the Best Explanation constraint is driven by an attempt to capture an idea that is unquestionably of importance in the debates about realism. It is another question, of course, whether the offered formulation really does capture the intended idea. Certainly, that formulation is, I think, variously unsatisfactory. But before we look at it again, I want to consider a very different account of the constraint which takes centre stage in David Wiggins' recent discussions of moral objectivity, both in *Needs, Values and Truth* and, more recently, in his "Moral Cognitivism, Moral Relativism and Motivating Moral Beliefs".[6]

I have suggested that the relevance, in the context of moral realism, of issues to do with convergence is best interpreted under the heading of Cognitive Command. Wiggins, however, views their relevance differently. He moots a constraint to the effect that

> If X is true, then X will under favourable circumstances command convergence, and the best explanation of the existence of this convergence will require the actual truth of X,[7]

elaborating the second part of that as follows:

> We have the truth-relevant sort of convergence where *the statement of the best explanation of the agreement in the belief* [that item t is F] *needs a premise to the effect that item t is indeed F, and the explanation would be simply invalidated by its absence.* (Wiggins' own emphasis)

For Wiggins, then, the explanandum to which the Best Explanation constraint is to be applied will not be the fact of practitioners of the discourse holding certain beliefs, as vaguely suggested by the first formulation of the constraint offered above. Rather, the

6. David Wiggins, "Moral Cognitivism, Moral Relativism and Motivating Moral Beliefs", *Proceedings of the Aristotelian Society* 91 (1990–91), pp. 61–86.
7. *Needs, Values, Truth*, p. 147.

explanandum will be the fact of convergence in such beliefs when it occurs.

Clearly, some such adjustment is called for, since, however "robust" a subject matter, one would not expect it to feature in the best explanation of true but *unwarranted* beliefs about it (on which one might expect, qua unwarranted, there would be no convergence). Nevertheless I think that Wiggins, by invoking convergence to accomplish the refinement, which might easily be secured in other ways,[8] effectively misses the chance to note the rather different set of issues to do with representation and Cognitive Command which questions about convergence raise.

However that may be, the most interesting contention in Wiggins' discussion is that, insofar as there is a legitimate constraint in the vicinity for which Harman was fumbling, it is one with which, when properly conceived, both ethics and mathematics, to take two widely disputed examples, may be seen to comply in exemplary fashion. The impression to the contrary, in Wiggins' view, derives from a misplaced emphasis on causality: the belief that "People think that P because P" can be an acceptable claim only where we may conceive of the fact, or state of affairs that P as situated in the causal swim, as it were, and thus as a potentially direct causal source of people's beliefs about it. The right question to ask, in Wiggins' view, is rather whether moral, or mathematical beliefs admit of what he calls *vindicatory explanation*—explanation of a subject's holding them which conforms to the following general schema:

> For this, that and the other reason (here the explainer specifies these), there is really nothing else to think but that P; so it is a

8. Granted, for instance, that there will not, in all probability, be any significant degree of convergence in unwarranted beliefs, an explanation of convergence, where it occurs, will presumably be available in any case in terms of the *warrantedness* of the belief in question. So if the actual truth of that belief is to play the envisaged explanatory role, it looks as though it had better be possible to invoke it at one remove, in the explanation of the availability of warrant for the belief—and a formulation in terms of that kind of explanation, with convergence no longer featuring as the explanandum, would then presumably accomplish the needed refinement.

fact that P; so given the circumstances and given the subject's cognitive capacities and opportunities and given his access to what leaves nothing else to think but that P, no wonder he believes that P.[9]

Consider, for instance, the belief of Wiggins' nine-year-old son and his classmates that $7 + 5 = 12$.

> The best explanation of why they all believe this is not that they have learnt and taken on trust the one truth "$7 + 5 = 12$" but (I hope and believe this):
> (i) As can be shown by the use of the calculating rules (and could in the end be rigorously demonstrated) it is a fact that $7 + 5 = 12$. There is nothing else to think but that $7 + 5 = 12$.
> (ii) The best explanation of my son and his classmates' shared belief is that they are going by the calculating rule that shows that there is nothing else to think but that $7 + 5 = 12$. If there is nothing else to think, then no wonder that, if their beliefs are answerable to the calculating rules, they agree in the belief that $7 + 5 = 12$.

The general form, then, of a vindicatory explanation of a subject's believing that P would appear to involve two claims. First, it will be contended that procedures of assessment appropriate to the discourse in which P is expressed leave, when properly applied, no option but the verdict that P; second, it will be claimed that the relevant subject's belief that P is formed and guided by the application of these procedures.

Wiggins' own conception of the realist project, in the moral case, is to find, however many awkward cases may be salient, at least some examples which show up favourably in the light of this constraint: examples—he quotes the claim that slavery is unjust and insupportable—which do indeed command a measure of convergence in belief, and such that the best explanation of that convergence is vindicatory in the sense just rehearsed. I think such a conception of the way a Best Explanation constraint should work

9. "Moral Cognitivism, Moral Relativism and Motivating Moral Beliefs", p. 66.

is arguably correct. In contrast, that is to say, with Cognitive Command, which is purportedly an a priori constraint on *any* dispute expressed within a seriously representational discourse, satisfaction of the Best Explanation constraint need not, in order to fulfil its intended interest and purpose, demand more than that opinions expressible within the discourse *sometimes* meet the condition imposed. For in any cases where they do, there at least it will be appropriate to think of the truth-conferring states of affairs as possessing the kind of autonomy which the constraint is supposed to test for. And once the point is in place for the good cases, it is not clear what obstacle there could be to so conceiving of such states of affairs as a *class,* even in cases where no tendency to convergence in opinion about them is actually apparent.

What is open to doubt, however, is whether Wiggins' idea of ineliminable citation in vindicatory explanations can really capture what the Best Explanation constraint is after. Misgivings arise as soon as we reflect that, although the words "So it is a fact that P" figure as an apparent bridge in Wiggins' original schematic account, nothing important seems to be lost if we omit them; thus,

> for this, that and the other reason (here the explainer specifies these) there is really nothing else to think but that P; so, given the circumstances and given the subject's cognitive capacities and opportunities and given his access to what leaves nothing else to think but that P, no wonder he believes that P.

Later in the paper[10] Wiggins writes,

> Vindicatory explanations are causal explanations but the causality that they invoke is not one that holds between minds and values or between minds and integers. That would be a gross misunderstanding of what is got across by the explanatory schema exemplified by: "There is nothing else to think but that $7 + 5 = 12$. So no wonder they think that $7 + 5 = 12$."

Vindicatory explanations thus do proceed, in Wiggins' view, by citing the causes of subjects' holding certain beliefs; but the causes

10. *Ibid.,* p. 80.

which they cite are not, and in many relevant cases could not simply consist in the truth-conferring states of affairs. Rather, presumably, what causes the children's belief that $7 + 5 = 12$ is what happens when they appropriately attentively apply the relevant arithmetical rules. What is cited in the vindicatory explanation is not the fact that $7 + 5 = 12$, but the fact that, in the light of proper application of relevant rules, there is nothing else to think but that $7 + 5 = 12$; which is to say that a duly careful and attentive application of the rules of assessment appropriate to the discipline leads ineluctably to the conclusion that one of its sentences commands assent. The truth-conferring state of affairs gets a mention only via the *embedded* occurrence of a clause which describes it within the "there is nothing else to think but that . . ." part of the explanation. And that part of the explanation, as Wiggins schematises and illustrates it, contains, so far as I can see, nothing essential to distinguish it from the claim that a proper observation of the standards of assertibility to which the discourse is subject mandates an acceptance of P.

This suggests that satisfaction of the Wiggins constraint actually takes us no further than minimal anti-realism; for the minimal truth aptitude of a discourse can be expected to involve an acknowledged core of standards which mandate certain verdicts and hence ensure that at least some convergences of opinion within it will admit of vindicatory explanation. The suggestion assumes, to be sure, that acceptability within a genuinely assertoric discourse cannot invariably be merely a *permissive* notion. That is: it must not be that whenever a particular statement is acceptable in the light of the standards of warrant which inform the discourse, someone can still refuse to accept it without contravention of those standards. But I am taking it that, whether on the grounds canvassed in the discussion note to Chapter 3 or on others, a region of discourse whose standards of warrant never actually *required* acceptance of a particular statement, no matter what the prevailing circumstances, could not coherently be conceived as dealing in determinate *assertoric* contents at all. Even if that assumption is wrong, I do not think that any of the discourses on which we are likely to want to focus attention in the course of realist/anti-realist debate is purely permissive in that sense. It is just not true, for instance, that absolutely anything can permissibly be found funny,[11] or regarded as revolting.

Wiggins' conception of the problematic of the situation, remember, requires only *some* favourable cases in order for a discourse as a whole to meet the standard of objectivity which the Best Explanation idea intends. Let us call a *demonstration* of a statement, relative to a discourse, any presentation of circumstances and considerations  such that, by the standards of proper assertibility informing the discourse in question, acceptance of the statement is then demanded if the standards are to be observed. For instance, the statement "The disaster at Chernobyl was not funny" might lend itself to such a demonstration. (But moral considerations are not the only kind of overriders in the case of comedy. My having two ears is, I take it, in present circumstances, simply not funny either.)[12] Clearly, no matter what discourse we are concerned with, some of its statements will, if it is not purely permissive, admit of demonstration in this sense. And a convergence about the status of such statements, if generated by response to the demonstration, will consequently allow of vindicatory explanation in Wiggins' sense. An explanation will be possible, that is to say, along the now familiar lines

(i) For this, that and any other reason (here the explainer runs a demonstration) it is mandatory to accept P—"there is really nothing else to think but that P".

(ii) Since the parties concerned are going by the relevant considerations, no wonder that they agree in the belief that P.

Perhaps the foregoing reflections overlook some aspect of the character which Wiggins wants or ought to want vindicatory explanations to have. But if not, we should conclude that Wiggins, in his attempt to escape from crudely causalist interpretations of the Best Explanation constraint, has merely supplanted them with a formulation which carries no realist teeth. We conclude

11. One conception of the finer detail of warrant for statements about comedy is outlined in the discussion note to Chapter 3.

12. Of course, that remark got a laugh in the course of the actual lecture! A safer example could have concerned the lectern in front of me.

this on the grounds, first, that minimal truth aptitude—subject to the qualification that the discourse in question not be purely permissive—ensures satisfaction of the Wiggins constraint; but, second, that minimal truth aptitude does not ensure that the reference to "the facts" in the Correspondence Platitude can carry the additional substance which the play with best explanation is, I suggested, most effectively interpreted as intended to secure.

## IV. Dropping Best Explanation

Let's reconsider the original formulation:

> A discourse is more than minimally truth-apt only if (or if? or iff?) mention must be made of the states of affairs which they concern in any best explanation of those of our beliefs expressed within it which are true.

We have not so far considered any of the objections which this thesis is likely to provoke. Perhaps the most immediate is that for anyone who believes in the unifiability of science, and believes moreover that science will ultimately be unified under physics, any *best* explanation will ultimately be a physical one. The only states of affairs mentioned in best explanations will thus be the states of affairs that correspond to the physical laws which those explanations involve, and the states of affairs depicted by the statements of initial conditions on which the explanatory use of those laws goes to work (which, of course, will have to be physical states of affairs, since otherwise physical law will not be applicable to them). Hence, on this view of the matter, only discourses dealing in physical states of affairs will pass the Best Explanation test. If the test is conceived as a necessary condition for a departure from minimalism, it thus amounts to no more than a thinly veiled insistence that only talk of the physical can deserve a realist account. By contrast, if the proposal is of the corresponding sufficient condition, what is offered is merely a test which will be contentious in the philosophy of science—disputed by anti-realists about theoretical physics—and which can have no immediate bearing on any discourse, such as morals, mathematics, or ordinary intentional psychology, of which we lack a physicalistic construal.

That's one line of difficulty for the Best Explanation test. But a different line argues to the contrary, and paradoxically, that theoretical science will *fail* the test. For consider any well-established but, of course, defeasible physical theory. Then ought not the best explanation of why it is held to be true to be *the same* whether it is actually subsequently defeated or survives indefinitely? After all, the causal antecedents of our accepting it are *already in place,* as it were, whatever the fate of the theory subsequently proves to be. Why should the best explanation of our holding a theory have to go beyond the citation of those causes and the invocation of whatever laws explain their belief-generating powers? And why should laws of the latter kind overlap at all with the ones putatively articulated in the theory which is the object of consideration? Yet in that case there is in general no reason whatever why the best explanation of our holding a scientific theory to be true should advert to any of the states of affairs that actually, let us suppose, confer truth upon it. In general, the best explanation of a theorist's holding particular scientific theoretical beliefs should confine consideration to his scientific inheritance, his observations, certain psychological laws, and features of his background psychology. Hence, in any case where the beliefs in question are path-breaking—not part of the scientific inheritance—there is no reason whatever why their subject matter should be involved in the explanation of their coming to be held (unless, perhaps, it is itself a psychological theory that is being constructed).

It was clearly not the intention of Harman, and of others who have followed him in the hunch that there is an important crux in this area, that the Best Explanation constraint should make trouble in this way for realism about theoretical natural science. The difficulty, of course, is that, as has rapidly emerged, it is actually very unclear what should count as a *best* explanation for the purpose of the intended constraint. Consider again the vapour trail in the Wilson cloud chamber. The scientist would have formed the belief "There goes a proton" even had the perceived vapour trail been caused by the passage of a particle (say, an x-on) so far unrecognised in physical science. One intuition about the idea of best explanation says that the best explanation of his belief should be invariant under this possibility—and indeed throughout any observationally similar circumstances in which he still forms a belief for what he will conceive as the same reasons. According to this intuition, the best explanation of his belief should consequently not make reference to protons, even when the passage of a proton figures among its actual causes. However an alternative intuition says that the best explanation of his belief should make reference to its *actual ultimate causes.* Accordingly, since, in the example as intended, the cause of the vapour trail, in any case where the belief formed is true, will be the actual passage of a proton, the best explanation of the belief should refer to the same. But this invites the rejoinder: why stop there? If explanations are generally made "better" by pushing back to ever ulterior events, processes and laws, why should not an even better explanation of the scientist's belief be given in which all mention of the proton once again disappears, and the cited initial conditions concern a yet more fundamental level of micro-material activity? In short: if its best explanation need concern only the immediate causes of the scientist's belief, why should the proton come into it? But if explanations are best only when ultimate, isn't it to be envisaged that the best explanation will, as it were, go past the proton? Either way, why so sure that mention of it must occur in the best explanation of the scientist's belief?

## V. Wide Cosmological Role

No doubt we could now respond by attempting to fashion construals of "best explanation" which would avoid this dilemma. But I would suggest that that would be to risk distraction, and that the play made with the idea of *best* explanation is now obscuring the intuitive point which the Harman constraint is, or ought to be, after. The fact, it seems to me, is that to ask in what terms the best explanation of subjects' holding a given belief should proceed is to invoke the idea of explanation in the wrong way. Rather than ask: what is the best explanation of subjects' holding the relevant beliefs?—does it need to advert to the states of affairs conferring truth on them?—we should be asking: *what in general can the citation of such states of affairs help to explain?*

In order to get this shift in focus, recall once more the parallel with the referents of pure abstract singular terms. Such an object can, I remarked, impinge upon us *only as* the referent of such a term. There is no question of it influencing the thought of someone who doesn't know what it is, or producing other kinds of effects on our consciousness, or on our bodies, or on non-human forms of life, or on inanimate matter. And analogues of each of these negative characteristics will belong to the referents of expressions of the form "the fact/state of affairs that P" so long as the legitimate uses of such expressions are restricted to occurrence within platitudinous paraphrases of the truth predicate, or within contexts—such as "he provided a demonstration of . . .", or "he is unaware of . . ."—where completion by the sentence "P" is inappropriate merely on grammatical grounds and a corresponding noun phrase is wanted instead. Such facts, or states of affairs, will display an inertia exactly corresponding to that of pure abstract objects: there will be no mode of cognitive or sensible interaction with such a state of affairs possible for a subject who lacks the concepts deployed in a statement of it; no wholly non-cognitive modes of interaction with such states of affairs will be possible at all; and they will have no causal powers. What follows is that it will not be possible to enlist such states of affairs in the direct empirical explanation either of anything non-anthropological or of anything to do with us which is independent of our exercise of the concepts under which we bring them.

The inertia of abstract objects is not, as it were, a fact of metaphysical nature which our inability to find use for certain kinds of context embedding their names merely reflects. To suppose otherwise is to get matters back to front. Abstract objects *owe* their inertia to the fact that the meanings of singular terms standing for them are fixed in such a way that no use is provided for the kinds of context whose truth would demand that the objects to which they involve reference are not inert in that kind of way. And it is the same, I am suggesting, with any genre of states of affairs whose whole being, as it were, is to serve as the reference of such uses of states-of-affairs-denoting singular terms *(state denoters)* as go no further than what is licensed by the currency of a minimal truth predicate. What the Best Explanation test is after—what, I suggested, makes something of the sort seem attractive—is the thought that in the case of some but not all discourses, a *much wider* range of uses of such terms is intelligible and appropriate, and a consequently more robust understanding of the Correspondence Platitude is imposed. The formulation we are after, then, has to do no more than directly ensure that this is so.

In his discussion of this matter in *The Nature of Morality,* Harman sometimes wrote as if moral facts may not properly be cited in the explanation of *anything* non-moral. He was therefore quite correctly taken to task by writers such as Nicholas Sturgeon,[13] who pointed out that our ordinary thought is quite comfortable with the idea that, for instance, a rebellion might be in part explained by the injustice of the prevailing social order, that a spectator's belief that certain children are doing something wrong might be explained in part by his seeing them doing something wrong, or that our belief that Hitler was morally depraved is based on things which he did precisely *because* he was morally depraved, so that his very depravity is part of the explanation of our believing that he was. Unquestionably, the citation of moral facts does play a part in a variety of ordinary explanatory contexts, including some in which the explananda are subjects' holding particular moral beliefs.

But what does this show? What we ought to ask, is: if we are satisfied that a discourse is minimally truth-apt, what, if any, types of explanatory context can *thereby* be expected to be significant and legitimate which feature uses of its distinctive vocabulary within the explanans or, more specifically, involve citation of the types of states of affairs to which the Correspondence Platitude entitles us

13. See Nicholas L. Sturgeon, "Moral Explanations", in D. Copp and D. Zimmerman, eds., *Morality, Reason and Truth* (Totowa, N.J.: Rowman and Allenheld, 1985), pp. 49–78. Sturgeon's debate with Harman is continued in a further exchange in N. Gillespie, ed., *Moral Realism: Proceedings of the 1985 Spindel Conference,* in *Southern Journal of Philosophy,* suppl. 24 (1986), pp. 57–78.

to regard its true statements as corresponding? The comparison with Fregean abstract objects might encourage us to have no expectations in this regard. But that would be too hasty. I already argued that Wiggins' species of vindicatory explanation will always be a possibility for such discourse. And there are other possibilities as well.

Wiggins' vindicatory explanations explain a group of subjects' convergence on a certain belief in terms of the fact (a) that, in the light of the relevant standards of warranted acceptability, a demonstration—in the rather general sense I introduced earlier—of that particular belief is available; and (b) that the subjects in question are going by those standards in forming their view. We ought now to note that a vindicatory explanation allows one kind of straightforward extension. Let F be a basic classificatory predicate—"funny", for instance, or "wicked"—distinctive of the discourse in question. And suppose that an item's being F admits, under appropriate circumstances, of demonstration in the sense we are concerned with. Now it may happen that a particular agent, or kind of object, is disposed to bring about or cause situations whose F-ness allows of demonstration in this way. And it may happen that, in such cases, we are inclined to transfer the epithet from the situations generated to their source and so to describe agents, for instance, as F or in cognate terms. In such a case we will have an explanatory chain which runs from (i) the source's being F to (ii) its doing or being disposed to do things whose F-ness can be demonstrated to (iii) our responding to those demonstrations by regarding such things as F to (iv) our regarding the source as F. Such an extension, then, of the kind of explanation envisaged by Wiggins can provide a perfectly acceptable natural explanation of subjects' believing that an agent is F in terms of the very fact that he is. Harman, therefore, should not have been in any doubt about that possibility. Rather, his point should have been that it is a possibility which is set up merely by a discourse's being minimally truth-apt, and by our willingness to transfer epithets to the dispositional source of acts or states of affairs which the discourse's basic predicates acceptably qualify. The Hitler example, for instance, has exactly this character. The proper conclusion from

such examples is accordingly not that moral facts are shown to be ⅄
on a par with natural ones as far as explanatory fruitfulness is
concerned, but that this sort of case is something for which we
should have been prepared just by recognising that moral discourse
is at least minimally truth-apt; and hence that if there are real
explanatory disanalogies between moral and natural facts, they will
emerge elsewhere.

A second harmless kind of case—where the propriety of explanations which mention the states of affairs dealt with by a contested
discourse can be comfortably acknowledged alongside the view that
the discourse is merely minimally truth-apt—is provided by the
injustice of the social order and the putatively consequential rebellion. At this point, it may even be possible to observe to the letter
Wittgenstein's injunction that philosophy should deal only in
assertions which no one will dispute! Here are some such. There is
a distinction between the injustice of a social order and the *sense of
injustice* which that order may foster in those who suffer under it,
or who observe it. There is also a distinction between the injustice
of a social order and those of its *non-moral features* which could
properly be cited in a demonstration of its injustice. Now, when
we speak, as in the rebellion example, as if the moral quality of a
situation were responsible for an agent's or group of agents'
behaviour—and thereby implicated in whatever further effects
their behaviour generates—we will not usually intend any claim,
I suggest, which involves an *exclusive focus* on that moral quality,
rather than on the associated judgemental or affective response, or
on the non-moral features to which a demonstration could appeal.
We will be content to acknowledge, in other words, that the
explanation might just as well proceed by adverting to agents'
*judgements* or *moral sense* of the situation (responses with which we
signal our agreement by using the preferred locution), or alterna-
ively, by adverting to those *non-moral features* of the situation to
which a vindication of their view could, we imply, quite properly
advert—features such as, in the case of slavery, the bitter, hopeless
hardship of the lives of the slaves, and their deprivation of all
opportunity for growth and fulfilment. Note, moreover, that the
latter kind of case can be extended to include in the range of

factors functional in the explanans further non-moral factors which, while not raw material for moral demonstrations, tend to go along with factors which are. A demonstration of injustice, for instance, might be able to restrict its attention to certain exploitative inequalities; it is a further consideration, not perhaps strictly required by such a demonstration, that those on the losing end of such inequalities tend—when the cake to be divided is of necessity small—to live lives of hardship. This sort of extension, bringing within the moral minimalist's compass such a generalisation as "Injustice tends to promote social instability", involves a kind of explanation which may always be possible where demonstration is possible, that is, where there is minimal truth aptitude.

I do not mean in the least to suggest by this that the type of explanatory claim illustrated by the rebellion example is misplaced. What I am saying is that if it is not misplaced, their equivalence for all practical purposes to explanations mentioning agents' reactions, or features apt to serve as a basis for a demonstration, of features tending to accompany features apt to serve as a basis for a demonstration, will ensure that corresponding explanatory claims can be expected to be in order in the case of all minimally truth-apt discourses.

Set these cases aside then. What other kinds of explanatory liaison are there which the states of affairs dealt with by a merely minimally truth-apt discourse might lack, and whose possession would impose a more substantial conception of the second term of the correspondence relation than anything required by the Correspondence Platitude? Let the *width of cosmological role* of the subject matter of a discourse be measured by the extent to which citing the kinds of states of affairs with which it deals is potentially contributive to the explanation of things *other than,* or *other than via,* our being in attitudinal states which take such states of affairs as object. I suggest that the idea which the Best Explanation constraint is really in pursuit of is that some discourses have, in these terms, a subject matter of relatively wide cosmological role. But the original constraint had it the wrong way round. The crucial question is not whether a class of states of affairs feature in the *best* explanation of our beliefs about them, but of *what else* there is, other than our beliefs, of which the citation of such states of affairs can feature in *good enough* explanations.

Let's try an exercise. Compare the Wetness of These Rocks, and the Wrongness of That Act. Reference to the wetness of the rocks can, uncontroversially, contribute towards explaining at least four kinds of thing:

(1) My perceiving, and hence believing, that the rocks are wet.
(2) A small (prelinguistic) child's interests in his hands after he has touched the rocks.
(3) My slipping and falling.
(4) The abundance of lichen growing on them.

The wetness of the rocks can be ascribed, that is, each of four kinds of consequence: cognitive effects, precognitive-sensuous effects, effects on us as physically interactive agents, and certain brute effects on inanimate organisms and matter. By contrast, the wrongness of that act, although citing it may feature in a vin-  dicatory explanation of my moral disapproval of the action, and hence of the further effects on the world which my disapproval may generate, would seem to have no part to play in the *direct* (propositional-attitude unmediated) explanation of any effects of the latter three sorts: precognitive-sensuous, interactive, and brute. It is true that the manner of speaking involved in the rebellion example would allow us to ascribe other than attitude-mediated affects to an evaluative state of affairs—in the case when we treat the evaluation as, in effect, encoding the natural features on which it is based, or features which accompany them in a law-like way. But without condemning such a locution as wrong, we must at least acknowledge that it blurs a distinction. And we don't need to blur distinctions in order properly to explain matters of types (2), (3) and (4) by citing the wetness of the rocks.

Although the pertinent details need further clarification and tidying, the overall shape of the constraint we want is now quite clear. There are some kinds of explanatory citation of the states of affairs with which a discourse deals which are licensed purely and simply by that discourse's minimal truth aptitude—by its exhibition of the appropriate syntax and discipline. Say that a subject

matter has *wide cosmological role* tout court just in case mention of
the states of affairs of which it consists can feature in at least some
kinds of explanation of contingencies which are not of that sort—
explanations whose possibility is not guaranteed merely by the
minimal truth aptitude of the associated discourse. What we have
just reviewed, then, is the makings of a prima facie case that the
moral lacks wide cosmological role.

Needless to say, if the case pans out in detail, that is bad news
for moral realism. But let me stress again that, from the pluralistic
perspective advocated here, it need not be disastrous news. It
would mean merely that one kind of strategy for substantiating
moral realism—the strategy of making out that moral facts are, as
it were, beefy enough to obstruct any purely platitudinous construal of moral truth as "correspondence to fact"—does not look
promising. But whether it ought then to be concluded that no
other strategy could fare better is a matter of the detail of inter-
relationships between the various realist/anti-realist cruces which
the pluralistic approach might want to recognise. And that detail
is for further investigation.

Two final points. First, although the wet rock example might
suggest otherwise, it is not my intention that the Wide Cosmological Role constraint should be satisfiable only by *causally active*
states of affairs, nor even that the explanations involved have to be
causal. The overarching point, remember, is that there be a *wider
range of intelligible and legitimate uses of the relevant state denoters than
can be generated merely by the minimal truth aptitude of a discourse.* In
principle, therefore, any additional kinds of context featuring the
state denoters are significant, and interesting further distinctions
may remain to be drawn depending on what the additional kinds
of uses are. Focussing on explanatory contexts is merely one salient
strategy if one picks up on the issue via the Harman/Sturgeon/
Wiggins debate about morals. It may transpire that, if we do
restrict attention to explanatory contexts, only discourses dealing
in causally active states of affairs will pass the test. But that, if it
is so, is a consequential matter and does not belong to the architec-
ture of the constraint. And indeed it is notable, in particular, that
the citation of *mathematical* facts does contribute, seemingly, to

other kinds of explanation than those which are of or via propositional attitudes. (It is because a prime number of tiles have been
delivered, for instance, that a contractor has trouble in using them
to cover, without remainder, a rectangular bathroom floor, even if
he has never heard of prime numbers and never thought about
how the area of a rectangle is determined.)

Finally, it should be noted that, whatever the fate of morals,
the states of affairs purportedly dealt with by discourse concerning
Lockean secondary qualities—colours, tastes, sounds, smells, pal-
pable textures and so on—do seem to exhibit the kind of
explanatory diversity called for. It is not a *conceptual* error to suppose that bulls are enraged by red rags, and colours do as a matter
of fact figure in the explanation of the behaviour of bees and but-
terflies, or small children without language, and certain purely
physical phenomena (it is not, doubtless, the most fundamental
explanation, but it *is* explanatory of the manifest colours on a
photographic negative to appeal, inter alia, to the colours of the
original object). Sounds startle babies and animals, and activate
reflexes like blinking. The smell of cheese in a trap may attract a
mouse. A cat sits by a fire because it's warm. And so on. The
effect of the Wide Cosmological Role constraint is not to create a
club which blackballs all but statements couched in the austere,
primary-quality vocabulary of theoretical science.

## DISCUSSION NOTE

*The basic minimalist stance was described as "anti-realist". But what
should any sensible moral realist ever want besides minimalism as it has
now emerged?*

This raises fundamental questions—about the *rewards* of
realism, where we can get it, and about the details of the relations
between those rewards and the various realism-relevant cruces here
distinguished—which I cannot attempt to take on here, even if I
thought I could defend stable views about them. But we can do
some summary score keeping. Successfully to defend moral
minimalism is to win through to the idea that moral discourse is

geared to the recognition and exchange of truths, and thus to see off any suggestion that it is beset by systematic error or is merely the sheepish expression of emotion masked by the wolfish syntax of genuine judgement. Minimalism will be consistent, moreover, with the prima facie quite robust kinds of reference to moral qualities and moral states of affairs on which this chapter has concentrated. Those are things that moral realists have wanted. And there is more. It is, so far as I can see, open to minimalism to maintain that the sensibilities on which moral discourse is founded are capable of *progress*—that morals can undergo significant development, and that, in response to our efforts, the story of our moral development can unfold better than it might otherwise have done.

*But:* the minimalist will have to admit that such ideas of progress, or deterioration, are ones for which we can have use only from *within* a committed moral point of view; and that the refinement of which our moral sensibilities are capable can only be a matter of the approaching of a certain equilibrium as appraised by the exercise of those very sensibilities. There will be no defensible analogue of the scientific realist's thought that the real progress of science is measured by the extent to which our theories represent a reality whose nature owes nothing to our natures or the standards that inform our conception of responsible discourse about it. It will not be possible to regard the disciplined formation of a moral view as a seriously representational mode of function, or as a mode of activity in which we respond to states of affairs which, precisely because they are at the service of explanations of other things, can be put to serious work in explaining the course assumed by those responses. Minimalism need not lapse into an amoral tolerance. The minimalist need not accept that differences of moral opinion which it is not possible to excuse as the product of some relevant vagueness may still involve nothing worthy of reproach. But he has to accept that such differences need involve nothing worth regarding as *cognitive* shortcoming. If one or the other opinion *must* deserve reproach in such a case, it will be for an irreducibly moral shortcoming, a failing which can be appreciated only from a committed moral point of view.

In general, the immediate price of minimalism about morals is that the gravity of moral judgement will lack an external sanction. No discourse-neutral notion of objectivity will give value to moral truth. When one is asked, "Why bother to try to arrive at correct moral opinion?", the only available answer will be: because such opinion informs better conduct—better, that is, from a moral point of view. The only value of moral truth will thus be an instrumental moral value. If we think there are, by contrast, intrinsic, general values associated with discovery, understanding and knowledge, we must recognise, I believe, that they belong with the application of these notions within discourses which deserve realism. It is, in any case, on this hard question—the varieties of worth that truth may have, and what they depend on—that the answer to the question, whether minimalism can assuage the desires of moral realism, depends.

# 6. Quietism

## I. Introduction

Quietism is the view that significant metaphysical debate is impossible. According to one version, realist and anti-realist tendencies both betray a muddled desire to step outside one's skin, as it were. Such tendencies derive, the thought goes, from the ill-conceived notion that reflection may somehow capture an Olympian standpoint from which the claim to objectivity of a linguistic practice—a "language game"—can be reviewed. But there is no such standpoint. Reflective description of the detail of language games is possible, but such description must be subordinate to the recognition that each is self-regulating and answerable only to standards immanent within it. No common metric against which they might be measured and compared is either desirable or exists.

I don't propose to argue for a view on the difficult exegetical question whether Wittgenstein really did take this "Wittgensteinian" view, or—beyond venturing one point—to consider the extent to which it would be consistent with his own philosophical practice: with things he says about avowals for instance, or mathematical sentences, or ethics, or the "hinge propositions" of *On Certainty*.[1] The point I will venture is that it is only if one over-

1. A catalogue of instances where Wittgenstein seems to fall into lines of thought that seemingly belong with the expressivist anti-realist tradition is pro-

looks a distinction that there will seem to be an *obvious* inconsistency between passages where Wittgenstein seems to want to look past the overtly assertoric cast of a range of sentences and the passages on which the quietist interpretation draws.[2] The distinction is that between two purposes for which the comparison between, say, mathematical statements and commands may be intended. It may be aimed, as by expressivism, to persuade us to reclassify certain sentences in terms of a framework of robust notions—*genuine* assertion, *genuine* truth, and so on—which supply the expressivist's stock-in-trade; it may be intended to persuade us, for instance, that mathematical statements really function as imperatives. On the other hand, it may be intended precisely to help *subvert* any such framework—to suggest that there is not the clean distinction to be made between genuinely truth-apt contents and "merely grammatical" assertions which the expressivist needs to work with. Rather, the suggestion can be, the "merely grammatical" notions are the only *general* notions of truth and assertoric content which we have, and beyond them lies only a plethora of differences which we need to notice and describe. A philosophical picture of what is going on in a discourse may, of course, be motivated by overlooking differences between it and others. So there will be space for appraisal of such pictures. But there is no space for debate about the applicability of metaphysically hypostatised notions of truth and assertoric content; and differences which merely call a philosophical picture

---

vided in Simon Blackburn's "Wittgenstein's Irrealism", in J. Brandt and R. Haller, eds., *Wittgenstein: Towards a Re-Evaluation* (Vienna: Holder-Pichler-Tempsky, 1990), pp. 13–26. Such instances are certainly more than occasional. The passages in the *Remarks on the Foundations of Mathematics* where Wittgenstein works with a comparison between mathematical statements and rules or commands are legion. The *Investigations* has been standardly read as advancing a non-assertoric conception of self-ascriptions of mental states. The *Lecture on Ethics*—admittedly an early work (1929)—is permeated by a contrast between judgements of absolute value and judgements of fact. And the treatment of "hinge propositions" in *On Certainty*, in particular the linguistically revisionary insistence that they are not properly viewed as objects of *knowledge*, is simply unintelligible unless we suppose its author believed that "grammatical" similarities—and especially those which provide the basis of the idea of minimal assertoric content—can mask distinctions in cognitive status.

   2. See, for instance, *Philosophical Investigations* §136 and surrounding.

into question must not be credited with a bearing on the very integrity of the language game concerned.

When Wittgenstein's position is interpreted along these lines, it is in no obvious way at odds with the approach which I have been outlining in this study. That approach grants that quietism makes at least one important contribution, viz. the insight that it *is* a metaphysical hypostasis of notions like truth and assertion to write their applicability within a discourse into the substance of a realist view about its subject matter. Rather, we should recognise that the satisfaction of certain minimal constraints of discipline and syntax carries assertoric content, truth aptitude, and, *ceteris paribus,* the justifiability of particular claims to truth in its train. To this extent, we can and should take discourses as diverse as film criticism and scientific cosmology as involving, for the most part, the attempt to say what is true, and as needing no metaphysical underpinning if they are to count as fit for that project. But I have also urged that this is not the end of the matter, that important differences relevant to realist intuition may yet exist between different "language games"; and I have tried to describe a number of specific ways in which something worth regarding as a realist/anti-realist debate might yet be had—a number of pivotal issues, including those of Cognitive Command, Width of Cosmological Role, the question whether the truth predicate in a discourse is evidentially unconstrained, and questions to do with the Euthyphro Contrast, whose interrelations remain to be explored in detail but each of which presents a relevant focus for debate about a particular discourse's suitability for an intuitive realism. Wittgenstein urged us not to let surface similarities between discourses cause us to overlook important differences. What I have been attempting is precisely to develop the beginnings of a framework in which one range of such differences can be logged and their significance appraised.

If a widespread opinion is correct, however, the appearance of consistency here is superficial. Many commentators who would disagree about the details would nevertheless agree that properly to have assimilated the ideas about rule following in the *Investigations* and the *Remarks on the Foundations of Mathematics* is to see that no distinctions of the kind which I have been trying to outline can be drawn and that a quietist stance concerning the traditional debates about realism is in the end effectively imposed. That claim—that the rule-following considerations serve, as Gareth Evans once impatiently expressed it, as a metaphysical wet blanket—is the focus of this chapter.

## II. McDowell's Wittgenstein

Although it has wide currency, explicitly argued statements of this idea are not easy to come by. But a version can be found in John McDowell's writings. Here is a characteristic passage.

> Consider the hardness of the logical "must". One is apt to suppose that the only options are, on the one hand, to conceive the hardness platonistically (as something to be found in the world as it is anyway: that is, the world as characterised from a standpoint external to our mathematical practices); or, on the other, (if one recoils from Platonism), to confine oneself to a catalogue of how human beings act and feel when they engage in deductive reasoning . . . On the second option, the hardness of the logical "must" has no place in one's account of how things really are; and there must be a problem about making room for genuine rationality in deductive practice, since we conceive that as a matter of conforming our thought and action to the dictates of the logical "must". If one recoils from Platonism into this second position, one has passed over a fully satisfying intermediate position, according to which the logical "must" is indeed hard (in the only sense we can give to that idea), and the ordinary conception of deductive rationality is perfectly acceptable; it is simply that we must avoid a mistake about the perspective from which the demands of the logical "must" are perceptible.[3]

3. John McDowell, "Non-Cognitivism and Rule-Following", in C. Leich and S. Holtzman, eds., *Wittgenstein: To Follow a Rule* (London: Routledge and Kegan Paul, 1981), pp. 141–162. The quotation is from page 156.

The overarching view of Wittgenstein's discussion of rules expressed in this passage and elsewhere in McDowell's writings[4] is that Wittgenstein accomplishes a constructive solution—the "fully satisfying intermediate position"—to a dilemma into which we are plunged by a misunderstanding of what it takes to generate a real constraint upon a practice, or to qualify our thought in some area as fully objective. The misunderstanding conceives of the requirements of a rule as, if they are to be genuinely objective, matters whose detail has to be settled, case by case, in full independence of any human propensity for reaction or judgement, so that the direction that the rule takes might in principle be appreciable from a perspective wholly external to ours—appreciable by a radically alien cognitive subject. This sublimation of rules leaves us with a pair of hopeless tasks: first, that of providing at least some sort of account of what, wholly independently of human propensity, determines the real direction followed by a rule; and second, that of saying something useful about how and why we might be presumed to be in cognitive touch with this "real direction". Recoiling from this platonistic Scylla,[5] one may find one's ship embroiled in the corresponding Charybdis: the rule-sceptical thought that there are really no such things as objective requirements, generated by rules, but only natural, unfettered propensities; that no real *following* of rules—no real objectivity in general—exists anywhere in our practices. The "fully satisfying intermediate position" is then to be earned by the reflection that all that is really wrong with Scylla is the notion that a truly objective constraint must be one whose dictates are appreciable from an "external perspective"—a perspective that stands apart from human reactive propensities and can thus command a view of the extent to which they keep us on track of the real requirements of the constraint. We have to learn the hard lesson that real objectivity cannot be *that*—as we recognise, in effect, when we recoil towards Charybdis. Rather, it is of the essence of a rule that it exists only within a practice which is

4. See especially his "Wittgenstein on Following a Rule", *Synthese* 58 (1984), pp. 325–363.

5. McDowell's image; "Wittgenstein on Following a Rule", pp. 341–342.

sustained by its participants sharing, as Stanley Cavell puts it in a passage applauded by McDowell,

> routes of interest and feeling, senses of humour, and of significance, and of fulfilment, of what is outrageous, of what is similar to what else, what a rebuke, what forgiveness, when an utterance is an assertion, when an appeal, when an explanation—all the whirl of organism Wittgenstein calls "forms of life".[6]

If, following McDowell, we call all that a "point of view", then the thought is that it is only from *within* a point of view that there is such a thing as recognising the requirements of a rule, and intentionally following them through.

No one can be blamed for wanting middle ground here. It is another (very good) question what exactly the "fully satisfying intermediate position" should be supposed to amount to. But my present concern is with the way in which McDowell applies his interpretation to the debate between moral cognitivism and its opponents. McDowell contends that the moral non-cognitivist is driven by a misbegotten construal of *ethical* fact and objectivity entirely of piece with the Platonism of Scylla. The moral non-cognitivist will be a philosopher labouring under the misapprehension that anything worth regarding as moral cognitivism has to make out how the relevant subject matter is *there,* so to speak, for any enquiring agent, independently of an evaluative "point of view". Since, as Wittgenstein teaches us, no subject matter is ever "there" in that kind of way, no disadvantageous comparison remains to be made. The appreciation of moral fact requires, to be sure, a moral point of view. But then, the appreciation of *any* fact requires a point of view.

A general model of realist/anti-realist debates is suggested by this perspective. The realist, prizing objectivity above all else, opts for Scylla; the anti-realist, recognising the hopeless constitutive and epistemological questions posed by such a view, overreacts,

6. Stanley Cavell, *Must We Mean What We Say?* (New York: Charles Scribners Sons, 1969), p. 52.

and winds up in Charybdis, effectively forfeiting the very subject matter whose objectivity the realist was concerned above all to conserve. The debate is then *undermined* by an application of the "fully satisfying intermediate position". There never was a real debate; only a misunderstanding of what the engagement of mind with an objective subject matter requires, and a misunderstanding of what it takes to avoid that misunderstanding. Nowhere, in the paper from which I quoted, does McDowell explicitly advance this as a correct general perspective on the matter, or explicitly rule out the possibility of realist/anti-realist debates among philosophers who are not labouring under the hyper-objectivist delusion of Scylla. Still, the more general claim puts *itself* forward.

But it is not, in my opinion, at all convincing. If McDowell's perspective is to undermine realist/anti-realist debate in general, it is necessary that in each instance the antagonists can be located, without misrepresentation, on the respectively appropriate horns of the Scylla–Charybdis dilemma. So realism has *always* to involve hyper-objectification, and anti-realism must *always* be fruitfully represented as a flight from hyper-objectification, into an abrogation of subject matter. And that simply isn't the way it has to go.

Take the case of Cognitive Command. The question whether it is a priori that differences of opinion formulable within a particular discourse will, prescinding from vagueness, always involve something worth regarding as a cognitive shortcoming has no evident intrinsic connection with a hyper-objectified conception of fact. It is a question to be settled by reference to what we conceive as the range of possible sources of such differences. As such it involves, naturally, ordinary conceptual reflection. But no view need be implicit about the *status* of such reflection—and certainly no commitment to the idea that its cogency should somehow depend on its being accessible to a "standpoint external to our reflective deliberations". If we decide that, say, visually assessable ascriptions of shape to material objects pass the test—that, for instance, a difference of opinion concerning whether a visible plane figure is approximately pear-shaped can be intelligible only as the product of inferior location, or abnormal visual function, or abnormal visual conditions, or inattention, or cognitive disfunction, or the vagueness involved in the predicate—surely we suffer no commitment thereby to the view that pear-shapedness is a "point-of-view"-independent quality, "there" for any shape-perceiving subject.

I have deliberately picked an example, of course, where a shape concept reflects a salience for human beings and, not inconceivably, might get no grip for other perceiving subjects. But the point is quite general: it is that whatever a "point of view" is, it can be allowed to condition the application of the concepts—in this case, "abnormal visual function" and the rest—which are used in the operation of a realism-relevant constraint.

A supporter of McDowell might rejoin that whatever distinctions can coherently be drawn under the aegis of Cognitive Command or the other constraints, they will be *our* distinctions; that it would be an error to suppose that contrasts in point of objectivity can be more robustly "there" than, say, the requirements of the rules of addition. But that should not prompt a *denial* that they are there ("in the only sense we can give to that idea"). That denial would have to depend on the thought that all such distinctions somehow embed the myth of Scylla. And that thought, it seems to me, merely misrepresents the detail of the various constraints on which we have been focussing.[7]

## III. The Basic Argument for Quietism

I do not think, therefore, that McDowell's Wittgenstein should be reckoned subversive of all realist/anti-realist debate. But there are other Wittgensteins to reckon with.

Consider Saul Kripke's well-known interpretation.[8] The contrasts with McDowell's account are very great. McDowell's Wittgenstein wants to point to an escape route from a misconceived philosophical debate. Kripke's Wittgenstein, by contrast, is a committed *participant* in that debate. For Kripke, the heart of the "rule-following considerations" is a sceptical paradox which pur-

7. This may need a qualification in the case of evidence transcendence, however. The matter is taken up below.

8. Saul A. Kripke, *Wittgenstein on Rules and Private Language* (Oxford: Basil Blackwell, 1982).

portedly overturns any possibility that rules and meanings embody real constraints. All that is then left is the attempt, by clinging to the (none too buoyant) "Sceptical Solution", to keep one's head above water in Charybdis.

The essence of Kripke's misconstrual, from McDowell's standpoint, is that it takes the destruction of Scylla as the heart of the dialectic on rules when, properly located, it is merely a lemma;[9] and then *advocates* the recoil to Charybdis, when the real character of Wittgenstein's concern, as McDowell conceives it, was to transcend the dilemma by disclosing a spuriously sublimated conception of fact and objectivity which is common to its horns.[10]

---

9. Differences of detail notwithstanding, my own early attempt at an interpretation of Wittgenstein's ideas on rules and their relevance to his philosophy of mathematics (in my *Wittgenstein on the Foundations of Mathematics* [London: Duckworth, 1980]) is subjected by McDowell to essentially the same complaint.

10. It is worth remarking that, even conceding McDowell's account of the historical Wittgenstein's intent, his reproach actually pays insufficient respect to the detail of Kripke's text. For it is far from clear whether the Sceptical Argument, if it accomplishes anything, can be confined to the destruction of Scylla.

Recall the way the development of the paradox actually goes. In the first instance a debate is constructed about a token claim concerning any past meaning of mine—say, the claim that by " + " I formally meant addition. My task is to defend this claim against a Sceptic. One would naturally suppose that even if I were to lose this debate, no conclusions about *reality* of meanings, rules etc. would be in prospect; the only conclusion licensed would be that the *epistemology* of claims about meaning is, under sceptical pressure, no more straightforward than the epistemology of the past, or of the material world, or of other minds has turned out to be. But that would be mistaken. Traditional forms of sceptical argument make much of what are taken to be our intrinsic cognitive predicament: it is contended that we are, necessarily, screened from *direct* knowledge of others' mental states, of the past and of the characteristics of matter, and are therefore restricted to inferences from behaviour, the present and our own experiences. A crucial contrast is thus that the debate with Kripke's Sceptic is to proceed under conditions of *cognitive idealisation:* in my attempt to win—to justify my claim that by " + " I formally meant addition—I am granted *perfect recall* of all aspects of my former behaviour and mental life. The governing strategic thought is precisely that, *were* there to be a fact about what I formally meant by " + ", it would somehow have to be constituted in aspects of my former behaviour and mental life, and ought therefore, under the idealisation, to be salient to me. If, therefore, *even* when so idealised, I still lose the debate, it follows that there can

Be that as it may, it is arguable that Kripke's Wittgenstein is committed to quietism in any case. for the irrealism about meanings, rules and their requirements imposed by the sceptical paradox—the thesis that there are "no facts of the matter" as far as rules and meanings are concerned—must necessarily inflate, it may seem, into a *global* irrealism: the thesis that there are no facts of the matter *anywhere*. It is the merest truism that whether any sentence is true is a function, in part, of what it says. If there are no substantial facts about what sentences say, there are no substantial facts about whether or not they are true. Thus, irrealism about meaning must enjoin an irrealism about truth, wherever the notion is applied. And irrealism about truth, wherever the notion is applied, is irrealism about all assertoric discourse.

---

indeed be no such fact. (And this conclusion is then easily developed to generate, successively, that there are no facts about what I presently mean, no facts about what anyone else presently means, nor, therefore, any facts about what any expression means, or in consequence about what uses comply with this meaning.)

This briefest outline of the overriding strategy of Kripke's Wittgenstein's Sceptical Argument is enough to bring out that no hyper-objectification of the nature of rules, or meanings, features in the argument *as a premise*. The conception of meaning-fact involved seems perfectly pretheoretical and ordinary. To be sure, there is an assumption involved: that facts about my former meanings are broadly psychological in a sense which would require them to show up in aspects of my former behaviour or conscious mental life; and that can be and, of course, has been contested. But while that assumption may be an error, it is not an error of sublimation. If anything is vulnerable to the Sceptical Paradox, a humanised Platonism is no less vulnerable than the hyper-objectified version.

McDowell's Scylla is simply not on the stage in Kripke's dialectic. Or at least, she is in no way implicated in the general strategy. To be sure, an implicit hyper-objectification might yet be involved if it turned out that the detail of the way the Sceptic putatively succeeds depended on denying his antagonist the resources of a "point of view". But that would not be a plausible contention in the present instance. It would represent the essential epistemology of first-person claims about former meanings as if they were inferential, based on the very data on which Kripke's dialectic concentrates, but as if such data would underdetermine which inference to draw unless the contribution of a "point of view" was brought into the reckoning. And the truth is that, for the most part, knowledge of former meanings, like knowledge of present ones, is *not* inferential and has no articulate epistemology.

This is a deceptively simple train of thought. A first reaction is that it relies heavily on the rhetoric of "no fact of the matter"; and that for anyone in sympathy with the broad framework which I have been advocating, such rhetoric will now have a somewhat oversimplicatory resonance. But that reaction is easily addressed. The irrealism established by Kripke's sceptical paradox, if it is sustained, comes to the contention that discourse about rules, meanings and what complies with them is at most minimally truth-apt—that nothing about such discourse merits movement away from minimalist anti-realism about it. And the globalising suggestion will be, then, that if this goes for meanings, it must go for ascriptions of truth as well, since they depend on meanings.

Someone who wanted to make a case for global minimalism along these lines would be heavily reliant, of course, both on the ability of minimalism about rules and meanings to control the sceptical paradox,[11] and on the cogency of the paradox itself. And many reasons for doubting the latter, and some for doubting the former, have emerged in recent literature. My interest in the line running from themes of Kripke's Wittgenstein to global minimalism is not that it sets up a competitive argument to that conclusion but that it illustrates the possibility of a more general strategy of subversion, free from reliance on the cogency of Kripke's paradox or any specific assumptions about the proper way to register its effect. The thought is simply this. *Whatever* exactly Wittgenstein's dialectic accomplishes, it surely imposes *some* kind of qualification to a realist conception of rules and meanings. And now, whatever that qualification is thought to be, it has to go through—since truth is a function of meaning—for ascriptions of truth as well. At the least, then, the rule-following considerations set an *upper bound* on the robustness of the realism which is available anywhere: the bound is set by the robustness of the realism which, after those considerations, it is appropriate to apply to judgements concerning meanings, rules and what complies with them. And if in addition we take it, as Kripke did, that Wittgenstein's argument imposes

11. That it can is, in effect, the characteristic claim of a proponent of the Sceptical Solution.

irrealism—or minimalism—about meanings and so on, then irrealism, or minimalism, is the upper bound everywhere.

## IV. Two Objections

There are two natural lines of resistance to this thinking. The first, already briefly touched on, is that it really does matter what the anti-realist claim about meanings consists in and how it is couched. Reflect that the claim that S is true may harmlessly be taken as equivalent to:

For some P: S says that P and P.

And now, if one's thinking proceeds in terms of the rhetoric of "no fact of the matter", it is indeed obscure how there could be a substantial fact of the matter whether a conjunction—a fortiori, a quantified conjunction—was true when there was no substantial fact of the matter whether one of its conjuncts was. But this move is hostage to the particular realism-divesting characteristic by which one takes it that meaning-discourse has been shown to be afflicted. It simply isn't obvious in general that, for any realism-motivating property F, the presence of a non-F statement in a conjunction, say, will suffice for the conjunction's not being F. To take perhaps the most obvious case: the presence in a conjunction of a statement about which one took a verificationist view would not enforce, without supplementary considerations, a verificationist view of the conjunction as a whole (since a conjunction might, obviously, be evidence-transcendent although not all its conjuncts were).

The second reservation about the generalised subversive thought is that, in the significance which it attaches to its conclusion—crudely, that whatever goes for meaning must go for truth, and hence for all truth-apt discourse—it lapses into a confusion between use and mention. It is correct, of course, that whether or not a sentence is true depends on its meaning; and that connection may suffice for the transferability of certain characteristics of claims about the meaning of a sentence—the characteristic, for instance, of having a subject matter about which a specific form of anti-realism is appropriate—to claims about the sentence's truth value. But claiming that a sentence is true is one thing, and making the claim expressed by an assertoric *use* of that sentence is another. The most that is immediately in prospect, therefore, is an "upper bound" to realism about *metalinguistic* claims of the form: S is true. No conclusion will be licensed, without further premises, about the status of the object-linguistic assertions obtainable by semantic descent from such claims.

I shall return to each of these misgivings after we have considered a very explicit train of thought recently presented by Paul Boghossian which, if sound, would enable the subversive to outflank them both—and to achieve the most cogent account thus far of how a minimalism about meaning must globalise.

## V. From Meaning-Minimalism to Global Minimalism

Boghossian writes as follows:

> consider a non-factualism solely about meaning—the view that, since there is no such property as a word's meaning something, and hence no such fact, no meaning-attributing sentence can be truth-conditional. Since the truth-condition of any sentence S is (in part anyway) a function of its meaning, a non-factualism about meaning will enjoin a non-factualism about truth-conditions: what truth-condition S possesses could hardly be a factual matter if that in virtue of which it has a particular truth-condition is not itself a factual matter. And so we have it that . . .
>
> (5)  For all S, P: "S has truth-condition P" is not truth conditional.
>
> However, since, courtesy of the disquotational properties of the truth predicate, a sentence of the form "S has truth-condition P" is true if and only if S has truth-condition P, and since (5) has it that "S has truth-condition P" is never simply true, it follows that
>
> (4)        For any S: "S" is not truth conditional.
>
> . . . It is then a fascinating consequence of a non-factualism about meaning, that it entails a *global* non-factualism; in this respect,

if no other, a non-factualism about meaning distinguishes itself from a similar thesis about *any* other subject matter.[12]

Boghossian's formulation notably kidnaps the word "true" to express whatever property provides the focus of dispute between "non-factualists" about a discourse and their realist opponents. Someone in sympathy with the approach followed in this study will want to protest at the philosophy of truth implicit in that. But there can be no real objection to Boghossian's use of the *word*. Our approach has been to focus the issue of realism on the question: what characteristics are possessed by a particular truth predicate beyond those it has to have if the discourse in which it operates is to rank as minimally truth-apt? It would be mere terminological legislation to ban use of "true" as an indicator that a predicate possessed such additional, realism-relevant properties—was "substantial". We can always assign some other term—say, "correctness"—to cover the merely minimal case. The thesis of the "non-factualist" about meaning can then become the contention that all discourse about meaning and cognate concepts is at most correctness-apt and is not in the market for any more substantial property.

Let's set out the argument more explicitly. It runs as follows. For any sentence S and propositional content P:

(i)      It is not the case that "S has the truth condition that P" has a truth condition.

That is a premise. Any theorist must accept it who holds that discourse about meaning, as well as cognate concepts, is apt only for correctness in the sense lately stipulated. For statements of the form "S has the truth condition that P" ascribe a semantic property to S, viz. a condition of substantial truth, and are unquestionably "cognate" in the intended sense. The argument then proceeds

(ii)      It is not the case that "S has the truth condition that P" is true;

—which putatively follows from (i), since only a sentence with a truth condition can, presumably, be true. Then

12. Paul A. Boghossian, "The Rule-Following Considerations", *Mind* 98 (1989), pp. 507–549. The quoted passage is from pp. 524–525.

which follows from (ii), "courtesy"—according to Boghossian—"of the disquotational properties of the truth predicate".

The conclusion, then, is that no matter what sentence S we select, no propositional content P correctly articulates a truth condition for it. Recalling that "truth" and "truth condition" are being understood in a substantial (more than minimal) sense throughout the argument, we then reflect that this is not a paradox but, precisely, the conclusion that no sentence is in the market for substantial truth—that is, precisely the global minimalist conclusion promised. QED?

There is some question whether global minimalism can be coherent. One worry would concern the content of the thesis: can the needed notion of substantial truth be fully intelligible if there are perforce no examples of it? A more serious concern would focus on the status of the argument for it. Won't a proponent want the argument to be *cogent?* And how can that be unless the claims essentially involved in running the argument at least exhibit Cognitive Command, and so are not merely minimally truth-apt? Boghossian expresses some sympathy with another discussion of mine[13] in which such concerns were expressed, and he himself attacks the coherence of meaning "non-factualism" elsewhere.[14] But his stated view about the present argument is that it is by no means obvious that there is anything unstable about its global conclusion, and hence that the argument stands as the disclosure not of any crisis for the meaning-minimalist but rather of a "fascinating consequence" of the position.

But that cannot be the right way of looking at the matter. Reflect that, by the principle—that only a sentence with a truth condition can be true—which sanctions the transition from (i) to (ii), we can move on from (iii) to

(iv)                    It is not the case that S is true;

13. Crispin Wright, "Kripke's Account of the Argument against Private Language", *Journal of Philosophy* 81 (1984), pp. 759–778.

14. In his essay "The Status of Content", *Philosophical Review* 99 (1989), pp. 157–183. For a brief review of Boghossian's main argument there, see the appendix to the present chapter.

and hence, substituting (i)—the argument's premise—for S, to

(v)             It is not the case that (i) is true.

Whence by another "courtesy of the disquotational properties of the truth predicate", we derive

(vi)      It is not the case that it is not the case that "S has
          the truth condition that P" has a truth condition.

Is that a *reductio* of (i)? This is not a silly question. When truth is understood as substantial, and contrasts with a more minimal surrogate—what we are temporarily calling correctness—denying the truth of something need not be inconsistent with affirming its correctness; and there will be a perfectly coherent notion of negation whose content is just the denial of truth. By contrast, a *reductio* of (i) will be something, presumably, which shows that it ought not to be asserted—that it is not even *correct*. A dilemma now arises for Boghossian's view of the argument. If the argument *is* a *reductio* of (i), it shows that meaning-minimalism is incoherent—if it shows anything. But if the argument is not a *reductio* of (i)—if the negation in (vi) is a denial of substantial truth rather than of correctness—then the original conclusion, at line (iii), no longer ranks as an expression of global minimalism, since (iii) will now be consistent with the *correctness* of claiming that some sentences have substantial truth conditions. The most that (iii), so interpreted, will require is that any statement of the taxonomy of the distinction between truth-apt discourses and discourses apt merely for correctness can itself be apt only for correctness.

So the "fascinating consequence" is not in prospect either way. What, if anything, is in prospect is a demonstration either that meaning-minimalism, as captured in premise (i), is self-defeating (which would certainly be interesting enough) or that it entails minimalism about the distinction between discourses which are apt for substantial truth and those which are not.[15]

15. This conclusion would still be uncomfortable in one of the ways in which global irrealism is: roughly, there is a strong desire that the philosophy in terms of which the taxonomy of the distinction between the substantially true and the merely correct is drawn be itself substantial.

But there are major problems with the argument in any case. We have distinct truth predicates simultaneously in play—"true" and "correct"—and corresponding predicates of falsity. It is of course essential to Boghossian's way of looking at the matter that truth should be, in this way, many-sorted. For he needs a truth predicate which can be withheld from discourses—precisely those about which what he calls the "non-factualist" stance is taken— even while recognising that they meet the syntactic and disciplinary conditions which qualify them as minimally truth-apt. But the range of the sentence quantifier in the argument is unrestricted, embracing both sentences which are apt for substantial truth, if there are any, and sentences which are merely minimally truth-apt. And this, obviously, has a potential bearing on the status of the principles, and especially Disquotation, by which the transitions in the argument proceed.

Let's look at the details. The move from (ii) to (iii) is a modus tollens on the right-to-left ingredient of the Disquotational Schema,

(I)                          A → "A" is true.

Can we safely assume that this principle is good—at least correct—when both truth and correctness are in play? Well, under what conditions, when both truth and correctness are in play, ought we to regard a conditional as at least correct? Various proposals are possible. But none will be acceptable, presumably, unless it determines that a conditional with a true or correct antecedent but a false or incorrect consequent is itself neither true nor correct. And in that case there is an obvious problem with the use made of (I). For the natural thought is that if A is merely correct, the claim that "A" is true at best *incorrectly* reports A's status. So, at least in that case, any instance of (I) is incorrect. And the case is, of course, the crucial one since, for the transition from (ii) to (iii), the relevant substituend for "A" is: "S has the truth condition that P"—a sentence apt, according to meaning-minimalism, only for correctness, not for truth.

The argument, it thus appears, simply overlooks that, when truth is many-sorted, and the assertion of a sentence may in principle lay claim to any of a variety of truth predicates, depending

on the type of sentence concerned, correct instances of the Disquotational Schema have to involve a truth predicate for which the
selected sentence is apt.

This objection is apt to seem decisive. But in fact it is not so.
For it assumes that when both truth and correctness are in play,
the matrix for the truth predicate must be *non-conservative:* that is,
that the value of "'A' is true" will drop to *false,* or *incorrect,* in all
cases save where A is assigned the value *true.* No doubt the
assumption is a natural one; if A is merely correct, and that is
distinct from its being true, then isn't the claim that it is true
simply *wrong?* But other ways of looking at the matter are possible,
and not entirely unmotivated. We already noted that when both
truth and correctness are in play, there will be a distinction
between negation proper—an operator transforming any true or
correct sentence into a false or incorrect one—and a negation
operator whose effect is to construct a true (or correct) sentence
just in case its argument fails of truth. The mooted objection takes
it, in effect, that "'A' is true" should be the complement of the
negation of A in the latter sense. But a perfectly sensible contrasting proposal is that it should, rather, complement the former
notion—the strict negation that takes us from at least correct
input to at least incorrect output and conversely. If we follow this
proposal, then, when A is merely correct, the evaluation of "'A' is
true" will likewise be correct; and, in general, the application of
the truth predicate to a sentence will be conservative both of at
least correctness and of at least incorrectness. So the correctness of
the Disquotational Schema will be reinstated, and the validity of
the transition from (ii) to (iii) in the argument restored.

But the bump comes up elsewhere in the carpet. For now there
is a difficulty with the principle that sanctions the transition from
(i) to (ii)—the seemingly incontestable principle that only a sentence with a truth condition can be true. Expressed as a conditional, this is the claim that

(II)         "A" is true $\rightarrow$ "A" has a truth condition.

And any conservative matrix for "'A' is true" puts this principle in
jeopardy in the case when A is not apt for truth, but is correct.
For then the conservative matrix will evaluate "'A' is true" as cor-

rect. But the consequent of (II)—the claim that "A" has a truth condition—will presumably be incorrect.

To see the specific difficulty, reflect that for the purposes of the transition from (i) to (ii), A is "S has the truth condition that P" and that, at this point in the argument—before the proof of the commitment to global minimalism is completed—it would of course be question-begging to assume that the meaning-minimalist may not coherently regard some sentences (sentences about the primary qualities of material bodies, for instance) as candidates for substantial truth. The ascription of a truth condition to such a sentence may thus, for all that may be assumed without question-begging, be correct. Hence, in the presence of a conservative matrix for "true", the claim

"S has the truth condition that P" is true

may be correct for such an S. But the whole basis of the argument is that meaning-minimalism has no option but to view

"S has the truth condition that P" has a truth condition

as invariably at least incorrect—otherwise there is no justification for the affirmation of (i) as a premise. The substitution of "S has the truth condition that P" for "A" in (II) thus, in the presence of a conservative matrix for "true" and the meaning-minimalist's own assumptions, generates a correct antecedent but an incorrect consequent. The conditional is therefore not at the service of the contraposition by which the argument proceeds.

In sum: if the matrix for "true" is non-conservative, then the Disquotational Schema fails in the crucial direction for the transition from (ii) to (iii); on the other hand, if the matrix is conservative, then, in the presence of premise (i), the principle that only a sentence with a truth condition is true breaks down (fails of correctness). Finally, if premise (i) is not granted, then there is, of course, no argument. Each way, the argument collapses.

## VI. The Intuitive Version Further Considered

What has collapsed, however, is just one attempt to explain rigorously how the rot is bound to spread, as it were; how whatever damage is inflicted on the objectivity of meaning and cognate matters by the rule-following considerations is bound to ramify without restriction of subject matter. And the general misgiving is apt to survive the failure of that particular attempt to render it rigorous. How can matters of fact ever have the hardness which is the defining aspiration of realism if a matter of fact is held to consist in the (substantial) truth of a propositional content, and matters of content have, in whatever precise way, "gone soft" after Wittgenstein?

Reflect again on the original intuitive version of the subversive train of thought. That version centred on the truism that the truth value of a statement as used in a particular context is a function of its meaning—of what, as used in that context, it says—and of the state of the world in relevant respects. Accordingly, if what the sentence says as used in a particular context (the condition which, so used, it imposes on the world) is somehow less than a fully robust matter, then—by the compelling principle that any deficiency, in point of objectivity, among the factors on which the resolution of a question depends must be transmitted to the answer to the question—it seems that the same must go for the claim that the sentence, as used on that particular occasion, is true.

I registered the doubt that, while the principle in question may indeed seem compelling when couched in terms of the language of "softness", "no fact of the matter", and their ilk, it is by no means clear whether every objectivity-relevant distinction goes along with it. We noted that evidence-transcendence is one immediate exception: that the presence of (defeasibly) decidable parameters among the factors determining the answer to a particular question need not, of course, ensure that the answer to the question is likewise (defeasibly) decidable. And it is the same with Euthyphro contrast: there is clearly provision for the possibility that while evaluation of at least some of the parameters affecting a question is determined as a function of best opinion, the overall answer to the question is something which even a best opinion can at most reflect and in whose determination it plays no constitutive role. But in other cases—and, crucially, in the case of Cognitive Command—matters stand differently. For when one's appraisal of the claim that S is true turns on an opinion about S's content as used in the particular context, divergent such appraisals may turn on differing such opinions. And if opinions about content and cognate matters fail of Cognitive Command, if no cognitive shortcoming need be involved in such a difference of opinion, then the same can hold for the claim that S is true. Accordingly, if it is right to suggest that Cognitive Command is the first and most basic of the hurdles that any advance from minimalism must surmount, then minimalism about meaning—if that is indeed what the rule-following considerations enjoin—has to involve minimalism about metalinguistic ascriptions of truth.

But the second objection mooted earlier still stands. For in order to globalise that thought, it seems we must now go via the semantic descent which Boghossian's argument promised to avoid. And no matter what realism-relevant properties are supposed to have been shown by the rule-following considerations to be lacking in meaning and cognate notions, it may seem just obvious that such descent cannot be expected to preserve that lack. Of course the question whether "P" is true in part turns on the semantic properties of the sentence "P"; but isn't it just a howler to suppose the same goes for the thought that P? The question whether the sentence "My lawn is green" is true depends on its meaning; but the question of the status of the *thought* that my lawn is green does not—in descending to the latter we have, as it were, gone past the contribution of meaning: all that remains is the worldly issue about the grass.[16]

It would be nice—for those who believe that the insights in Wittgenstein's discussion of rules ought to be reconcilable with the validity of a wide class of realist/anti-realist debates—if this simple defensive point were decisive. But it is hard to shake off the suspicion that it merely encourages us to bury our heads in the sand. *How* could the claim that P escape the fate of its meta-linguistic counterpart if the latter's fate is sealed just by the involvement of content? Language is not a mere clothing for thought: we

---

16. Boghossian is accused of overlooking this distinction by Simon Blackburn in "Wittgenstein's Irrealism"; but the charge is quite misconceived, since Boghossian's argument is explicitly to a metalinguistic conclusion, and involves no element of semantic descent.

have no wordless contact with the thought that P. If we are to assess it, it has somehow to be given to us *symbolically*. And our assessment will then be a function of the content which we find in its symbolic mode of presentation and of what we take to be the state of the world in relevant respects. If your and my sole language is English, then, in order to assess my claim that my lawn is green, it will be no less necessary for you to form a judgement about the content of the sentence "My lawn is green" as uttered by me than if I'd said that "My lawn is green" is true. We have no grip on the question of the truth status of a claim which doesn't make it into the question whether a tokening of a sentence is true.

Essentially the same point could be expressed like this. The difference between what is involved in forming an opinion about whether "P" is true, and forming an opinion about whether or not P, is not that in the former but not the latter case one has to take into consideration not merely worldly states of affairs but—at least usually—considerations of content as well, whereas in the latter one can restrict one's attention to the world, as it were. The essential epistemology of a well-founded opinion is the same in either case. In the case of the metalinguistic claim, it goes via appreciation of the semantic properties of the particular language to which the mentioned sentence belongs. But in the case of the object-linguistic claim assessment also proceeds, perforce, via appreciation of the semantic properties of *a* language—viz. whatever the language is, in which the thought to be considered is expressed.

It remains, of course, that a disagreement about whether "P" is true may precisely issue from a disagreement about the semantic attributes of "P"; whereas *we shall not describe* a disagreement between users of the same language as concerning whether or not it is the case that P unless we take it that there is no disagreement about the semantic attributes of the sentence used to express the claim in dispute. But can that reflection really carry a superior objectivity for the object-linguistic dispute, or a more robustly cognitive epistemology for the object-linguistic claim?

Consider a rough parallel. Suppose a subcommunity of *comic empathisers*—people whose senses of humour coincide so perfectly that whenever they have a disagreement about comedy, and vagueness (in any of the ways provided for by the Cognitive Command constraint) is not to blame, the explanation will be that they differ in their opinions about some non-comic matter. And now let *comedy** be a concept of the comic which is parochial to the empathisers' sense of humour—a concept whose fully self-reliant exercise is possible only for one of the empathisers. With such a concept to hand, then, merely by characterising a difference of opinion as concerning whether or not something is funny*, rather than funny simpliciter, we can cut off the option of excusing it by appeal to irreducible differences in senses of humour. Hence, the kind of case which poses a problem for the Cognitive Command of ordinary discourse about what is funny will not pose a problem for the Cognitive Command of comedy*. Yet the mix of the cognitive and the affective in the basis for opinions about comedy* is exactly the same as it is for opinions about comedy. If discourse about comedy* does exert Cognitive Command and ordinary discourse about comedy does not, isn't that merely an artifact of creative accounting, as it were—objectivity for cheap?

The general form of the point is this. Suppose a class of predications are such that it can never be a priori excluded that disagreement about one of them originates in some variation in a particular non-cognitive disposition of the disputants. Then there will be no obstacle to defining a range of concepts, cognate to those distinctive of the predications in question, such that nothing counts as a disagreement about the application of one of *these* concepts unless the disputants *share* the relevant non-cognitive disposition. By describing a disagreement as focussed upon the application of one of these latter concepts, we can thus preempt the possibility that it has one particular kind of non-cognitive source. Nevertheless, the operation of the non-cognitive disposition is no less involved in the application of the new concepts than in that of the old. It is not that we now stand on firmer ground, or engage more "robust" matters. The difference is only in what we have determined to be the appropriate mode of description of any disagreements that arise.[17]

17. I think that the illusion of security to be gained by semantic descent in this context is partially fostered by an intuitive Platonism about propositional

John McDowell once wrote:

> When we say "'Diamonds are hard' is true if and only if dia-
> monds are hard", we are just as much involved on the right-hand
> side as the reflections on rule-following tell us we are. There is
> a standing temptation to miss this obvious truth, and to suppose
> that the right-hand side somehow presents us with the possible
> fact, pictured as a non-conceptualised configuration of things in
> themselves.[18]

---

contents and the manner in which their truth values are determined. The
Platonism comes out like this. Just as whether a *sentence* is true depends both on
its meaning and on how matters stand in the relevant worldly respects, so, we
may say, whether a *proposition* is true depends on its content and the relevant
state of the world. But in contrast with the relation between a sentence and its
meaning, the content of a proposition *individuates it*—and individuates it, moreover, in a fashion which is supposed to be transparent to the reflective subject.
So it seems there is no space for a cognitive accomplishment at the level of
propositions akin to the recognition of the meaning of a sentence—so no space
for an enquiry into the objectivity of that accomplishment, or into the status of
the subject matter to which it purports to respond. But against this, it seems
just plain obvious that the reaction-dependence of rules, the ceaseless involvement of our sub-cognitive natures in our step-by-step appreciation of the
requirements of rules which Wittgenstein emphasises, cannot be at ease with
the mythology of the epistemically transparent yet fully substantial propositional
object. Moreover, even if it could, that would not ensure that a restriction of
the attention to "worldly" matters would then encompass everything relevant to
the question of the truth or falsity of such an object. For recognising the truth
of a proposition, even when it is conceived as a fully transparent object, involves
not merely some sort of cognitive acquaintance with what is, as a matter of fact,
a truth-conferring state of affairs but the recognition of an *internal* relation
between the two—a relation essential to the identity of each of its terms. The
proposition could not be *that* proposition unless it was made true by *that* state
of affairs; the state of affairs could not be that state of affairs unless it made true
that proposition. But the inchoate realism about internal relations, characteristic
of Platonist thinking in the philosophy of mathematics and much of our ordinary thinking about logical inference, is widely and I think rightly perceived as
something on which the rule-following considerations most centrally bear.
Whatever is accomplished by the ideas about rules for the objectivity and the
epistemology of so far unacknowledged internal relations generally, is accomplished for the idea of the so far unratified truth of a proposition.

18. "Wittgenstein on Following a Rule", p. 352.

The foregoing makes vivid, I believe, the point of this remark. By describing the matter at issue as being whether diamonds are hard, rather than whether "Diamonds are hard" is true, we rule out as inappropriate any explanation of a difference of opinion about it in terms of divergent understanding of the mentioned sentence. But an activity of the understanding—whether targeted on that sentence or on some other sentence—is inextricably involved in any engagement with the issue, just as among the empathisers the sense of humour is inextricably involved in engagement with issues of comedy*. If, after Wittgenstein's discussion, we are persuaded that the better comparison is of the active understanding with the sense of humour, rather than with a representational faculty like perception, then is not the moral to be drawn that something irreducibly *human and subcognitive* actively contributes to our engagement with any issue at all—a contribution explicitly allowed for when the issue is formulated metalinguistically, yet which does not go away when an object-linguistic formulation is preferred but is merely presumed shared among thinkers who engage the issue in question?

Now, however, we seem effectively to have rejected each of the objections that stood in the way of the intuitive line of subversive thought. As far as the first is concerned, we have granted that not every anti-realism relevant property would be transferable from claims about meaning to claims about truth. But lack of Cognitive Command is one that will. If the rule-following considerations show that judgements about meanings and what, conditionally, constitutes compliance with them fail of Cognitive Command, the same must hold for claims about sentences' truth. And once things get that far, it seems—so far as the second objection is concerned— that it would be at best an extremely uneasy tactic to attempt to hold subversion at bay by play with the distinction between metalinguistic ascriptions of truth and their object-linguistic counterparts. The intuitive argument is thus no trivial sophism; and the spectre of global minimalism is with us still.

## VII. Saving the Debates?

How to proceed? Well, whatever the real force of the foregoing considerations, they at least cannot make matters *worse* for claims in general than they are for their metalinguistic counterparts—the statement that P cannot have been shown thereby to be a *weaker* candidate for something better than minimalism than the statement that "P" is true. So a clean way to think about the matter is to ask: what scope remains for realist/anti-realist debate precisely about such metalinguistic claims? Can there still be well-defined such debates once we duly recognise the implication of questions concerning the objectivity of the content of the mentioned sentence, and the consequent bearing, whatever exactly it is, of the rule-following considerations?

The answer is that, possibly with one exception, we can certainly save *versions* of the various cruces which I have been concerned to highlight in this study. To illustrate. If a case can be made that a certain class of judgements—let P be a representative—exert Cognitive Command, then the same case is available for the claim that any difference of opinion concerning whether "P" is true, where not excused by vagueness (in any of the relevant ways) or by *divergent understandings of the meaning of "P" or confusion concerning any matters knowable a priori on the basis of knowledge of the meaning of "P"*, must involve something worth regarding as a cognitive shortcoming. Similarly, where the states of affairs apt to confer truth on a class of judgements exhibit the width of cosmological role which I suggested was the crux which the Best Explanation constraint was after, then the *non-semantic* states of affairs which enter into the determination of the truth value of the claim that "P" is true will do the same. Finally, where a measure of co-variance is ensured, a priori, between the truth values of a class of judgements and the verdicts of best opinions concerning them, under such further conditions that the relation between the truth of such a judgement and a favourable best opinion about it should be regarded as a constitutive one rather than merely as a matter of "tracking", then *among subjects agreed in their understanding of "P" and in all matters knowable a priori on the basis of that understanding*, best opinion will bear the same constitutive relation to the distribution of truth values among the corresponding metalinguistic judgements.

The exception is Evidence Transcendence. Not that there is any difficulty about *formulating* the crux in metalinguistic mode. If it is a potentially evidence-transcendent truth that P, then it is a potentially evidence-transcendent truth that "P" is true. The difference is that, in apparent contrast with the situation of the metalinguistic versions just sketched of Cognitive Command, Wide Cosmological Role and the issues to do with the Euthyphro Contrast, the rule-following considerations here seem to bear directly on the question whether any class of judgements can pass the test, even after its metalinguistic reformulation. Their apparent bearing is very immediate, and curiously seldom appreciated. How can a sentence be undetectably true unless the rule embodied in its content—the condition the world has to satisfy to confer truth upon it—can permissibly be thought of as extending, so to speak, of itself into areas where we cannot follow it and there determining, without any contribution from us or our reactive natures, that a certain state of affairs complies with it? Are not the presuppositions of that conception exactly those of the thought that what constitutes proper application of an arithmetical rule, say, at some so far unconsidered point in a series of such applications, is a matter settled autonomously, by the rule itself, independently of whether we ever will or could form a judgement on the matter? What is Wittgenstein stigmatising when he sneers at the myth of "superrigid machinery", or the "superlative conception" of rules,[19] if not precisely that: the idea that such purely conceptual matters of accord and discord have no ontological dependence on any facts to do with human nature? More specifically: what conception of such matters can both allow them to be determinate in ways which human beings cannot, perhaps in principle, acknowledge and yet leave space for the idea that their very constitution somehow depends on contingencies of human subcognitive propensity? For anyone inclined to doubt that there can be a satisfactory positive answer to that question, the possibility should loom large that the rule-following considerations resolve the issue between Dummett's realist and his opponent.

In none of the other three cases, however, does the application of the relevant constraint, reformulated so as to apply at the

19. See especially *Philosophical Investigations* §§190–197.

metalinguistic level, seem likely to be prejudiced by the dialectic about rule following. In particular, it seems most unlikely that any grounds will emerge for thinking that the reformulated constraints are never satisfied by any discourse—which is what it would take for the threat of global minimalism to be realised. But the metalinguistic constraints were so formulated that a class of statements will comply with them just in case the corresponding object-linguistic claims comply with the constraints as originally formulated. So we may affirm that some at least of the debates about realism, so far from being undercut, or sweepingly resolved in a minimalist direction, may be so formulated that the rule-following considerations have no direct bearing on their outcome.

But these sketchy remarks do not, of course, settle the question. There is a residual concern to which they do not speak. There are actually four ways the rule-following considerations might threaten to undermine realist/anti-realist debate. They might somehow prevent its very formulation—get in the way of a satisfactory statement of what is at issue. Or they might disclose mistaken assumptions held in common by the antagonists—McDowell's conception of the matter. Or they might globally prejudice the outcome in favour of minimalism. The most that can have been provided—and what, I would like to think, has indeed been provided—by our discussion to this point are formulations which meet these three concerns, ensuring in particular that the classification of discourses as apt only for minimalism or as satisfying further realism-relevant conditions will not be sensitive to variations in the view taken of the objectivity of content. But that leaves altogether unaddressed the further source of concern. Realism about a discourse involves the conviction that, in its proper practice, we attain to a desirable objectivity. How is the aspiration to objectivity *ever* to be satisfied if our response to an issue, arising in whatever discourse, can never be freed from a dependence upon propensities of spontaneous reaction—those involved in the appreciation of content—whose own status in point of objectivity is called into question? More generally, the fourth concern is whether, even if the key distinctions can be formulated in ways that allow the status of a discourse to be determined independently of the rule-following dialectic, their serviceability as vehicles for the expression of realist intuition may not be so severely compromised by a proper understanding of that dialectic that there is no longer any *point* to the taxonomy which they might enable us to construct.

Well, let someone who thinks that is so make the case. The point I have wanted to argue is that the case still needs making in detail, in the light both of a more pluralistic and fine-grained conception of the realist/anti-realist debates than has been commonplace—a conception which I hope I have begun to outline—and a much better understanding of those "rule-following considerations" than any so far accomplished in the vague and unsatisfactory treatments offered even by the best writing on the topic. Too many admirers of Wittgenstein's later philosophy have been beguiled by the idea that it might contain at its core the resources to unravel metaphysical debate—"to give philosophy peace". That should be the very last conclusion for a critical philosophy to draw—certainly not one to jump to. And I doubt if it's true.

# Appendix. On an Argument against the Coherence of Minimalism about Meaning

In section III of "The Status of Content", Paul Boghossian offers an argument whose effect, if sustained, would be, importantly, that minimalism about meaning is incoherent.[20] The argument is not, as one might expect, that meaning-minimalism leads to global minimalism and that the latter is incoherent anyway. Rather, the meaning-minimalist, Boghossian contends, is committed to contradictory theses independently of any inflation into global minimalism. Specifically, he can offer no coherent account of the behaviour of the truth predicate. For he ought to accept each[21] of the following claims:

(5) The predicate "has the truth condition that P" does not refer to a property;

(6) For any sentence S and propositional content P, "S has the truth condition that P" is not truth conditional.

20. The official target of Boghossian's argument is an irrealism ("non-factualism") about meaning and content generally. But Boghossian's irrealist will grant that discourse about such matters can quite properly assume an assertoric cast, and that a notion of correct assertibility will operate over it. There is no relevant dissimilarity between meaning-irrealism, so conceived, and meaning-minimalism to enable Boghossian's argument to succeed against the former but not the latter.

21. Later in the paper Boghossian canvasses the possibility of a meaning-irrealism constituted by (5) alone; but I won't be concerned with that here.

And these are actually inconsistent, since (5) entails

(7) "True" does not refer to a property,

whereas (6) entails the negation of (7).

We do well first to consider why a meaning-minimalist should accept (5) and (6). To be sure, the commitment to (6) is hardly in doubt if, as in section V above, we reserve "correct" as the truth predicate for minimally truth-apt sentences, and "true" as the truth predicate for discourses which satisfy some further realism-relevant constraint. For the minimalist thesis is then precisely that content-discourse in general, and hence ascriptions of truth conditions in particular, lack truth conditions. But what of (5)? Why should the minimalist—or the irrealist for that matter—accept that predicates of the form "has the truth condition that P" refer to no property?

The answer has to be that corresponding to the distinction between truth-apt and merely correctness-apt discourse will be a distinction between two types of predication, one associated with the generation of statements possessed of substantial truth conditions and the other generating only correctness-apt statements. The claim that a predicate "refers to a property" is then to be understood as placing it in the former group. When (5) is so construed, there is no question about the meaning-minimalist's commitment to it—and indeed no clear contrast between (5) and (6).

Let us then consider the two putatively conflicting entailments. Why, first, should it be supposed that (5) entails (7)? Boghossian cites his indebtedness to me for the (putative) reason. It is an application of the very vague thought that "non-factuality" among the determinants of an issue must divest the issue of factuality, and the reflection that S's truth condition, if it has one, is among the determinants of its truth value. Recast for our present concern, the question is whether a predicate G can "refer to a property"— can generate truth-conditional contexts—if whether it applies depends in part on whether another predicate, F, applies which generates only correctness-apt contexts. The matter is difficult, but fortunately we have in effect already reviewed it at the start of section VI above, where we noted that, whatever may be said about other realism-relevant characteristics, claims of truth will be divested of Cognitive Command if claims about content—and hence about truth conditions—are so. So we may conclude that the entailment from (5) to (7) will go through if Cognitive Command is necessary for the possession of substantial truth conditions.

Why does Boghossian think, though, that (6) entails the negation of (7)? The intuitive train of thought here is that since sentences of the form "S has the truth condition that P" are significant declarative sentences, the claim that they are not in the market for truth and falsity demands something other than a deflationary notion of truth (since any significant declarative sentence is apt for deflationary truth and falsity). And if truth is non-deflationary, then "true" must refer to a substantial property of statements—since it is one which a stably correctly assertible statement can lack.

I think there is nothing importantly amiss with this train of thought either. The difficulty with Boghossian's argument is to ensure that the two lemmas connect—to show that the conclusion of the first is indeed inconsistent with the conclusion of the second. Isn't the argument just punning on "refers to a property"? The sense in which, according to (5), "true" *fails to refer* to a property is that predications of it fail to generate contexts with substantial truth conditions; the sense in which "true" *does refer* to a property is that, by (6)—and indeed on any view which allows stably correctly assertible sentences not to be truth-apt—it allows of no broadly deflationary construal and therefore presumably marks some sort of real achievement, as it were. One feels a tension; but is there really any inconsistency?

Yes, there is—provided a very natural assumption is made. The assumption is that the accomplishment of any "real achievement" has to be something which may be marked by a *true* statement, so that "S is true" has to be a statement-form which is apt for truth. But if that is so, the same goes, presumably, for "non-achievement" (mere correctness). Dropping the metaphor, then, the assumption comes to the contention that the taxonomy of the distinction between merely correctness-apt discourses and those which are apt for truth should itself be a substantial matter: that the statements which classify discourses on one side or the other should be truth-apt. But of course, nakedly so expressed, it is clear that the assumption is not one which the meaning-minimalist can make, since how a discourse fares under that distinction is a function of the species of *content* its statements possess, and thus—by the principle which informs the argument from (5) to (7)—cannot be a substantial matter.

That may seem unsatisfactory. But it is the disclosure of an incoherence only if we take it that the very existence of a distinction between the truth-apt and the merely correctness-apt demands that its details may be recorded by *truths*. That is an assumption to which Boghossian in effect commits himself by presupposing that

> Whether truth is robust or deflationary constitutes the biggest decision a theorist of truth must make. But decide he must. It is an assumption of the present paper that the concept of truth is *univocal* as between these two conceptions, that a concurrent commitment to *both* a robust and a deflationary concept of truth would be merely to pun on the word "truth". We should not confuse the fact that it is now an open question whether truth is robust or deflationary for the claim that it can be both. There is no discernible plausibility in the suggestion that the concept of a correspondence between language and the world and the concept of a language-bound operator of semantic ascent might both be versions of the same idea.[22]

Boghossian here misleads himself by the concluding sentence. The question is not whether the concept of truth might incorporate both those notions, nor even whether distinct such concepts might be in play over a single discourse. The question is whether distinct truth predicates may be in play over distinct discourses. Boghossian discloses no objection to the suggestion that they may. But the issue is the crux of the matter. For it is clear in advance, independently of the detail of Boghossian's argument, that if the meaning-minimalist has the resources only of a single notion—undifferentiated "truth"—by means of which to express his views, he will have to allow that the existence of a distinction between

22. "The Status of Content", p. 165, n. 17.

"minimal" and "substantial" discourses, *however* characterised, will depend on something's being true of the latter which is not true of the former. So if he then goes on to say that the distinction consists in the fact that the statements of "substantial" discourses possess truth conditions, whereas those of minimal discourses do not, he has committed himself to the view that the distinction is constituted in a province—content—about which, on his own admission, there is nothing true to say. And in that case he has indeed tied his own shoelaces together. The solution, Boghossian's plea for univocity notwithstanding, is to recognise that the meaning-minimalist *must* work with a pluralist conception of truth. In particular, he has to insist that distinction between the truth-apt and the merely correctness-apt is one whose details, since founded in semantic contrasts, may be recorded only by *correct* statements. "S is true", "S has the truth condition that P", "S is correct", "S has the correctness condition that P"—all these are statement-forms whose instances are, for the meaning-minimalist, only correctness-apt.[23]

23. It might seem that the meaning-minimalist has another option, namely to retain a monistic view of truth and seek to characterise the distinction between minimal and substantial discourses in quite other terms than those of truth-conditionality. But this is not really another option (provided the alternative characterisation locates the distinction in *some* sort of contrast in species of content). Will minimal discourses turn out to be truth-apt, on the alternative proposal, or will they not? If they do not, then since it remains that they will be subject to *some* notion of stable correct assertibility, the theorist *will be* recognising a plurality of truth predicates—his monism will be merely verbal. If, on the other hand, minimal discourses will be truth-apt on the alternative proposal, then however that alternative goes, there can be no good objection to a terminological revision whereby the word "true" is annexed to the combination of truth (monistically understood) plus substantiality, while "correct" is reserved for the combination truth-plus-minimality. And then the point will stand, for just the reason outlined in the text: that the taxonomy of the distinction between the minimal and the substantial cannot, on pain of incoherence, be supposed by the meaning-minimalist to be capable of more than *correct* statement. In general, so long as the distinction between the minimal and the substantial is grounded in species-content, the meaning-minimalist will be forced to regard the taxonomy of the distinction as capable only of a minimal characterisation.

There *is* a discomfort about this position, touched on earlier. The meaning-minimalist will have to hold that the question whether meaning-minimalism is to be accepted is a question apt only for a correct answer, and so not an answer exerting Cognitive Command. This means that the view must lack a certain kind of *cogency:* whatever arguments might support it, it will be possible to decline them without cognitive shortcoming. So we learn something useful from consideration of Boghossian's discussion. But there is no simple contradiction inherent in the view along the lines Boghossian tries to describe.[24]

24. Although Boghossian charges that the meaning-minimalist is committed to contradictory claims about the predicate "true", we can represent his basic thought more simply if we focus on the predicate ". . . has the truth condition that P". The thesis of meaning-minimalism may be represented as

(M)          "S has the truth condition that P" is not truth-
             conditional.

Boghossian would have us argue that (M) is contradictory somewhat as follows:

(1) The predicate ". . . has the truth condition that P" is *robust*—since, by (M), it fails to apply to at least one type of significant declarative sentence (namely, "S has the truth condition that P").

(2) The predicate ". . . has the truth condition that P" is *not robust*—since, by (M), predications of it do not generate sentences with substantial truth conditions.

But the contradiction is an artifact of description—the assumption, quite unsupported, that there is any characteristic of predicates, "robustness" which doesn't belong to a predicate unless that predicate generates truth-conditional sentences but does belong to "true" and all cognate predicates such as ". . . has the truth condition that P", provided they apply selectively among stable correctly assertible declarative sentences. The meaning-minimalist should rejoin that the contradiction lies not with (M) but with conditions imposed on "robust" which are implicitly inconsistent with (M). All he is committed to is that predications and denials of truth-conditionality are not themselves truth-conditional.

# Index

# Index

Constitutive independence, p. 81

M. Johnston on projectivism, p. 109-110
     "     on "dispositional theories of value", p. 135

Cognitivism p. 146

Minimalism, pp. 24-25

Surface-assertoric discourse, p. 29

characterization of realism, p. 92

causal inertia, p. 192